Lecture Notes in Computer Science 15400

Founding Editors

Gerhard Goos
Juris Hartmanis

Editorial Board Members

Elisa Bertino, *Purdue University, West Lafayette, IN, USA*
Wen Gao, *Peking University, Beijing, China*
Bernhard Steffen, *TU Dortmund University, Dortmund, Germany*
Moti Yung, *Columbia University, New York, NY, USA*

The series Lecture Notes in Computer Science (LNCS), including its subseries Lecture Notes in Artificial Intelligence (LNAI) and Lecture Notes in Bioinformatics (LNBI), has established itself as a medium for the publication of new developments in computer science and information technology research, teaching, and education.

LNCS enjoys close cooperation with the computer science R & D community, the series counts many renowned academics among its volume editors and paper authors, and collaborates with prestigious societies. Its mission is to serve this international community by providing an invaluable service, mainly focused on the publication of conference and workshop proceedings and postproceedings. LNCS commenced publication in 1973.

Marco Console · Boris Konev
Editors

Reasoning Web

Declarative Artificial Intelligence: Knowledge, Rules, Logic

19th International Summer School 2023
Oslo, Norway, September 21–24, 2023
Tutorial Lectures

Editors
Marco Console ⓘ
Sapienza, University of Rome
Rome, Italy

Boris Konev ⓘ
University of Liverpool
Liverpool, UK

ISSN 0302-9743 ISSN 1611-3349 (electronic)
Lecture Notes in Computer Science
ISBN 978-3-031-80282-9 ISBN 978-3-031-80283-6 (eBook)
https://doi.org/10.1007/978-3-031-80283-6

© The Editor(s) (if applicable) and The Author(s), under exclusive license
to Springer Nature Switzerland AG 2025

This work is subject to copyright. All rights are solely and exclusively licensed by the Publisher, whether the whole or part of the material is concerned, specifically the rights of translation, reprinting, reuse of illustrations, recitation, broadcasting, reproduction on microfilms or in any other physical way, and transmission or information storage and retrieval, electronic adaptation, computer software, or by similar or dissimilar methodology now known or hereafter developed.
The use of general descriptive names, registered names, trademarks, service marks, etc. in this publication does not imply, even in the absence of a specific statement, that such names are exempt from the relevant protective laws and regulations and therefore free for general use.
The publisher, the authors and the editors are safe to assume that the advice and information in this book are believed to be true and accurate at the date of publication. Neither the publisher nor the authors or the editors give a warranty, expressed or implied, with respect to the material contained herein or for any errors or omissions that may have been made. The publisher remains neutral with regard to jurisdictional claims in published maps and institutional affiliations.

This Springer imprint is published by the registered company Springer Nature Switzerland AG
The registered company address is: Gewerbestrasse 11, 6330 Cham, Switzerland

If disposing of this product, please recycle the paper.

Preface

The "Reasoning Web School" (RW) is an annual event organised under the umbrella of the "Declarative AI" conference. The 2023 edition was hosted by the Oslo Metropolitan University, Norway. This year, the event returned to in-person attendance following the 2020–2022 editions held virtually due to the Covid-19 pandemic. The program contained eight three-hour courses given over four days. We were fortunate to have excellent speakers and course subjects. The broad, but not exclusive theme of RW 2023 was "Declarative Artificial Intelligence: Knowledge, Rules, Logic." The courses were as follows:

- Evgeny Kharlamov, Bosch Center for Artificial Intelligence, Germany and University of Oslo, Norway.
    Declarative AI for Industry: Methods, Applications, Trends
- Martin Giese, University of Oslo, Norway.
    Ontologies vs Constraints
- Andreas Pieris, University of Edinburgh, UK.
    Termination of Reasoning
- Michael Thomazo, Inria, France.
    Compact Query Rewritings for Ontology-Based Query Answering
- Filip Murlak, University of Warsaw, Poland.
    Graph Queries and Description Logics
- Riccardo Rosati Sapienza, University of Rome, Italy.
    Controlled Query Evaluation in Description Logic Ontologies
- Ana Ozaki, University of Oslo & University of Bergen, Norway.
    Learning from Neural Networks with Queries and Counterexamples
- Christian Straßer and Kees van Berkel, Ruhr University Bochum, Germany and Institute for Logic and Computation, TU Wien, Vienna, Austria
    Proof-Theoretic Approaches in Logical Argumentation

We are grateful to all the speakers who contributed to the success of the Reasoning Web School 2023. Five of these contributions resulted in chapters published in this volume. All the chapters received at least one anonymous review, providing feedback and recommendations to improve the quality of the presentation.

We are grateful to the Scientific Advisory Board for contributing ideas to shape the School Program. We are thankful to Oslo Met and particularly to Ahmet Soylu for hosting a wonderful event. Last but not least, we appreciate Springer's traditional and valuable support for the publication of the lecture notes.

August 2024
Marco Console
Boris Konev

Organization

School Chairs

Marco Console   Sapienza, University of Rome, Italy
Boris Konev   University of Liverpool, UK

Scientific Advisory Board

Danushka Bollegala   University of Liverpool, UK
Diego Calvanese   Free University of Bozen, Italy
Georg Gottlob   University of Oxford, UK
Domenico Lembo   Sapienza, University of Rome, Italy
Leonid Libkin   University of Edinburgh, UK
Vladimir Lifschitz   University of Texas at Austin, USA
Arild Waaler   University of Oslo, Norway
Guohui Xiao   University of Bergen, Norway

Lecturers

Kees van Berkel   Ruhr University Bochum, Germany
Martin Giese   University of Oslo, Norway
Evgeny Kharlamov   Bosch Center for Artificial Intelligence, Germany
                                           and University of Oslo, Norway
Filip Murlak   University of Warsaw, Poland
Ana Ozaki   University of Bergen, Norway
Andreas Pieris   University of Edinburgh, UK and University of
                                           Cyprus, Cyprus
Riccardo Rosati   Sapienza, University of Rome, Italy
Christian Straßer   Ruhr University Bochum, Germany
Michael Thomazo   Inria, France

Contents

Compact Query Rewritings for Ontology-Based Query Answering 1
   Michaël Thomazo

Finite-Model Reasoning for Graph Queries and Description Logics 23
   Filip Murlak

Controlled Query Evaluation in Description Logic Ontologies 54
   Gianluca Cima, Domenico Lembo, Lorenzo Marconi, Riccardo Rosati, and Domenico Fabio Savo

Actively Learning from Machine Learning Models with Queries
and Counterexamples 61
   Ana Ozaki

A Tutorial in Proof-Theoretic Approaches to Logical Argumentation 78
   Kees van Berkel and Christian Straßer

Author Index 115

Compact Query Rewritings for Ontology-Based Query Answering

Michaël Thomazo[✉]

Inria, DI ENS, ENS, CNRS, University PSL, Paris, France
michael.thomazo@inria.fr

Abstract. Ontology-based query answering is an important reasoning problem at the core of logic-based data integration. Formally, the problem takes as input a database instance I, a set of existential rules $\mathcal{R}$, and a Boolean conjunctive query q, and asks whether $I, \mathcal{R} \models q$. The query entailment problem thus defined is usually reduced towards a query evaluation problem, either through *materialization* of entailed atoms, or through *query rewriting*. In these lecture notes, we present a couple of query rewriting algorithms, and discuss an approach whose aim is to avoid a blow-up in the size of the rewritings in cases that are typically present in real-world, namely in the presence of (large) role and concepts hierarchies.

Keywords: Ontology-Based Query Answering · Query Rewriting

1 Introduction

The way that data is stored and accessed by organizations and companies has radically changed over the past couple of decades. Traditionally, data has been stored in highly-structured relational databases, and assumed to be a complete description of the relevant information. Today, data is often extracted from the Web, distributed, heterogeneous, and the completeness assumption made previously cannot reasonably be made anymore. This triggered the birth of a research field at the intersection of data management and knowledge representation and reasoning, where a user aims at querying data while taking general knowledge into account, under an open-world semantics. The vision is to rely on a shared vocabulary, coined an *ontology*, to integrate data from several data sources and to perform automated reasoning. The challenge is then to query the data while taking the ontology into account, according to a formal semantics defined by first-order logic.

The pros of adding this logical layer is to clearly specify the meaning of the terms, to help the user to express their information need in a vocabulary they are familiar with, and to provide more complete sets of answers. The challenge is that instead of a classical query evaluation task (does q hold in a specific model?), we now consider a query entailment task (does q hold in any model of the data and of the ontology?). As expected, the complexity of this entailment task is hugely dependent on the type of knowledge that we express through the ontology.

An important research effort has been dedicated to investigate the trade-off between the complexity of query answering and the expressivity of the used ontology. Two main formalisms for expressing the latter have been considered: that of Description Logics [4], and that of existential rules [5], also known as Datalog$^\pm$ [13]. Depending on which classes of description logics or existential rules are considered, different approaches may be applicable. In these notes, we will consider existential rules to represent ontologies. They are first-order formula of the shape $\forall \mathbf{x} \forall \mathbf{y}(B(\mathbf{x},\mathbf{y}) \rightarrow \exists \mathbf{z} H(\mathbf{y},\mathbf{z}))$, where B and H are conjunctions of atoms, respectively called the body and the head of the rule. For instance, it may allows to state that "every actor plays a role in some movie", which could be expressed by

$$\forall x \ \mathsf{MovieActor}(x) \rightarrow \exists y \ \mathsf{PlaysIn}(x,y) \wedge \mathsf{Movie}(y)$$

The decision problem we will focus on in these notes is the problem of conjunctive query entailment for a knowledge base, that is, given a database I, a set of existential rules $\mathcal{R}$ and a Boolean conjunctive query q, does it hold that $I, \mathcal{R} \models q$?

Without further restriction, this problem is undecidable. A tool of choice to impose restrictions on $\mathcal{R}$ ensuring decidability is the notion of *universal model* of I and $\mathcal{R}$. A universal model of I and $\mathcal{R}$ is a model U of I and $\mathcal{R}$ such that for any model M of I and $\mathcal{R}$, there exists a homomorphism from U into M. It has been shown that a universal model can be built by an iterative procedure, called the *chase*, that "applies" rules in a fair fashion until no more rules are applicable. Denoting by $\mathsf{chase}(I, \mathcal{R})$ the result of the chase of I and $\mathcal{R}$, it holds that

$$I, \mathcal{R} \models q \Leftrightarrow \mathsf{chase}(I, \mathcal{R}) \models q.$$

While chase computation is a rather intuitive notion, it suffers from several drawbacks, among which: *(i)* its computation may never halt *(ii)* even in halting case, its size may be prohibitively large for allowing an efficient computation *(iii)* whenever data changes, the chase must be updated accordingly, which is a costly operation. These limitations are partially overcome through a dual approach, called query rewriting. Instead of modifying the data to ensure that consequences are materialized, one computes, given $\mathcal{R}$ and q, another query q' such that $I, \mathcal{R} \models q$ if and only if $I \models q'$. This approach is the focus of these notes, with the following questions in mind: how can we compute a rewriting, given q and $\mathcal{R}$? Given that such rewritings are typically of size exponential with respect to the input query, can we reduce their size in real-world cases? What are the limitations of such an approach? How to extend the approach to more expressive cases?

These notes are structured as follows: we first introduce the formal definitions required to describe the problem and the approach in Sect. 2. Section 3 focuses on the abstract notion of rewritability, present some alternative definitions, and discuss its applicability. We then discuss in Sect. 4 a first query rewriting algorithm, whose termination guarantee does not depend on syntactic criteria, but on the existence of a UCQ-rewriting: it is thus optimal in its applicability, and we will also show that it enjoys some optimality property: it outputs the smallest possible UCQ-rewriting. This optimality result is however too weak to ensure the efficiency of the approach, and we thus extend the search space in Sect. 5, allowing a more liberal use of disjunction in the rewritings. This allows to circumvent a combinatorial explosion typically arising in practice. We conclude by discussing the problem of query optimization and related work regarding Datalog rewritings.

2 Preliminaries

2.1 Some Basic Notions

Let us consider $\mathbf{P}, \mathbf{C}$ and $\mathbf{V}$ three infinite countable disjoint sets of respectively predicates, constants and variables. Each predicate $p \in \mathbf{P}$ is associated with a positive integer, called the *arity* of p. A *term* is either a constant or a variable. As a convention, we will denote constants by $a, b, c, \ldots$ and variables by $x, y, z, \ldots$ An *atom* is of the form $p(t_1, \ldots, t_k)$, where p is of arity k and t_i is a term for any i. The terms of an atom a are denoted by $\mathsf{term}(a)$, and its variables by $\mathsf{var}(a)$. An instance is a (possibly infinite) set of atoms. A database is a finite instance. A conjunctive query is an existentially closed conjunction of atoms. We extend the functions term and var to instances (and databases, conjunctive queries...) in the natural way. Given two sets of atoms A and B, a *homomorphism* from A to B is a function π from $\mathsf{term}(A)$ to $\mathsf{term}(B)$ such that for any constant c, $\pi(c) = c$ and $\pi(A) \subseteq B$. A Boolean conjunctive query q evaluates to true on an instance I (denoted by $I \models q$) if there is homomorphism from q to I. Of particular interest in these notes is the notion of existential rules.

Definition 1 (Existential Rule). *An existential rule (or simple rule) $R = (B, H)$ is a closed formula of shape*

$$\forall x_1, \ldots, \forall x_p (B \to \exists z_1, \ldots, \exists z_q \ H),$$

where B (the body of R, denoted by $\mathsf{body}(R)$) and H (the head of R, denoted by $\mathsf{head}(R)$) are two finite conjunctions of atoms on $(\mathbf{P}, \mathbf{C})$, $\mathsf{var}(B) = \{x_1, \ldots, x_p\}$, $\mathsf{var}(H) \setminus \mathsf{var}(B) = \{z_1, \ldots, z_q\}$. The set of variables appearing both in the body and the head of R is called the frontier of R, and is denoted by $\mathsf{fr}(R)$.

An instance I is a model of an existential rule R (we say that R is satisfied in I) if for any homomorphism from $\mathsf{body}(R)$ to I there exists a homomorphism π' from $\mathsf{head}(R)$ to I such that $\pi(x) = \pi'(x)$ for any $x \in \mathsf{fr}(R)$. An instance I' is a model of I if $I \subseteq I'$, and a model of $\mathcal{R}$ if it is a model of any rule $R \in \mathcal{R}$.

Note that ontologies are also quite often formally represented using description logics, and that some description logics (such as $\mathcal{EL}$ [3] or members of the

DL-Lite family [15]) are at the core of standards for the semantic web[1]. Not all description logic axioms are expressible by existential rules (even slightly extended with harmless features such as *denial constraints*): for instance, the $\mathcal{ALC}$ concept inclusion $\neg A \sqsubseteq B$ is not expressible by existential rules. The choice of existential rules in these notes is mainly driven by two facts: existential rules are used in a large share of the literature; and the non-expressibility of concept inclusions such as $\neg A \sqsubseteq B$ permits the existence of universal models, which is a core tool for reasoning that we present now.

To keep notations light, we will often treat conjunctions (or disjunctions) of atoms as sets of atoms, replace $\wedge$ by commas, and omit quantifiers in rules. The quantification of rules remain unambiguous, as every variable appearing only a rule body is existentially quantified, while all the others are universally quantified.

2.2 The Ontology-Based Query Answering Problem

The problem we focus on in these notes is that of *ontology-based query answering* (OBQA). Formally, it takes as input an instance I, a set of existential rules $\mathcal{R}$ and a Boolean[2] conjunctive query q, and asks whether

$$I, \mathcal{R} \models q,$$

that is, does q evaluates to true on every model of I and $\mathcal{R}$. This problem is known to be undecidable [8], but is semi-decidable. The main semi-decision procedure relies on the *chase* [7]. The intuition behind the chase is to "complete" the instance, that is, to add tuples to the instance to ensure that all rules are satisfied. To do so in the least specific way, whenever the body of a rule hold without the head being satisfied accordingly, to add (in the most general way possible) atoms allowing the head to hold. We formalise this intuition through the notion of *trigger*.

Definition 2 (Trigger). *Let I be an instance and $\mathcal{R}$ be a set of rules. A trigger (w.r.t. $\mathcal{R}$, usually omitted) t on I is a pair (R, π) where π is a homomorphism from $\mathsf{body}(R)$ into I. t is active if π cannot be extended into a homomorphism from $\mathsf{head}(R)$ into I.*

Example 1 (Trigger). Let us consider the rule $R = r(x, y) \rightarrow r(y, z)$, and the instance $I_1 = \{r(a, b)\}$. The pair (R, π) where $\pi(x) = a$ and $\pi(y) = b$ is an active trigger on I_1. The same trigger is not active on the instance $I_2 = \{r(a, b), r(b, b)\}$.

Whenever a trigger is active, the corresponding rule can be applied in the following fashion.

Definition 3 (Rule Application). *Let I be an instance and $t = (R, \pi)$ be an active trigger on I. The application of t on I according to π produces a fact*

---
[1] https://www.w3.org/TR/owl2-profiles/.
[2] The non-Boolean case can be reduced to the Boolean case.

$\alpha(I, R, \pi) = I \cup \pi^{\mathsf{safe}}(\mathsf{head}(R))$, where $\pi^{\mathsf{safe}}(x) = x$ if $\pi(x)$ is defined and a fresh variable otherwise.

Example 2. Continuing the previous example, (R, π) can be applied on I_1, yielding $I'_1 = I_1 \cup \{r(b, y_1)\}$.

Definition 4 (Derivation). *Let I be an instance and $\mathcal{R}$ be a set of rules. A derivation (with respect to $\mathcal{R}$) from I is a (possibly infinite) sequence $I = I_0, I_1, \ldots, I_k, \ldots$ such that for all $i \geq 1$, there are a rule R and a homomorphism π from $\mathsf{body}(R)$ to I_{i-1} such that $I_i = \alpha(I_{i-1}, R, \pi)$.*

Proposition 1 (Soundness and Completeness of Derivations). *Let I be an instance, $\mathcal{R}$ be a set of existential rules and q be a Boolean conjunctive query. Then $I, \mathcal{R} \models q$ if and only if there exists a finite derivation whose result I' is such that $I' \models q$.*

A derivation is a *chase* sequence if it is *fair*, which intuitively means that no rules application is indefinitely postponed.

Definition 5 (Chase Sequence). *A derivation $I = I_0, \ldots, I_k, \ldots$ (w.r.t $\mathcal{R}$) is a chase sequence if for any j, if t is an active trigger (w.r.t. $\mathcal{R}$) on I_j, there exists an $i > j$ such that t is not active on I_j.*

It will be convenient, especially with respect to query rewritability later on, to apply rules in a breadth-first fashion.

Definition 6 *($\mathsf{chase}_k(I, \mathcal{R})$). We define the kth step of the breadth-first chase by induction on k:*

- $\mathsf{chase}_0(I, \mathcal{R}) = I$
- $\mathsf{chase}_{i+1}(I, \mathcal{R}) = \bigcup_{R, \pi \in T} \alpha(\mathsf{chase}_i(I, \mathcal{R}), R, \pi)$,

where T is the set of active triggers (w.r.t. $\mathcal{R}$) on $\mathsf{chase}_i(I, \mathcal{R})$ and fresh variables are not shared across rule applications.

Note that Definition 5 introduces a notion that is known in the literature as *restricted chase sequence*. Other definitions exist,[3] but the technical details in these definitions are not required here. While the chase is an intuitive process to solve ontology-based query answering, it has some drawbacks. First, it may not terminate, even in seemingly simple cases, as witnessed by the following example.

Example 3. Let us consider again $R = r(x, y) \rightarrow r(y, z)$ and $I_1 = \{r(a, b)\}$. The sequence $I_1, I_2, \ldots, I_n, \ldots$, where $I_2 = I_1 \cup \{r(b, x_1)\}$ and for $i \geq 3$, $I_i = I_{i-1} \cup \{r(x_{i-2}, x_{i-1})\}$ is an infinite derivation (and the only one up to variable renaming).

---

[3] The interested reader can consult [23] for definitions and the study of the termination of the different variants.

Second, even in cases where the chase terminates, it may not be practical to compute it. For instance, *maintaining* the chase in presence of updates is a complex task, which is especially important in settings where data has a high-update rate. For these reasons, alternative algorithms have also been considered, and we introduce in the next section the notion of *rewriting*.

3 Rewritability and Relationship with the Chase

3.1 $\mathcal{L}$-Rewritability

The goal behind rewriting is similar to that of the chase: to reduce a query entailment problem to a query evaluation problem. That is, instead of checking whether q evaluates to true on every model of $\mathcal{R}$ and I, checking whether some query (q in the previous section) evaluates to true on a given interpretation (in the previous section, the result of the chase). However, instead of modifying the instance, the query rewriting approach focuses on the query. We reduce ontology-based query answering to checking whether I is a model of some query $q_\mathcal{L}$. The challenge is thus to find out which $q_\mathcal{L}$ to define, in function of q and $\mathcal{R}$. The conditions we want on $q_\mathcal{L}$ are formalized through the notion of *rewritability*.

Definition 7. *Let $\mathcal{L}$ be a query language. A query q is $\mathcal{L}$-rewritable w.r.t. to a rule set $\mathcal{R}$ if and only if there exists $q_\mathcal{L} \in \mathcal{L}$ such that for any instance I, $I, \mathcal{R} \models q$ if and only if $q_\mathcal{L}$ evaluates to true on I.*

The notion of rewritability is parametrized by a query language $\mathcal{L}$. As query language, one can consider conjunctive queries, but CQ-rewritability of ontology-based queries is very restricted. Hence, more expressive query languages are usually studied, such as union of conjunctive queries (UCQ), first-order logic (FO), non-recursive Datalog, and Datalog. Let us recall the notion of Datalog queries.

Definition 8 (Datalog). *A Datalog rule is an existential rule whose set of existential variables is empty. Given a set of Datalog rules, one can define a relation $<$ on predicates such that $p < q$ if and only if there exists a rule R such that p appears in $\mathsf{body}(R)$ and q appears in $\mathsf{head}(R)$. A Datalog program is said non-recursive if there are no cycles in the transitive closure of $<$.*

3.2 UCQ-Rewritability: Alternative Definitions

Most rewriting algorithms in the literature have generated UCQ-rewritings. As it often happens with central notions, the class of rule sets that ensure the existence of UCQ-rewritings has however been defined in a variety of ways, which we quickly recall here. A first interesting notion is the notion of bounded derivation depth property.

Definition 9 (Bounded Derivation Depth Property). *A rule set $\mathcal{R}$ has the bounded derivation depth property if the following property holds:*

$$\forall q \; \exists k \; \forall I \quad I, \mathcal{R} \models q \iff \mathsf{chase}_k(I, \mathcal{R}) \models q$$

It has been shown that a rule set enjoys the bounded derivation depth property if and only if there exists a UCQ-rewriting for any query [26].

Another related notion is that of *FO*-rewritability, where we are not only interested in rewritings that are conjunctive queries, but where we allow to use the more general first-order queries. However, as it is clear that sound and complete rewritings of conjunctive queries under existential rules must be closed under homomorphism, it is a consequence of a paper from Rossman [29] that the existence of an FO-rewriting implies the existence of a UCQ-rewriting. Note that *UCQ*-rewritability, *FO*-rewritability and non-recursive-Datalog-rewritability are three equivalent notions only as long as the *size* of the rewritings are not considered. The impact of the chosen query language on the worst-case size of the rewritings has been studied in, e.g. [20].

A natural problem, given a query language $\mathcal{L}$, a query q and a rule set $\mathcal{R}$ is whether q is $\mathcal{L}$-rewritable with respect to $\mathcal{R}$. This is however undecidable for classical query languages [5]. For that reason, syntactic conditions have been proposed to ensure the existence of an $\mathcal{L}$-rewriting: for first-order rewritability, one can cite linearity, multi-linearity, stickiness, acyclicity of the graph of rule dependencies among others [5, 12, 14].

A Short Note on Query Containment. Before turning our attention to the computation of UCQ-rewritings, let us recall an important notion, that of query containment.

Definition 10 (Query Containment). *A Boolean query q_1 is contained in another Boolean query q_2 if whenever q_1 evaluates to true on I, then q_2 evaluates to true on I.*

Query containment is undecidable for first-order queries, but in the case of conjunctive queries, there exists a simple check, as explicited below.

Theorem 1 (Homomorphism Theorem). *Let q_1 and q_2 be two Boolean conjunctive queries. Then q_1 is contained in q_2 if and only if there exists a homomorphism from q_2 to q_1.*

This implies that deciding if q_1 is contained in q_2 is an NP-complete problem: given the typically small size of the considered conjunctive queries, it is thus still feasible to perform these checks. Such a check will be performed many times in the piece-based rewriting algorithm that we present in the next section, and is important for the termination of the rewriting algorithm. Note that the same problem is undecidable when considering Datalog queries instead of conjunctive queries [30].

4 Generating UCQ Rewritings

This section is devoted to the problem of computing a UCQ-rewriting of q with respect to $\mathcal{R}$. The classical way to compute such rewritings is to start from the original query, and perform all possible "atomic" rewritings of that query with respect to the rule set, before reiterating the process with the generated queries until reaching a fixpoint [1,21,25,28,32]. To help the reader to build an intuition, we start by explaining such an "atomic" rewriting process for the simple case of Datalog, that is, of rules that do not contain any existentially quantified variables in their head. We then show that naively generalizing this approach to general existential rules fails, and present the piece-based rewriting algorithm. We then explore the relationships between the piece-based rewriting algorithm, and other approaches inspired from the description logics community, showing that both algorithms are essentially the same. We finish by a discussion on the *optimality* of the obtained rewritings.

4.1 Datalog Unfolding

Rewriting for Datalog (and later for existential rules) is based on the notion of *unification*. Intuitively, an atom *unifies* with the head of a rule R when it can possibly be generated by an application of R. We assume that Datalog rules have been normalized by having a single atom in the head (which can be done without loss of generality).

Definition 11 (Datalog Unification). *Let q be a conjunctive query, and R be a Datalog rule. A* unifier *of q with R is a pair $\mu = (a, u)$, where a is an atom of q and u is a substitution of $\mathsf{var}(a) \cup \mathsf{var}(\mathsf{head}(R))$ by $\mathsf{term}(\mathsf{head}(R)) \cup \mathbf{C}$ s.t. $u(a) = u(\mathsf{head}(R))$.*

As illustrated in Example 4, one-step rewritings are defined in such a way that they perform the "converse" operation to a rule application.

Definition 12 (Datalog One-Step Rewriting). *Let q be a conjunctive query, R be a Datalog rule, and $\mu = (a, u)$ be a unifier of q with R. The* one-step rewriting *of q w.r.t. to μ, denoted by $\beta(q, R, \mu)$ is $u(\mathsf{body}(R) \cup (q \setminus a))$*

Example 4 (Datalog Unification and Rewriting). Let us consider $q_e = t(x_1, x_2) \wedge s(x_1, x_3) \wedge s(x_2, x_3)$, and $R = s_1(x, y) \rightarrow s(x, y)$. A Datalog unifier of q_e with R is $\mu_d = (s(x_1, x_3), \{u(x_1) = x, u(x_3) = y\})$. The one-step rewriting q'_e of q_e according to μ_d is the following query:

$$t(x, x_2), s_1(x, y), s(x_2, y).$$

Let us notice that this query is equivalent to

$$t(x_1, x_2), s_1(x_1, x_3), s(x_2, x_3),$$

where x has been renamed by x_1 and y by x_3. In the following, we will allow ourselves to use such variable renamings without prior notice.

If we consider $I_e = \{t(a,b), s_1(a,c), s(b,c)\}$, R is applicable on I_e by mapping (among other choices) x to a and y to c. q_e can be mapped to the resulting instance, while q'_e can be mapped to I_e.

Note that the one-step rewriting operator is just a step towards the computation of UCQ-rewritings: this would have to be iterated, as presented in Sect. 4.3. We first present how to tackle existentially quantified variables in rule head, before presenting an algorithm for computing UCQ-rewritings.

4.2 Existentials

Note that the rewriting operation defined for Datalog rules is not readily applicable when one is considering existential rules. We illustrate this through the following example.

Example 5 (False Unification). Let us again consider $q_e = t(x_1, x_2) \wedge s(x_1, x_3) \wedge s(x_2, x_3)$, and $R' = f(x) \rightarrow \exists y\ s(x, y)$. A Datalog unification of q_e with R' is $\mu_{\text{err}} = (s(x_1, x_3), (u(x_1) = x, u(x_3) = y))$. According to Definition 12, the rewriting of q_e with R' would be

$$q_r = t(x, x_2) \wedge f(x) \wedge s(x_2, y).$$

However, q_r is not a sound rewriting of q_e, which can be checked by computing the chase starting from q_r considered as an instance.

Two workarounds have been proposed in the literature, while remaining in the function-free fragment of first-order logic. The first one consists in restricting the applicability of the rewriting operator, by allowing the unification of existential variables with variables which have a single occurrence in the considered query. Doing only this would make lose completeness of the rewriting procedure. Hence, another operation, which consists in unifying atoms of the same predicate, is added to regain completeness. This approach is among other used by PerfectRef [15]. Two limitations are unfortunate with such an approach: first, it is applicable only to rules whose head have been normalized to have a single atom. While this is not a problem in terms of expressive power (see [19] for a study of normalization procedure and their impact on chase termination and query rewritability), it increases the size of the obtained rewritings, which hinders performance. Another performance issue is that a lot of unnecessary unifications may be created.

These limitations are avoided by the other approach [25], which use a slightly different notion of unifiers, namely piece-unifier – which is, of course, slightly more complex (both to define and to compute).

Definition 13 (Piece-Unifier). *Let q be a conjunctive query and R be a rule. A piece-unifier of q with R is a pair $\mu = (q', u)$ with $q' \subseteq q, q' \neq \emptyset$, and u a substitution of $\mathsf{fr}(R) \cup \mathsf{var}(q')$ by $\mathsf{term}(\mathsf{head}(R)) \cup \mathbf{C}$ such that:*

1. for all $x \in \mathsf{fr}(R)$, $u(x) \in \mathsf{fr}(R) \cup \mathbf{C}$;
2. for all $x \in \mathsf{sep}_q(q')$, $u(x) \in \mathsf{fr}(R) \cup \mathbf{C}$;
3. $u(q') \subseteq u(\mathsf{head}(R))$;

where $\mathsf{sep}_q(q')$, called the *separating variables*, denotes the set of variables that belongs both to q' and to $q \setminus q'$.

Definition 14 (Rewriting). *Given a conjunctive query q, a rule R and a piece-unifier $\mu = (q', u)$ of q with R, the rewriting of q according to μ, denoted by $\beta(q, R, \mu)$ is $u(\mathsf{body}(R) \cup \bar{q}')$, where $\bar{q}' = q \setminus q'$.*

Example 6. Let us again consider $q_e = t(x_1, x_2) \wedge s(x_1, x_3) \wedge s(x_2, x_3)$, and $R' = f(x) \to \exists y\ s(x, y)$. $\mu_{\mathsf{err}} = (s(x_1, x_3), (u(x_1) = x, u(x_3) = y))$ is not a piece-unifier of q_e with R', as x_3 is a separating variable and is unified with an existential variable of R'. On the other hand, $\mu = (\{s(x_1, x_3), s(x_2, x_3)\}, (u(x_1) = u(x_2) = x, u(x_3) = y)$ is a piece-unifier: the separating variables are x_1 and x_2, which are unified with the frontier variable x. The associated rewriting is $t(x, x) \wedge f(x)$.

Definition 15 (Rewriting (w.r.t. $\mathcal{R}$)). *Let q be a conjunctive query and $\mathcal{R}$ be a set of existential rules. A rewriting of q (w.r.t. $\mathcal{R}$) is a conjunctive query q_k that is obtained by a finite sequence $q = q_0, \ldots, q_k$ such that for all $i \in \{0, \ldots, k-1\}$, there is $R_i \in \mathcal{R}$ and a piece-unifier μ_i of q_i with R_i such that $q_{i+1} = \beta(q_i, R_i, \mu_i)$.*

The next proposition, a proof of which can be found in [5], states the soundness and completeness of $\mathcal{R}$-rewritings. Intuitively, the proof relies on an equivalence between performing a single rule application on a database, and performing a one-step rewriting of a query.

Proposition 2. *Let q be a conjunctive query, $\mathcal{R}$ be a set of existential rules, and I be an instance. Then $I, \mathcal{R} \models q$ if and only if there exists a rewriting q' of q w.r.t. $\mathcal{R}$ such that $I \models q'$*

4.3 A Piece-Based Rewriting Algorithm

Before introducing a first rewriting algorithm, we introduce the notion of *cover* of a set of conjunctive queries, which is intuitively a minimal subset having the same semantics.

Definition 16. *Let $\mathcal{Q}$ be a set of conjunctive queries. A cover of $\mathcal{Q}$ is a set $\mathcal{Q}^c$ such that:*

1. *for any $q \in \mathcal{Q}$, there exists $q' \in \mathcal{Q}^c$ such that q is contained in q';*
2. *there is no pair of distinct queries q, q' in $\mathcal{Q}^c$ such that q is contained in q'.*

Algorithm 1 computes, given a conjunctive query q and a set of existential rules $\mathcal{R}$, a set $\mathcal{Q}_F$ that is a UCQ-rewriting of q with respect to $\mathcal{R}$. Of course, such a computation can only halt when there exists a finite UCQ-rewriting of the input query. A set of queries to be explored ($\mathcal{Q}_E$) is initialized to $\{q\}$. At each iteration of the while loop, every possible rewriting of q with a rule of $\mathcal{R}$ is computed, and stored in a set $\mathcal{Q}_t$ of temporary queries. A cover of the queries generated so far is computed, and any query that has not been explored yet is put in the next iteration of $\mathcal{Q}_E$.

Data: A conjunctive query q, a rule set $\mathcal{R}$
Result: The minimal UCQ-rewriting of q w.r.t. $\mathcal{R}$ if it exists
$\mathcal{Q}_F := \{q\}$;
$\mathcal{Q}_E := \{q\}$;
while $\mathcal{Q}_E \neq \emptyset$ do
$\quad$ $\mathcal{Q}_t = \emptyset$;
$\quad$ for $q_i \in \mathcal{Q}_E$ do
$\quad\quad$ for $R \in \mathcal{R}$ do
$\quad\quad\quad$ for μ piece-unifier of q_i with R do
$\quad\quad\quad\quad$ $\mathcal{Q}_t = \mathcal{Q}_t \cup \beta(q, R, \mu)$;
$\quad\quad\quad$ end
$\quad\quad$ end
$\quad$ end
$\quad$ $\mathcal{Q}^c := \text{cover}(\mathcal{Q}_F \cup \mathcal{Q}_t)$;
$\quad$ $\mathcal{Q}_E = \mathcal{Q}^c \setminus \mathcal{Q}_F$;
$\quad$ $\mathcal{Q}_F = \mathcal{Q}^c$;
end
return $\mathcal{Q}_F$;

Algorithm 1: A Breadth-First Rewriting Algorithm

It is clear that any element of $\mathcal{Q}_F$ is a sound rewriting of q with respect to $\mathcal{R}$. What is less trivial is that whenever Algorithm 1 terminates, it outputs a sound and complete UCQ-rewriting of q with respect to $\mathcal{R}$. This relies on the *prunability* [25] of the considered rewriting operator.

Definition 17 (Prunability). *A rewriting operator β is said* prunable *if for any set of rules $\mathcal{R}$ and for any q_1, q_2, q_2' such that q_2 is contained in q_1, if q_2' is a one-step rewriting of q_2, then either q_2' is contained in q_1 or there exists a one-step rewriting q_1' of q_1 such that q_2' is contained in q_1'.*

Intuitively, this property allows us to explore (that is, to rewrite) only the most general queries obtained during the rewriting process. Prunability of several rewriting operations is discussed in [25] – perhaps surprisingly, some natural rewriting operations are not prunable, with the implication that it is not always possible to remove "redundant" conjunctive queries before termination of a rewriting algorithm. This is unfortunate, as removing such queries may help termination, and, as discussed in the following subsection, is also very useful from an optimality point of view.

4.4 A Note on Optimality of UCQ-Rewriting Algorithms

Let us finish this section by discussing the output of UCQ-rewriting algorithms. Let us assume that the same pair $(q, \mathcal{R})$ is given as input to two different UCQ-rewriting algorithms. How is it possible to compare the *quality* of their output?

Assuming that they respectively output q_1 and q_2, how can we say that one rewriting is better than the other? Naturally, one wants both rewritings to be sound and complete. A goal has as well been to try to *minimize* the size of the obtained rewritings (see for instance the evaluation of [24]), where by minimizing one means to output UCQ-rewritings that consists of as few conjunctive queries as possible. In this section, we study more precisely the structure of such minimal rewritings, and show that any sound and complete algorithm can be transformed, by some post-processing of its result, into an algorithm outputting an optimal rewriting (in terms of number of conjunctive queries in the output UCQ).

Proposition 3. *Let $\mathcal{R}$ be a set of existential rules, q be a conjunctive query that admits a finite sound and complete UCQ-rewriting $\mathcal{Q}$ with respect to $\mathcal{R}$. Any cover of $\mathcal{Q}$ is of minimal cardinality among sound and complete rewriting sets of q with respect to $\mathcal{R}$.*

Proof. Let $\mathcal{Q}_1$ and $\mathcal{Q}_2$ be two arbitrary finite sound and complete rewriting sets of q with respect to $\mathcal{R}$. Let $\mathcal{Q}_1^c$ (resp. $\mathcal{Q}_2^c$) be a cover of $\mathcal{Q}_1$ (resp. $\mathcal{Q}_2$). $\mathcal{Q}_1^c$ are also sound and complete, and are of smaller cardinality. We show that they have the same cardinality. Let $q_1 \in \mathcal{Q}_1^c$. There exists $q_2 \in \mathcal{Q}_2^c$ such that $q_1 \models q_2$. If not, q would be entailed by $F = q_1, \mathcal{R}$ since $\mathcal{Q}_1^c$ is a sound rewriting of q (and q_1 maps to itself), but no element of $\mathcal{Q}_2^c$ would map to F. This would show that $\mathcal{Q}_2^c$ is not complete, which is absurd. Similarly, there exists $q_1' \in \mathcal{Q}_1^c$ such that $q_2 \models q_1'$. Thus $q_1 \models q_1'$, which implies that $q_1' = q_1$, by definition of a cover. This implies that for any $q_1 \in \mathcal{Q}_1^c$, there exists an equivalent q_2 in $\mathcal{Q}_2^c$. Such a q_2 is unique (otherwise, this would violate the fact that $\mathcal{Q}_2^c$ is a cover). The function associating q_1 with q_2 is thus a bijection from $\mathcal{Q}_1^c$ to $\mathcal{Q}_2^c$, which shows that these two sets have the same cardinality.

5 Compacting Rewritings

Proposition 3 provides a way to define and compute the optimal UCQ-rewriting of a query that is UCQ-rewritable. In this section, we explore the consequences of this optimality for real-world ontologies, which mainly consists of role and concept hierarchies. It is thus of utmost importance to efficiently process such rules. After noticing that they may easily lead to UCQ-rewritings of unreasonable size, we introduce the query language of *semi-conjunctive queries*, and their union. Their expressive power is the same as of union of conjunctive queries, but they may be much more concise. We then revisit in Sect. 5.3 the theory of piece-unifiers to support semi-conjunctive queries (of a restricted shape), enabling us to get a rewriting algorithm with good properties.

5.1 A Common Source of Blow-Up

Hierarchies are ubiquitous in real world ontologies. Unfortunately, they tend to make the size of UCQ-rewritings drastically grow, as witnessed by the following example.

Example 7. Let $\mathcal{R}_n = \{R_i\}_{1 \leq i \leq n}$, where $R_i = r_i(x,y) \to r_{i-1}(x,y)$. Let q_n be the following query: $\bigwedge_{i=1}^{n} r_0(x_i, x_{i+1})$. The optimal UCQ-rewriting of q_n with respect to $\mathcal{R}_n$ contains $(n+1)^n$ conjunctive queries.

Proposition 3 implies that the above rewriting is indeed optimal with respect to UCQs, as this rewriting is its own cover, and each query in this UCQ is minimal. Hence, even in very simple and common cases, rewriting towards UCQs may lead to queries that are prohibitively large. Even for small values of n, the generated queries may be too large to be accepted as input by databases systems on which we want to evaluate it. This motivates the use of more expressive query languages as target. An interesting question would be to find out how concisely a target query language can express the rewriting of a query with respect to an ontology. This question has been (partially) studied for specific ontology languages and target query languages [10, 20].

5.2 Dealing with Hierarchies

The language we will focus on is called *unions of semi-conjunctive queries*. Intuitively, a semi-conjunctive query is very similar to a conjunctive query, except that each "atom" is now allowed to be a disjunction of atoms.

Definition 18. *A semi-conjunctive query (SCQ) is a closed logical formula of the form:*

$$\exists x\, D_1 \wedge D_2 \wedge \ldots D_n,$$

where D_i is a disjunction of atoms (for any i), and x is the set of variables that appear in the formula.

An SCQ s evaluates to true over an instance I if there exists π from var(s) to term(I) such that for any $D_i \in s$, there exists $a \in D_i$ such that $\pi(a) \in I$. SCQs are especially interesting to deal with hierarchies, as illustrated in the following example.

Example 8. Continuing Example 7, an SCQ-rewriting of q_n with respect to $\mathcal{R}_n$ is:

$$\bigwedge_{i=1}^{n} \bigvee_{j=0}^{n} r_j(x_i, x_{i+1}),$$

Any conjunctive query is a semi-conjunctive query, and a semi-conjunctive query is equivalent to a union of conjunctive queries – in particular, to the union of its *selections*, which is a conjunctive query obtained by choosing an atom in each disjunction of the semi-conjunctive query.

Definition 19 (Selection). *Let s be an SCQ. A selection of s is a conjunctive query $q = \bigwedge_{d \in s} i(d)$, where i is a function that maps each $d \in s$ to some $i(d) \in d$ (where d is considered as a set of atoms).*

Example 9 (Selection). Let $s = (r_0(x,y) \vee r_1(x,y)) \wedge (r_0(y,z) \vee r_1(y,z))$. s has four selections, which are:

- $r_0(x,y) \wedge r_0(y,z)$
- $r_0(x,y) \wedge r_1(y,z)$
- $r_1(x,y) \wedge r_0(y,z)$
- $r_1(x,y) \wedge r_1(y,z)$

We will need some restrictions on the considered semi-conjunctive queries to perform the technical development.

Definition 20 (Shared Variable). *Let s be an SCQ. A shared variable of s is a variable of two atoms a and b such that a and b belong to two different conjunctions of s.*

Definition 21 (Well-Formed SCQ). *An SCQ s is* well-formed *if for any shared variable x of s and any disjunction d of s, either x does not appear in d, or x is an argument of every atom of d.*

Example 10 (Well-Formed SCQs). $(r_0(x,y) \vee r_1(x,y)) \wedge (r_0(y,z) \vee r_1(y,z))$ is well-formed, as y is the only shared variable and appear in every atom. On the other hand, $(p(x) \vee r_1(x,y)) \wedge (r_0(y,z) \vee r_1(y,z))$ is not well-formed: y is shared and appears in the disjunction $(p(x) \vee r_1(x,y))$, but not in the atom $p(x)$.

We will only consider well-formed SCQs in the remaining of this presentation, without further mentioning it. This is not a restriction, as we rewrite conjunctive queries (which are well-formed SCQs), and our rewriting operations perserve well-formedness of SCQs.

5.3 Unification for SCQs

We now present the COMPACT algorithm, which uses a modified version of piece-based unifier to deal with union of semi-conjunctive queries rather than conjunctive queries.

Definition 22 (Piece-Unifier). *Let s be an SCQ and R be a rule. A piece-unifier of s with R is a triple $\mu = (s', q', u)$ with s' being a non empty subset of the disjunctions of s, q' a selection of s', and u a substitution of $\mathsf{fr}(R) \cup \mathsf{var}(s')$ by $\mathsf{term}(\mathsf{head}(R)) \cup \mathbf{C}$ such that:*

1. *for all $x \in \mathsf{fr}(R)$, $u(x) \in \mathsf{fr}(R) \cup \mathbf{C}$*
2. *for all $x \in \mathsf{sep}_s(s')$, $u(x) \in \mathsf{fr}(R) \cup \mathbf{C}$*
3. *$u(q') \subseteq u(\mathsf{head}(R))$*

where $\mathsf{sep}_s(s') = \mathsf{var}(s') \setminus \mathsf{var}(s \setminus s')$.

Example 11. Let $s = t(x_1, x_2) \wedge (s_1(x_1, x_3) \vee s(x_1, x_3)) \wedge (s_1(x_2, x_3) \vee s(x_2, x_3))$. $\mu = (s', q', u)$ is a unifier of s with $R_3 = f_1(x) \to s_1(x, y)$, where:

- $s' = (s_1(x_1, x_3) \lor s(x_1, x_3)) \land (s_1(x_2, x_3) \lor s(x_2, x_3))$
- $q' = s_1(x_1, x_3) \land s_1(x_2, x_3)$
- $u(x_1) = u(x_2) = u(x) = x, u(x_3) = u(y) = y$.

To define the result of a rewriting according to a piece-unifier for SCQs, we need to distinguish between two different cases for the considered unifier. The first one, and the most different with respect to classical piece-based rewriting, is when a unifier is *local*. Locality is a syntactic criteria which covers all the case of concept and role hierarchies. This leads to the introduction of disjunction in rewritings (in a way that is local to the considered disjunction, hence the name). Non-local unifiers are treated in a standard way.

Definition 23 (Local Unifier). *Let s be an SCQ, R be an atomic-body rule, and $\mu = (s', q', u)$ be a unifier of s with R. μ is local if q' is restricted to a single atom, and if the restriction of u to $\mathsf{term}(q')$ is injective and does not map a variable to a constant.*

Example 12. The unifier in Example 11 is not local, since two disjunctions are unified at one.

Let μ_L be the unifier of $s = t(x_1, x_2) \land (s_1(x_1, x_3) \lor s(x_1, x_3)) \land (s_1(x_2, x_3) \lor s(x_2, x_3))$ with $R_4 = t(x, y) \to r(y, x)$, defined by $\mu_L = (t(x_1, x_2), t(x_1, x_2), (u(x_1) = y, u(x_2) = x))$. μ_L is a local unifier.

In order to ensure that linear rewritings cannot lead (by themselves) to non-termination, we need one more technical definition, that of X-entailment.

Definition 24 (X-entailment). *Let I be a set of atoms, and X be a set of variables. Let a be an atom. a is X-entailed by I if there is a homomorphism π from a to I such that if $x \in \mathsf{var}(a) \cap X$, then $\pi(x) = x$.*

Example 13. Let $I = \{r(x, y), p(x, u)\}$. The atom $p(x, v)$ is $\{x\}$-entailed by I, but $r(y, x)$ is not.

We can now introduce the notion of local rewriting, which is the crucial part to define more concise rewritings than UCQs.

Definition 25 (Local Rewriting). *Let $s = \bigwedge_{i=1}^n d_i$ be an SCQ, R be an atomic-body rule and $\mu = (s' = \{d_k\}, q', u)$ be a local piece-unifier of R with s. The local rewriting of s with respect to R and μ (denoted by $\gamma_L(s, R, \mu)$) is $d'_k \land \bigwedge_{i \neq k} u(d_i)$, where $d'_k = u(d_k) \lor u(\mathsf{body}(R))$, if $u(\mathsf{body}(R))$ is not $\mathsf{sep}_{d'_k \land \bigwedge_{i \neq k} u(d_i)}(\{u(d_k)\})$-entailed by $u(d_k)$, and s otherwise. We define the natural bijection b between disjunctions of s and disjunctions of s' by $b(d_k) = d'_k$ and $b(d) = u(d)$ otherwise.*

Example 14. Let μ_L be the unifier of s with R_4 as defined in Example 12. The rewriting of s with respect to μ_L is:

$$(t(x_1, x_2) \lor t(x_2, x_1)) \land (s_1(x_1, x_3) \lor s(x_1, x_3)) \land (s_1(x_2, x_3) \lor s(x_2, x_3))$$

The other case is that of non-local unifiers. Note that a unifier is non-local (among other cases) whenever it unifies with a rule that does not have an atomic body. For non-local rewritings, the definition is basically the same as in the UCQ case: remove the unified parts of the query, and apply the substitution to the image of the body and to the non-unified part of the query.

Definition 26 (Non-Local Rewriting). *Let $s = \bigwedge_{i=1}^{n} d_i$ be an SCQ, R be a rule, and $\mu = (s' = \{d_1, \ldots, d_k\}, q', u)$ be a non-local unifier of R with s. The non-local rewriting of s with respect to R and μ (denoted by $\gamma_{NL}(s, R, \mu)$) is $u(\mathsf{body}(R)) \wedge \bigwedge_{i=k+1}^{n} u(d_i)$.*

Example 15. Let μ_{NL} be the unifier of $q_{NL} = t(x_1, x_2) \wedge (s_1(x_1, x_3) \vee s(x_1, x_3)) \wedge (s_1(x_2, x_3) \vee s(x_2, x_3))$ with $R_2 = f(x) \rightarrow \exists y \; s(x, y)$ defined by $\mu_{NL} = ((s(x_1, x_3) \vee s_1(x_1, x_3)) \wedge (s(x_2, x_3) \vee s_1(x_1, x_3)), s(x_1, x_3) \wedge s(x_2, s_3), u_{NL}(x_1) = u_{NL}(x_2) = x, u_{NL}(x_3) = y)$. μ_{NL} is not a local unifier, as it unifies two disjunctions at one. The rewriting of q_{NL} with respect to μ_{NL} is:

$$f(x) \wedge t(x, x).$$

5.4 The COMPACT Algorithm

Now that we have defined notions of unification and of rewriting of a semi-conjunctive query with respect to an existential rule, we can put things together to define a sound and complete rewriting algorithm. It is very similar to Algorithm 1, with the main difference being that queries are first *saturated* with respect to local unifiers before being rewritten according to non-local ones. An SCQ s is saturated with respect to local-unifiers if any local rewriting of s is equal to s. This saturation is doomed to exist by definition of local rewritings, because of the condition of non-X-entailment of the added atom.

We thus first introduce Algorithm 2, which computes the saturation of an SCQ with respect to local unifiers.

Data: An SCQ s, a set of existential rules $\mathcal{R}$
Result: A saturation of s with respect to local unifiers
$s_0 := \mathsf{null}$;
$s_n := s$;
while $s_0 \neq s_n$ **do**
$\quad s_0 := s_n$;
$\quad$ **for** *every rule $R \in \mathcal{R}$* **do**
$\quad\quad$ **for** *every local unifier μ of s_n with R* **do**
$\quad\quad\quad s_n := \gamma_L(s_n, R, \mu)$;
$\quad\quad$ **end**
$\quad$ **end**
end

Algorithm 2: LU-Saturation

We illustrate Algorithm 2 in Example 16.

Example 16. We apply Algorithm 2 on $q_e = t(x_1, x_2) \wedge s(x_1, x_3) \wedge s(x_2, x_3)$ and $\mathcal{R}_e$. $R_1 = p(x) \wedge h(x) \rightarrow s(x, y)$ has two atoms in its body, and thus no local unification is possible. Any unification of q_e with $R_2 = f(x) \rightarrow s(x, y)$ unifies x_3 with an existentially quantified variable, thus should unify two atoms at once, and thus no local unification of q_e with R_2 exists. $R_3 = f_1(x) \rightarrow s_1(x, y)$ does not generate atoms of relevant predicate. There is a local unifier of q_e with $R_4 = t(x, y) \rightarrow t(y, x)$, which unifies $t(x_1, x_2)$. This modifies s_n to:

$$(t(x_1, x_2) \vee t(x_2, x_1)) \wedge s(x_1, x_3) \wedge s(x_2, x_3).$$

Two further local unifications of s_n with $R_5 = s_1(x, y) \rightarrow s(x, y)$ exist, which leads to the SCQ:

$$(t(x_1, x_2) \vee t(x_2, x_1)) \wedge (s(x_1, x_3) \vee s_1(x_1, x_3)) \wedge (s(x_2, x_3) \vee s(x_2, x_3)).$$

It is easy to check that there are no further local unifiers.

Algorithm 3 uses LU-saturation as a subroutine. We illustrate the behavior of Algorithm 3 in Example 17.

Data: A CQ s (thus an SCQ), a set of existential rules $\mathcal{R}$
Result: A sound and complete USCQ-rewriting of s w.r.t. $\mathcal{R}$
$\mathcal{S}_F := \{s\}$;
$\mathcal{S}_E := \{s\}$;
while $\mathcal{S}_E \neq \emptyset$ do
$\quad \mathcal{S}_t := \emptyset$;
$\quad$ for *every* $s' \in \mathcal{S}_E$ do
$\quad\quad s' = \text{LU-SATURATION}(s', \mathcal{R})$;
$\quad\quad$ for *every rule* $R \in \mathcal{R}$ do
$\quad\quad\quad$ for *every non-local unifier* μ *of* s' *with* R do
$\quad\quad\quad\quad \mathcal{S}_t = \mathcal{S}_t \cup \gamma_{NL}(s', R, \mu)$
$\quad\quad\quad$ end
$\quad\quad$ end
$\quad$ end
$\quad \mathcal{S}_t = \text{cover}(\mathcal{S}_F \cup \mathcal{S}_t)$;
$\quad \mathcal{S}_E = \mathcal{S}_t \setminus \mathcal{S}_F$;
$\quad \mathcal{S}_F = \mathcal{S}_t$;
end
return $\mathcal{S}_F$;

Algorithm 3: Compact

Example 17. We run Algorithm 3 on q_e and $\mathcal{R}_e$. We first LU-saturate q_e, modifying it to

$$(t(x_1, x_2) \vee t(x_2, x_1)) \wedge (s(x_1, x_3) \vee s_1(x_1, x_3)) \wedge (s(x_2, x_3) \vee s(x_2, x_3)).$$

as explained in Example 16. We now create new SCQs, resulting from non-local unifications of q_e with some rule of $\mathcal{R}_e$. q_e is unifiable with $R_1 = h(x) \wedge q(x) \to s(x,y)$, by considering the selection $s(x_1, x_3) \wedge s(x_2, x_3)$. The resulting SCQ is $s_e^1 = h(x) \wedge q(x) \wedge t(x,x)$. By considering the same selection, q_e is unifiable with $R_2 = p(x) \to s(x,y)$, which results in $q_e^2 = p(x) \wedge t(x,x)$. q_e is unifiable with $R_3 = p_1(x) \to s_1(x,y)$ (with corresponding selection $s_1(x_1, x_3) \wedge s_1(x_2, x_3)$), resulting in $q_e^3 = p_1(x) \wedge t(x,x)$. Last, q_e is unifiable with R_5 with selection $s(x_1, x_3) \wedge s(x_2, x_3)$, resulting in $q_e^4 = s_1(x,y) \wedge t(x,x)$.

Algorithm 3 does not generate any further rewriting at this step. As q_e^4 is covered by q_e, q_e^4 is discarded. All other SCQs are pairwise incomparable, and no further unifications are possible: Algorithm 3 stops and output $\{q_e, q_e^1, q_e^2, q_e^3\}$.

The proof of soundness and completeness of Algorithm 3 is made by establishing links with piece-based unifiers, rather than directly linking them with the chase.

Lemma 1. *Let s be an SCQ, R be an existential rule, and μ be a unifier of s with R. Then for any selection q' of $\gamma_L(s, R, \mu)$ (or $\gamma_{NL}(s, R, \mu)$ if μ is not local), there exists a selection q of s such that q' is a rewriting of q.*

Lemma 2. *Let s be an SCQ, q be a selection of s, and R be a rule. For any rewriting q' of q with R, there exists a rewriting s' of s with R and a selection q'' of s' such that q' is equivalent to q''.*

Having these two lemmas in place, one can readily show the following.

Theorem 2. *Algorithm 3 computes a sound and complete rewriting for any query q and any rule set $\mathcal{R}$ whenever there exists a finite UCQ-rewriting.*

Non-Optimality with respect to the number of SCQs In the case of UCQs, we showed that Algorithm 1 outputs an optimal rewriting in terms of number of conjunctive queries. While this may not be a good evaluation criteria, as already discussed, it is still worth noting that this is not the case of Algorithm 3, as witnessed by the following example.

Example 18. Let $\mathcal{S}$ be a set of SCQs containing exactly the following queries:

- $(t(x_1, x_2) \vee t(x_2, x_1)) \wedge (s(x_1, x_3) \vee s_1(x_1, x_3)) \wedge (s(x_2, x_3) \vee s_1(x_2, x_3))$;
- $t(x,x) \wedge h(x) \wedge q(x)$;
- $t(x,x) \wedge (p(x) \vee p_1(x))$.

It is easy to check that $\mathcal{S}$ is equivalent to the output of COMPACT on the running example, but of strictly smaller cardinality in terms of SCQs in the disjunction.

It would still be interesting to try to generate as few SCQs as possible, given that the containment check between SCQs is quite costly – this is not a "simple" homomorphism check as in the case of CQs. The interested reader can consult [31], where a first such optimization is proposed, by considering only *prime* non local unifiers (which are unifiers that cannot be decomposed into a set of local unifiers).

6 Conclusion

We considered the problem of ontology-based query answering, which is a core problem in the setting of data integration through a logical layer. Whereas a classical approach relies on the materialization of all possible consequences, we focused on an approach based on query rewriting, which avoids some of the pitfalls dues to materialization. We presented two algorithms. First, we presented a piece-based rewriting algorithm, which computes a rewriting towards a union of conjunctive queries when a conjunctive query q and a rule set $\mathcal{R}$ is given as input, granted that such a finite rewriting exists. Upon the remark that large hierarchies of concepts and roles are ubiquitous in real-world ontologies, we then presented COMPACT, which deals specifically with such axioms to avoid a common source of combinatorial blow-up.

From a practical point of view, the optimization of such queries is still an open problem. Indeed, whereas a lot of work has been done in relational databases to perform efficiently joins, the interplay between join and unions that arises in union of conjunctive queries is beyond the capabilities of current optimizers. There is a huge potential for improvement, which has been partially explored [11]. From a more theoretical point of view, it would be interesting to delineate for which query languages similar algorithms can be devised, that is: for which query language $\mathcal{L}$ can we find an algorithm that is guaranteed to find an $\mathcal{L}$-rewriting of a query q with respect to a rule set $\mathcal{R}$ whenever such an $\mathcal{L}$-rewriting exist? Path-based query languages (see [33] for a survey), which has decidable query containment [16] and Datalog, which is a target for numerous rewriting algorithms [2,6,9,17,18,22,27] are a natural target for such questions.

Acknowledgments. The author thanks the anonymous reviewer for their numerous constructive comments.

References

1. Acciarri, A., et al.: Quonto: querying ontologies. In: Veloso, M.M., Kambhampati, S. (eds.) Proceedings, The Twentieth National Conference on Artificial Intelligence and the Seventeenth Innovative Applications of Artificial Intelligence Conference, July 9–13, 2005, Pittsburgh, Pennsylvania, USA, pp. 1670–1671. AAAI Press/The MIT Press (2005). http://www.aaai.org/Library/AAAI/2005/isd05-001.php
2. Ahmetaj, S., Ortiz, M., Simkus, M.: Rewriting guarded existential rules into small datalog programs. In: Kimelfeld, B., Amsterdamer, Y. (eds.) 21st International Conference on Database Theory, ICDT 2018, March 26–29, 2018, Vienna, Austria. LIPIcs, vol. 98, pp. 4:1–4:24. Schloss Dagstuhl - Leibniz-Zentrum für Informatik (2018). https://doi.org/10.4230/LIPICS.ICDT.2018.4
3. Baader, F.: Terminological cycles in a description logic with existential restrictions. In: Gottlob, G., Walsh, T. (eds.) IJCAI-03, Proceedings of the Eighteenth International Joint Conference on Artificial Intelligence, Acapulco, Mexico, August 9–15, 2003, pp. 325–330. Morgan Kaufmann (2003). http://ijcai.org/Proceedings/03/Papers/048.pdf

4. Baader, F., Calvanese, D., McGuinness, D.L., Nardi, D., Patel-Schneider, P.F. (eds.): The Description Logic Handbook: Theory, Implementation, and Applications. Cambridge University Press (2003)
5. Baget, J., Leclère, M., Mugnier, M., Salvat, E.: On rules with existential variables: walking the decidability line. Artif. Intell. **175**(9–10), 1620–1654 (2011). https://doi.org/10.1016/j.artint.2011.03.002
6. Bárány, V., Benedikt, M., ten Cate, B.: Rewriting guarded negation queries. In: Chatterjee, K., Sgall, J. (eds.) Mathematical Foundations of Computer Science 2013 - 38th International Symposium, MFCS 2013, Klosterneuburg, Austria, August 26–30, 2013. Proceedings. Lecture Notes in Computer Science, vol. 8087, pp. 98–110. Springer (2013https://doi.org/10.1007/978-3-642-40313-2_11
7. Beeri, C., Vardi, M.Y.: The implication problem for data dependencies. In: Even, S., Kariv, O. (eds.) Automata, Languages and Programming, 8th Colloquium, Acre (Akko), Israel, July 13–17, 1981, Proceedings. Lecture Notes in Computer Science, vol. 115, pp. 73–85. Springer (1981https://doi.org/10.1007/3-540-10843-2_7
8. Beeri, C., Vardi, M.Y.: A proof procedure for data dependencies. J. ACM **31**(4), 718–741 (1984). https://doi.org/10.1145/1634.1636
9. Berger, G., Gottlob, G., Pieris, A., Sallinger, E.: The space-efficient core of vadalog. ACM Trans. Database Syst. **47**(1), 1:1–1:46 (2022). https://doi.org/10.1145/3488720
10. Bienvenu, M., Kikot, S., Kontchakov, R., Podolskii, V.V., Zakharyaschev, M.: Ontology-mediated queries: combined complexity and succinctness of rewritings via circuit complexity. J. ACM **65**(5), 28:1–28:51 (2018). https://doi.org/10.1145/3191832
11. Bursztyn, D., Goasdoué, F., Manolescu, I.: Teaching an RDBMS about ontological constraints. Proc. VLDB Endow. **9**(12), 1161–1172 (2016). https://doi.org/10.14778/2994509.2994532, http://www.vldb.org/pvldb/vol9/p1161-bursztyn.pdf
12. Calì, A., Gottlob, G., Kifer, M.: Taming the infinite chase: query answering under expressive relational constraints. J. Artif. Intell. Res. **48**, 115–174 (2013). https://doi.org/10.1613/jair.3873
13. Calì, A., Gottlob, G., Lukasiewicz, T.: A general datalog-based framework for tractable query answering over ontologies. J. Web Semant. **14**, 57–83 (2012). https://doi.org/10.1016/J.WEBSEM.2012.03.001
14. Calì, A., Gottlob, G., Pieris, A.: Query rewriting under non-guarded rules. In: Laender, A.H.F., Lakshmanan, L.V.S. (eds.) Proceedings of the 4th Alberto Mendelzon International Workshop on Foundations of Data Management, Buenos Aires, Argentina, May 17–20, 2010. CEUR Workshop Proceedings, vol. 619. CEUR-WS.org (2010). https://ceur-ws.org/Vol-619/paper12.pdf
15. Calvanese, D., De Giacomo, G., Lembo, D., Lenzerini, M., Rosati, R.: Tractable reasoning and efficient query answering in description logics: the DL-Lite family. J. Autom. Reason. **39**(3), 385–429 (2007). https://doi.org/10.1007/s10817-007-9078-x
16. Calvanese, D., De Giacomo, G., Lenzerini, M., Vardi, M.Y.: Containment of conjunctive regular path queries with inverse. In: Cohn, A.G., Giunchiglia, F., Selman, B. (eds.) KR 2000, Principles of Knowledge Representation and Reasoning Proceedings of the Seventh International Conference, Breckenridge, Colorado, USA, April 11–15, 2000, pp. 176–185. Morgan Kaufmann (2000)
17. Carral, D., Dragoste, I., Krötzsch, M.: The combined approach to query answering in horn-alchoiq. In: Thielscher, M., Toni, F., Wolter, F. (eds.) Principles of Knowledge Representation and Reasoning: Proceedings of the Sixteenth International Conference, KR 2018, Tempe, Arizona, 30 October–2 November 2018, pp.

339–348. AAAI Press (2018). https://aaai.org/ocs/index.php/KR/KR18/paper/view/18076
18. Carral, D., González, L., Koopmann, P.: From horn-sriq to datalog: a data-independent transformation that preserves assertion entailment. In: The Thirty-Third AAAI Conference on Artificial Intelligence, AAAI 2019, The Thirty-First Innovative Applications of Artificial Intelligence Conference, IAAI 2019, The Ninth AAAI Symposium on Educational Advances in Artificial Intelligence, EAAI 2019, Honolulu, Hawaii, USA, January 27–February 1, 2019, pp. 2736–2743. AAAI Press (2019). https://doi.org/10.1609/AAAI.V33I01.33012736
19. Carral, D., Larroque, L., Mugnier, M., Thomazo, M.: Normalisations of existential rules: not so innocuous! In: Kern-Isberner, G., Lakemeyer, G., Meyer, T. (eds.) Proceedings of the 19th International Conference on Principles of Knowledge Representation and Reasoning, KR 2022, Haifa, Israel, July 31–August 5, 2022 (2022). https://proceedings.kr.org/2022/11/
20. Gottlob, G., Kikot, S., Kontchakov, R., Podolskii, V.V., Schwentick, T., Zakharyaschev, M.: The price of query rewriting in ontology-based data access. Artif. Intell. **213**, 42–59 (2014). https://doi.org/10.1016/j.artint.2014.04.004
21. Gottlob, G., Orsi, G., Pieris, A.: Query rewriting and optimization for ontological databases. ACM Trans. Database Syst. **39**(3), 25:1–25:46 (2014). https://doi.org/10.1145/2638546
22. Gottlob, G., Schwentick, T.: Rewriting ontological queries into small nonrecursive datalog programs. In: Brewka, G., Eiter, T., McIlraith, S.A. (eds.) Principles of Knowledge Representation and Reasoning: Proceedings of the Thirteenth International Conference, KR 2012, Rome, Italy, June 10–14, 2012. AAAI Press (2012). http://www.aaai.org/ocs/index.php/KR/KR12/paper/view/4510
23. Grahne, G., Onet, A.: Anatomy of the chase. Fundam. Informaticae **157**(3), 221–270 (2018). https://doi.org/10.3233/FI-2018-1627
24. Imprialou, M., Stoilos, G., Grau, B.C.: Benchmarking ontology-based query rewriting systems. In: Hoffmann, J., Selman, B. (eds.) Proceedings of the Twenty-Sixth AAAI Conference on Artificial Intelligence, July 22–26, 2012, Toronto, Ontario, Canada, pp. 779–785. AAAI Press (2012). https://doi.org/10.1609/AAAI.V26I1.8215
25. König, M., Leclère, M., Mugnier, M., Thomazo, M.: Sound, complete and minimal UCQ-rewriting for existential rules. Semantic Web **6**(5), 451–475 (2015). https://doi.org/10.3233/SW-140153
26. Leclère, M., Mugnier, M., Ulliana, F.: On bounded positive existential rules. In: Lenzerini, M., Peñaloza, R. (eds.) Proceedings of the 29th International Workshop on Description Logics, Cape Town, South Africa, April 22–25, 2016. CEUR Workshop Proceedings, vol. 1577. CEUR-WS.org (2016). https://ceur-ws.org/Vol-1577/paper_31.pdf
27. Marnette, B.: Resolution and datalog rewriting under value invention and equality constraints. CoRR arXiv:1212.0254 (2012)
28. Pérez-Urbina, H., Horrocks, I., Motik, B.: Efficient query answering for OWL 2. In: Bernstein, A., et al. (eds.) The Semantic Web - ISWC 2009, 8th International Semantic Web Conference, ISWC 2009, Chantilly, VA, USA, October 25–29, 2009. Proceedings. Lecture Notes in Computer Science, vol. 5823, pp. 489–504. Springer (2009). https://doi.org/10.1007/978-3-642-04930-9_31
29. Rossman, B.: Homomorphism preservation theorems. J. ACM **55**(3), 15:1–15:53 (2008). https://doi.org/10.1145/1379759.1379763
30. Shmueli, O.: Equivalence of DATALOG queries is undecidable. J. Log. Program. **15**(3), 231–241 (1993). https://doi.org/10.1016/0743-1066(93)90040-N

31. Thomazo, M.: Conjunctive query answering under existential rules - decidability, complexity, and algorithms. Ph. D. thesis, Montpellier 2 University, France (2013). https://tel.archives-ouvertes.fr/tel-00925722
32. Trivela, D., Stoilos, G., Chortaras, A., Stamou, G.: Resolution-based rewriting for horn-SHIQ ontologies. Knowl. Inf. Syst. **62**(1), 107–143 (2020). https://doi.org/10.1007/S10115-019-01345-2
33. Wood, P.T.: Query languages for graph databases. SIGMOD Rec. **41**(1), 50–60 (2012). https://doi.org/10.1145/2206869.2206879

Finite-Model Reasoning for Graph Queries and Description Logics

Filip Murlak[✉]

University of Warsaw, Warsaw, Poland
f.murlak@uw.edu.pl

Abstract. The task of query entailment consists in determining if a given query holds in every extension of a given structure that satisfies a given set of constraints. In knowledge representation, traditionally, this includes both finite and infinite extensions. In many contexts, however, it is desirable to consider only finite extensions. In this tutorial we present a handful of techniques that can be used to move from the unrestricted to the finite case. We illustrate these techniques by proving a series of decidability results for various classes of queries, ultimately arriving at unions of conjunctive regular path queries, which are the theoretical core of practical graph query languages. For the constraint language we use description logics, which are popular ontology formalisms used in knowledge representation and are capable of expressing most constraints relevant in graph databases. The methods we discuss are applicable to various description logics, but for the simplicity of the exposition we work with the basic logic $\mathcal{ALC}$.

Keywords: Conjunctive regular path queries · Query entailment · Description logics · Finite-model reasoning

1 Introduction

Some of the fundamental problems in database theory and knowledge representation can be seen as instances of the query entailment problem. While *query evaluation* asks whether a given query holds in a given structure, in the task of *query entailment* one needs to determine if the query holds in every model of a given theory that extends the given structure. The input structure represents the raw data, as stored in a database; the theory captures the context of the problem, such as a set of database constraints or an ontology; and the query extracts specific information.

The recent proliferation of graph databases has brought the database community and the knowledge representation community closer together, as some of the key problems studied in these communities involve the same structures—labelled graphs—and the same or very similar combinations of formalisms for theories

---

Supported by NCN grant 2018/30/E/ST6/00042.

© The Author(s), under exclusive license to Springer Nature Switzerland AG 2025
M. Console and B. Konev (Eds.): Reasoning Web. Declarative Artificial Intelligence: Knowledge, Rules, Logic, LNCS 15400, pp. 23–53, 2025.
https://doi.org/10.1007/978-3-031-80283-6_2

and queries. One such combination is description logics and conjunctive regular path queries. Description logics [1] are a family of formalisms based on fragments of first order logic, akin to modal logics; they are among the most prominent ontology languages and they are capable of expressing most constraints relevant in graph databases. Conjunctive regular path queries [3] are an extension of conjunctive queries (primitive positive first-order formulas) in which regular expressions over binary predicates can be used as atoms; they are the core of practical query languages used in the Semantic Web and in graph databases.

What distinguishes the two communities is the approach to infinity: knowledge representation embraces infinite models, whereas database theory focuses on finite models. While many problems have been solved over unrestricted models long ago, their finite-model counterparts have seen progress only recently and many questions remain open. This tutorial presents key techniques behind this progress [6–10] and discusses current challenges.

2 Preliminaries

2.1 Graphs

We fix an enumerable set Γ of node labels and an enumerable set Σ of edge labels. We model graph databases as labeled directed graphs in which nodes can have multiple labels, while edges have a single label. Parallel edges are allowed, as long as they have different labels.

We present such graphs as relational structures over unary relation symbols Γ and binary relation symbols Σ. That is, a graph G is a pair $\bigl(dom(G), \cdot^G\bigr)$ where $dom(G)$ is the set of nodes of G and the function $\cdot^G$ maps each $A \in \Gamma$ to a set $A^G \subseteq dom(G)$ and each $r \in \Sigma$ to a binary relation $r^G \subseteq dom(G) \times dom(G)$. A node v *has label* A iff $v \in A^G$ and *node u is an r-successor of node v* iff $(v, u) \in r^G$.

Graph G is *finite* if $dom(G)$ is finite and A^G and r^G are empty for all but finitely many $A \in \Gamma$ and $r \in \Sigma$.

Graph G is a *subgraph* of graph G', written $G \subseteq G'$, if $dom(G) \subseteq dom(G')$, $A^G \subseteq A^{G'}$ and $r^G \subseteq r^{G'}$ for all $A \in \Gamma$ and $r \in \Sigma$.

The *restriction* of graph G to $U \subseteq dom(G)$ is the subgraph G' of G such that $dom(G') = U$, and $A^{G'} = A^G \cap U$, $r^{G'} = r^G \cap (U \times U)$ for all $A \in \Gamma$ and $r \in \Sigma$.

We use $\bar{A}$ for *complement node labels*: we say a node has label $\bar{A}$ iff it does not have label A and let $\bar{A}^G = dom(G) \setminus A^G$, $\Gamma_0^- = \{\bar{A} \mid A \in \Gamma_0\}$, $\Gamma_0^\pm = \Gamma_0 \cup \Gamma_0^-$ for every $\Gamma_0 \subseteq \Gamma$.

2.2 Queries

Let $\mathcal{V}$ be an enumerable set of variables. We work with *conjunctive regular path queries* (CRPQs) of the form

$$q = A_1(x_1) \wedge \cdots \wedge A_k(x_k) \wedge \varphi_1(y_1, z_1) \wedge \ldots \wedge \varphi_m(y_m, z_m),$$

where $x_1, \ldots, x_k, y_1, \ldots, y_m, z_1, \ldots, z_m \in \mathcal{V}$, $A_1, \ldots, A_k \in \Gamma^\pm$, and $\varphi_1, \ldots, \varphi_m$ are regular expressions over the alphabet $\Gamma^\pm \cup \Sigma$, using concatenation, union, and Kleene star. We write $var(q)$ for the set of variables used in q.

A *match* of q in a graph G is a function $\pi \colon var(q) \to dom(G)$ such that for every atom $A(x)$ in q, $\pi(x) \in A^G$, and for every atom $\varphi(y, z)$ in q there are $\ell_1, \ldots, \ell_n \in \Gamma^\pm \cup \Sigma$, and $v_0, \ldots, v_n \in dom(G)$ for some $n \in \mathbb{N}$ such that

1. $v_0 = \pi(y)$ and $v_n = \pi(z)$;
2. for all $i \in \{1, \ldots, n\}$, either $\ell_i \in \Sigma$ and $(v_{i-1}, v_i) \in (\ell_i)^G$ or $\ell_i \in \Gamma^\pm$ and $v_{i-1} = v_i \in (\ell_i)^G$;
3. the word $\ell_1 \ldots \ell_n$ matches the regular expression φ.

We say that q is *satisfied* in G and write $G \models q$ if there is a match of q in G. We also use *unions* of CRPQs (abbreviated as UCRPQs) represented as sets of CRPQs $Q = \{q_1, \ldots, q_k\}$ and extend the notion of satisfaction to UCRPQs in the natural fashion. We write Γ_Q and Σ_Q for the sets of node and edge labels used in Q. By regular path queries, abbreviated as RPQs, we mean binary atoms of CRPQs. A query is *test-free* if it does not use labels from $\Gamma^\pm$ in regular expressions. A query is *simple* if it only uses regular expressions of the forms r and $(r_1 + r_2 + \cdots + r_n)^*$ with $r, r_1, r_2, \ldots, r_n \in \Sigma$.

2.3 Description Logics

We work with graph properties expressed in the *description logic* $\mathcal{ALC}$ [1]. In description logics, elements of Γ and Σ are called *concept names* and *role names*, respectively. $\mathcal{ALC}$ allows building more complex concepts with the following grammar:

$$C ::= \bot \mid \top \mid A \mid \neg C \mid C \sqcap C \mid C \sqcup C \mid \exists r.C \mid \forall r.C,$$

where $A \in \Gamma^\pm$, $r \in \Sigma$, and $n \in \mathbb{N}$. We extend the interpretation function $\cdot^G$ to complex concepts as follows:

$$\bot^G = \emptyset, \quad \top^G = dom(G), \quad (\neg C)^G = dom(G) \setminus C^G,$$
$$(C_1 \sqcap C_2)^G = C_1^G \cap C_2^G, \quad (C_1 \sqcup C_2)^G = C_1^G \cup C_2^G,$$
$$(\exists r.C)^G = \{u \in dom(G) \mid \text{some } r\text{-successor of } u \text{ has label } C\},$$
$$(\forall r.C)^G = \{u \in dom(G) \mid \text{all } r\text{-successors of } u \text{ have label } C\}.$$

Statements in description logics have the form of *concept inclusions (CIs)*,

$$C \sqsubseteq D$$

where C and D are concepts. A graph G *satisfies* $C \sqsubseteq D$, in symbols $G \models C \sqsubseteq D$, if $C^G \subseteq D^G$. A set $\mathcal{T}$ of CIs is traditionally called a *TBox*. We write $\Gamma_\mathcal{T}$ and $\Sigma_\mathcal{T}$ for the sets of concept and role names used in $\mathcal{T}$. A graph G *satisfies* $\mathcal{T}$, written as $G \models \mathcal{T}$, if $G \models C \sqsubseteq D$ for each $C \sqsubseteq D \in \mathcal{T}$. A node v in G *satisfies* $C \sqsubseteq D$ if $v \in C^G$ implies $v \in D^G$; v *satisfies* $\mathcal{T}$ if it satisfies each $C \sqsubseteq D \in \mathcal{T}$.

An $\mathcal{ALC}$ TBox can be *normalized*; that is, up to introducing auxiliary concept names, it can be expressed equivalently in the same logic using only CIs of the forms
$$K \sqsubseteq L, \quad A \sqsubseteq \exists r.B, \quad A \sqsubseteq \forall r.B,$$
where $A, B \in \Gamma^{\pm}$, $r \in \Sigma$, K is $\top$ or an intersection of concept names and complement concept names, and L is $\bot$ or a union of concept names and complement concept names (see e.g. [11, Prop. 1]). CIs of the form $A \sqsubseteq \exists r.B$ are called *participation constraints*. For a normalized TBox $\mathcal{T}$, we write $\mathcal{T}_\exists$ for the set of all participation constraints in $\mathcal{T}$, and $\mathcal{T}_\forall$ for $\mathcal{T} \setminus \mathcal{T}_\exists$.

Example 1. Suppose that we represent family relations using node labels Person, Parent, Male, Female, Mother, Father and edge label childOf. Then, the following TBox states that all males and females are persons, all fathers and mothers are parents, each person is a child of a person, a person that has a child is a parent, male parents are fathers, and female parents are mothers, fathers are male, and mothers are female:

$$\begin{aligned}
\text{Male} \sqcup \text{Female} &\sqsubseteq \text{Person}, & \text{Male} \sqcap \text{Parent} &\sqsubseteq \text{Father}, \\
\text{Father} \sqcup \text{Mother} &\sqsubseteq \text{Parent}, & \text{Female} \sqcap \text{Parent} &\sqsubseteq \text{Mother}, \\
\text{Person} &\sqsubseteq \exists\text{childOf.Person}, & \text{Father} &\sqsubseteq \text{Male}, \\
\top &\sqsubseteq \forall\text{childOf.Parent}, & \text{Mother} &\sqsubseteq \text{Female}.
\end{aligned}$$

The TBox is not in the normal form, but it is very easy to normalize it: it suffices to split Male $\sqcup$ Female $\sqsubseteq$ Person into Male $\sqsubseteq$ Person and Female $\sqsubseteq$ Person, and similarly for Father $\sqcup$ Mother $\sqsubseteq$ Parent.

Note that the TBox above says neither that each person is a male or a female, nor that a person cannot be both. These constraints could be expressed using

$$\text{Person} \sqsubseteq \text{Male} \sqcup \text{Female} \quad \text{and} \quad \text{Male} \sqcap \text{Female} \sqsubseteq \bot.$$

The TBox also does not say that a child of a person is a person. This could be expressed using
$$\exists\text{childOf.Person} \sqsubseteq \text{Person}.$$

This CI is not in the normal form, but it can be equivalently expressed as

$$\overline{\text{Person}} \sqsubseteq \forall\text{childOf.}\overline{\text{Person}}.$$

Finally, the TBox does not say that every parent has a child. This is not expressible in $\mathcal{ALC}$, but it becomes expressible if we extend $\mathcal{ALC}$ with the ability to speak about inverse edges. We would then write Parent $\sqsubseteq \exists\text{childOf}^-.\top$. This extension yields a logic called $\mathcal{ALCI}$, one of a rich family of description logics build upon $\mathcal{ALC}$ (more about them in Sect. 9). ◂

2.4 Graph Homomorphisms and Simple Preservation Properties

A *homomorphism* h from graph G to graph G', written $h : G \to G'$, is a function $h : dom(G) \to dom(G')$ such that $u \in A^G$ iff $h(u) \in A^{G'}$ and $(u,v) \in r^G$ implies $(h(u), h(v)) \in r^{G'}$ for all $u, v \in dom(G)$, $A \in \Gamma$, and $r \in \Sigma$. That is, h preserves the presence of edges and both the presence and the absence of node labels. Graph G *maps homomorphically* into graph G', written $G \to G'$, if there exists a homomorphism from G to G'. Note that a subgraph G of graph G' does not necessarily map homomorphically into G', because in G' nodes may have additional labels.

Graph homomorphisms, as defined here, have some relatively strong preservation properties, which we now briefly discuss. The first one is a direct consequence of the definition, but it is nevertheless worth formulating explicitly, as we will be relying on it throughout the paper. It involves the notion of type, defined below.

A *type* is a finite subset of $\Gamma^{\pm}$ that contains at most one of A and $\bar{A}$ for all $A \in \Gamma$. A *type over* $\Gamma_0 \subseteq \Gamma$ is a type that is a subset of $\Gamma_0^{\pm}$. A node u *is of type* τ *in* G if $u \in A^G$ for all $A \in \tau$. In particular, every node is of type $\emptyset$.

Lemma 1. *For every homomoghism $h : G \to G'$, type τ, and node v in G,*

$$v \text{ is of type } \tau \text{ in } G \quad \textit{iff} \quad h(v) \text{ is of type } \tau \text{ in } G'.$$

From Lemma 1 it follows immediately that homomorphisms preserve concept inclusions of the from $K \sqsubseteq L$, where K and L do not involve edge labels:

$$v \text{ satisfies } K \sqsubseteq L \quad \textit{iff} \quad h(v) \text{ satisfies } K \sqsubseteq L.$$

We also have the following global preservation properties, but this time only one implication holds.

Lemma 2. *If $G \to G'$, then*

- *$G' \not\models Q$ implies $G \not\models Q$ for every UCRPQ Q;*
- *$G' \models \mathcal{T}_\forall$ implies $G \models \mathcal{T}_\forall$ for every $\mathcal{ALC}$ TBox $\mathcal{T}$.*

3 The Entailment Problem

Given a finite graph G, a TBox $\mathcal{T}$, and a query Q, we say that Q is *entailed* by G and $\mathcal{T}$, written as

$$G, \mathcal{T} \models Q,$$

if $G' \models Q$ for every graph G' such that $G' \models \mathcal{T}$ and $G \subseteq G'$. A *counter-model* for $G, \mathcal{T}$, and Q is a graph H such that $H \supseteq G$, $H \models \mathcal{T}$, and $H \not\models Q$. That is, $G, \mathcal{T} \models Q$ iff there is no counter-model for $G, \mathcal{T}$, and Q. We say that Q is *finitely entailed* by G and $\mathcal{T}$, written as

$$G, \mathcal{T} \models_{fin} Q,$$

if there is no *finite* counter-model. (The traditional formulation uses a finite set of ground facts, called the ABox, instead of G.)

Example 2. Does the TBox $\mathcal{T} = \{\text{Person} \sqsubseteq \exists\,\text{childOf}.\,\text{Person}\}$ model reality well? Suppose we know that at least one person exists; that is, the input graph G consists of a single node v with label Person. Then, over finite models we can conclude that somebody is their own ancestor,

$$G, \mathcal{T} \models_{\text{fin}} \exists x\ \text{childOf}^+(x, x)\,,$$

because in every finite extension G' of G that satisfies $\mathcal{T}$, following the childOf edges starting from v we will close a cycle at some point. Over unrestricted models, on the other hand, the query is not entailed,

$$G, \mathcal{T} \not\models \exists x\ \text{childOf}^+(x, x)\,,$$

because the infinite chain of childOf edges starting in v is an extension of G' that satisfies $\mathcal{T}$, yet does not satisfy the query. Should we then embrace infinite models or rethink our modelling?

This example is intentionally paradoxical. From two apparent truths ("Every person is a child of a person" and "There has been only finitely many persons") it derives an apparent falsity ("Somebody is their own ancestor"). One might be tempted to interpret this as an argument in favour of reasoning over unrestricted models. However, it is actually the first of these "truths" that is at fault. In the tree of life, the transition between different species is the effect of gradual changes caused by accumulating genetic mutations guided by natural selection. If we could backtrack from any living person through the generations of their ancestors, we would see these gradual changes reverting, leading to organizms we would no longer recognize as persons. Eventually, we would see forms of life for which even the notion of child is vague.

Thus, finite model reasoning allowed us to identify a modelling error. The error is unexpected, because the faulty assertion actually holds *locally*. Indeed, we would not be able to detect the difference between finite and unrestricted models using local queries, such as conjunctive queries (we prove this in Sect. 6). CRPQs, however, are not local and if we want to use them, we have to distinguish between finite and unrestricted models. ◂

The *entailment problem* is to decide if $G, \mathcal{T} \models Q$ for given G, $\mathcal{T}$, and Q. The *finite entailment problem* is to decide if $G, \mathcal{T} \models_{\textit{fin}} Q$ for given G, $\mathcal{T}$, and Q. Throughout the paper we will be focusing on decidability, not worrying about the complexity of the described algorithms. This will allow us to keep the arguments relatively high-level without resorting to hand-waving.

While the objective of this paper is to showcase key techniques in finite entailment, it is beneficial to the reader's morale to set ourselves a concrete goal. We will be aiming at the following theorem.

Theorem 1. *The finite entailment problem for UCRPQs and $\mathcal{ALC}$ is decidable.*

We achieve this goal in 5 steps, each illustrating a different technique:

- in Sect. 4 we show how to eliminate the input graph by replacing it with a single node, for both finite and unrestricted entailment;

- in Sect. 5 we solve unrestricted entailment of UCRPQs;
- in Sect. 6 we solve finite entailment of UCQs, by reduction to unrestricted entailment of UCQs;
- in Sect. 7 we solve finite entailment of simple UCRPQs, by reduction to finite entailment of UCQs;
- in Sect. 8 we solve finite entailment of UCRPQs, by reduction to finite entailment of simple UCRPQs.

Before we move on to the first step of the plan, let us make a small preliminary simplification step. We call a CRPQ *connected* if for every pair of variables there is a path of binary atoms connecting them. By a *connected component* of a CRPQ q we mean a maximal connected subquery of q. Connected components of q form a partition of the atoms of q, with different connected components using disjoint sets of variables. Every CRPQ is equivalent to the conjunction of its connected components and every UCRPQ Q is equivalent to the conjunction of all UCRPQs $Q_1, \ldots, Q_m$ that can be obtained by picking exactly one connected component from each CRPQ in Q. In consequence,

$$G, \mathcal{T} \models Q \quad \text{iff} \quad G, \mathcal{T} \models Q_i \text{ for all } i = 1, 2, \ldots, m$$

and similarly for $\models_{fin}$. Hence, from now on we focus on (unions of) connected CRPQs.

4 Handling Data: Star-Like Graphs and Factorization

As a first step of our five-point plan we eliminate the input graph from the problem. More precisely, we reduce the general problem to a special case involving only input graphs consisting of a single isolated node. For convenience, we assume that the input is a unary type, rather than a node. This gives us some additional flexibility, because τ can also contain complement node labels.

A graph *realizes* type τ if it contains a node of type τ. We write

$$\tau, \mathcal{T} \models Q$$

if every graph that realizes τ and satisfies $\mathcal{T}$ also satisfies Q. Similarly,

$$\tau, \mathcal{T} \models_{fin} Q$$

if every finite graph that realizes τ and satisfies $\mathcal{T}$ also satisfies Q.

To reduce to the special case we apply the following general strategy:

1. show that if there is any counter-model, there is also one of a special shape;
2. show how to find counter-models of the special shape.

Star-Like Graphs

A *star-like* graph H consists of k disjoint graphs $H_1, \ldots, H_k$ (called *peripheral parts*) and a graph H^0 (called *the central part*) that shares exactly one node with each H_i for $i = 1, \ldots, k$ and the shared node has identical labels in both parts.

Proposition 1 (star-like counter-model property). *For every finite graph G, $\mathcal{ALC}$ TBox $\mathcal{T}$, and UCRPQ Q, $G, \mathcal{T} \not\models Q$ iff some star-like graph whose central part is G, possibly with additional node labels, is a counter-model.*

Proof. Suppose that $G, \mathcal{T} \not\models Q$. Then there is G' such that $G' \supseteq G$, $G' \models \mathcal{T}$, and $G' \not\models Q$. Consider the star-like graph H defined as follows. For the central part we take graph G, but for each node v in G we include all labels that v has in G'. Then, for each node v in G, we add as a peripheral part an isomorphic copy of G' with v as the unique shared node. Clearly, $H \to G'$. By Lemma 2, $H \not\models Q$ and $H \models \mathcal{T}_\forall$. For a participation constraint $A \sqsubseteq \exists r.B$ in $\mathcal{T}$, note that each node in H belongs to a peripheral part, and each peripheral part satisfies $\mathcal{T}$, because it is an isomorphic copy of G'. Hence, for each node with label A we will find a witnessing r-successor with label B. Thus, $H \models \mathcal{T}$. □

In order to decide if such a star-like counter-model H exists, we separate the existence of the central part from the existence of suitable peripheral parts. To this end, we replace global conditions $H \models \mathcal{T}$ and $H \not\models Q$ with local conditions over parts of H. We refer to this technique as *factorizing* the TBox $\mathcal{T}$ and the query Q. Factorizing the TBox is easy, but the query requires some work.

Factorizing the TBox

Rather than working with star-like graphs, we introduce a more general notion, which will come handy later.

A *bubble cover* of a graph G is a set of induced subgraphs of G, called *bubbles*, such that the union of all bubbles is G and every two bubbles share at most one node. The *bubble graph* of a bubble cover is an undirected graph whose nodes are the bubbles, and two bubbles are adjacent iff they are not disjoint. A bubble cover is *acyclic* if its bubble graph is acyclic, and *connected* if its bubble graph is connected. The bubble graph of a connected acyclic bubble cover is a tree; in such case we use the term *bubble tree*. The parts of a star-like graph G constitute a connected acyclic bubble cover of G: the central part is the only internal node in the corresponding bubble tree and the peripheral parts are leaves.

Lemma 3. *For an $\mathcal{ALC}$ TBox $\mathcal{T}$, a graph G, and a bubble cover of G, $G \models \mathcal{T}$ iff every bubble satisfies $\mathcal{T}_\forall$ and every node in G satisfies each participation constraint in $\mathcal{T}$ in at least one of the bubbles that contain it.*

Proof. We prove the right-to-left implication by contraposition. That is, we assume that $G \not\models \mathcal{T}$ and show that the bubble cover does not satisfy the condition in the statement of the lemma. We consider three cases.

Suppose that a CI of the form $K \sqsubseteq L$ is violated in G. Then some node in G does not satisfy the CI. This node belongs to some bubble and has the same labels in the bubble as in the whole graph G. Hence, the node does not satisfy the CI in the bubble either.

Similarly, suppose that a CI of the form $A \sqsubseteq \forall r.B$ is not satisfied in G. Then, there is an r-edge in G from a node with label A to a node without label B. This edge belongs to some bubble, which in consequence does not satisfy the CI either.

Finally, suppose that a CI of the form $A \sqsubseteq \exists r.B$ is not satisfied in G. Then, there exists a node v with label A that has no r-successor with label B in G. But then the same is true in every bubble that contains v. Hence, v does not satisfy the CI in any bubble.

This completes the proof of the right-to-left implication. For the converse implication the argument is similar. □

Factorizing the Query

A query Q is *factorized* if for every two graphs G_1 and G_2 sharing a single node (with identical labels in both graphs),

$$G_1 \cup G_2 \models Q \quad \text{iff} \quad G_1 \models Q \text{ or } G_2 \models Q.$$

For example, $A(x) \wedge r(x,y) \wedge B(y)$ is factorized, but $A(x) \wedge r^*(x,y) \wedge B(y)$ is not factorized.

For factorized queries, replacing the global condition $H \models Q$ with a local one is easy: a factorized query holds in a star-like graph H iff it holds in any of its parts. Again, we prove a more general property.

Lemma 4. *For every connected acyclic bubble cover of a graph G, a factorized UCRPQ holds in G iff it holds in any of the bubbles.*

Proof. The bubble graph of a connected acyclic bubble cover is a tree. The image of a match of a UCRPQ in G, together with witnessing paths, is a finite subgraph of G. Consequently, there is a finite subtree of the bubble tree such that the UCRPQ also holds in the corresponding subgraph of G. Hence, it suffices to show the claim for finite bubble trees. We proceed by induction on the size of the bubble tree. If the bubble tree consists of a single bubble, we are done. Otherwise, pick a leaf bubble B. Because Q is factorized, it holds either in B or in the subgraph of G corresponding to the subtree obtained by removing the leaf bubble B. In the first case we are done immediately, in the second case we use the induction hypothesis to obtain a single bubble that satisfies Q. This completes the proof of the left-to-right implication. The converse implication holds trivially for any UCRPQ. □

We would like to replace the input Q with a factorized $\widehat{Q}$. We cannot hope for $\widehat{Q}$ to be equivalent to Q, because being factorized is a semantic property. If we start from a query Q that is not factorized, like $A(x) \wedge r^*(x,y) \wedge B(y)$, each equivalent query is not factorized either. However, a weaker guarantee suffices. A query $\widehat{Q}$ is *almost equivalent* to query Q if for every graph G,

Q holds in G iff $\widehat{Q}$ holds in every graph equal to G up to $\Gamma_{\widehat{Q}} \setminus \Gamma_Q$.

Lemma 5. *If $\widehat{Q}$ is almost equivalent to Q, and neither $\mathcal{T}$ nor G use labels from $\Gamma_{\widehat{Q}} \setminus \Gamma_Q$, then $G, \mathcal{T} \models Q$ iff $G, \mathcal{T} \models \widehat{Q}$. The same holds for $\models_{fin}$.*

Proof. Suppose that H is a counter-model for Q. Then, by the definition of almost equivalence, some $\widehat{H}$ equal to H up to $\Gamma_{\widehat{Q}} \setminus \Gamma_Q$ does not satisfy $\widehat{Q}$. As neither G nor $\mathcal{T}$ use labels from $\Gamma_{\widehat{Q}} \setminus \Gamma_Q$, it follows that $\widehat{H}$ is a counter-model for $\widehat{Q}$.

For the converse implication, observe that because $\widehat{Q}$ is almost equivalent to Q, $G \models Q$ implies $G \models \widehat{Q}$. Consequently, every counter-model for $\widehat{Q}$ is also a counter-model for Q. □

The key idea behind the construction of $\widehat{Q}$ is to exchange information about partial matches of Q in G_1 and G_2 by means of fresh node labels in the shared node, with some disjuncts of $\widehat{Q}$ detecting errors in the encoded information and others putting partial matches together. Let us see an example.

Example 3. Let Q consist of a single CRPQ

$$A(x) \wedge r^*(x,y) \wedge B(y).$$

For $\widehat{Q}$ we can take the union of the following CRPQs:

$$A(x) \wedge \bar{C}_A(x), \quad C_A(x) \wedge r^*(x,z) \wedge \bar{C}_A(z), \quad C_A(z) \wedge C_B(z),$$
$$\bar{C}_B(z) \wedge r^*(z,y) \wedge C_B(y), \quad \bar{C}_B(y) \wedge B(y).$$

Intuitively, $\widehat{Q}$ detects if label C_A is missing in a node r-reachable from A or label C_B is missing in a node from which B is r-reachable, or some node has both label C_A and label C_B.

Let us see that $\widehat{Q}$ is almost equivalent to Q. For a graph G, let $\widehat{G}$ be obtained from G by placing label C_A in all nodes reachable from a node with label A, and label C_B in all nodes from which a node with label B can be reached. Then, $G \models Q$ iff $\widehat{G} \models C_A(z) \wedge C_B(z)$. All the remaining CRPQs in $\widehat{Q}$ are not satisfied in $\widehat{G}$. In any other graph equal to G up to labels C_A and C_B, one of the remaining CRPQs from $\widehat{Q}$ will hold. It follows that $\widehat{Q}$ is almost equivalent to Q.

Now, let us see that $\widehat{Q}$ is factorized. Consider graphs G_1 and G_2 sharing a single node (with the same labels in both these graphs). Suppose that $G_1 \cup G_2 \models \widehat{Q}$. If one of the CRPQs that does not involve binary atoms can be matched in $G_1 \cup G_2$, then it can also be matched in G_1 or in G_2 (because the shared node has the same labels in both graphs). For the remaining two CRPQs the argument is symmetric. Suppose for example that $C_A(x) \wedge r^*(x,z) \wedge \bar{C}_A(z)$ can be matched in $G_1 \cup G_2$. Then, on the path witnessing this there is an edge from a node with label C_A to a node without label C_A. This edge alone is a witnessing path for $C_A(x) \wedge r^*(x,z) \wedge \bar{C}_A(z)$. As the edge belongs either to G_1 or to G_2, in one of these graphs $C_A(x) \wedge r^*(x,z) \wedge \bar{C}_A(z)$ can be matched. Hence, $\widehat{Q}$ is indeed factorized.

Let us point out that complement node labels play a crucial role here: without them, constructing $\widehat{Q}$ would not be possible. ◂

The general construction is a bit tedious, but not fundamentally different from the one in Example 3.

We say a regular expression φ' is a *quotient* of a regular expression φ if there are languages U and V such that a word w matches φ' iff there are $u \in U$ and $v \in V$ such that uwv matches φ.

Theorem 2 ([9]). *For each connected UCRPQ Q one can construct effectively a connected factorized UCRPQ $\widehat{Q}$ almost equivalent to Q. Moreover, each regular expression in $\widehat{Q}$ is a quotient of a regular expression from Q.*

The additional property is very useful, because it ensures that factorization preserves many different classes of queries. For instance, if Q is a UCRPQ or test-free, so is $\widehat{Q}$, because the alphabet used in a quotient of a regular expression φ is always a subset of the one used in φ. Each quotient of r is equivalent to $\emptyset$ or r itself. Similarly, each quotient of $(r_1 + r_2 + \cdots + r_n)^*$ is equivalent to $\emptyset$ or $(r_1 + r_2 + \cdots + r_n)^*$. Since regular expressions of the form $\emptyset$ can be eliminated from queries, if Q is a UCQ or simple, we can assume that so is $\widehat{Q}$.

Eliminating the Input Graph

We are now ready to put the pieces together.

Proposition 2. *For every finite graph G, $\mathcal{ALC}$ TBox $\mathcal{T}$, and UCRPQ Q, Q is not (finitely) entailed by G and $\mathcal{T}$ iff for some graph $\widehat{G}$ obtained from G by adding labels from $\Gamma_{\mathcal{T}} \cup \Gamma_{\widehat{Q}}$,*

- *$\widehat{G} \not\models \widehat{Q}$, $\widehat{G} \models \mathcal{T}_\forall$, and*
- *each maximal type τ over $\Gamma_{\mathcal{T}} \cup \Gamma_{\widehat{Q}}$ realized in $\widehat{G}$ can be realized in a (finite) model of $\mathcal{T}$ that does not satisfy $\widehat{Q}$.*

Proof. Without loss of generality we can assume that labels from $\Gamma_{\widehat{Q}} \setminus \Gamma_Q$ are not used in G and $\mathcal{T}$. By Lemma 5, $G, \mathcal{T} \not\models Q$ iff $G, \mathcal{T} \not\models \widehat{Q}$. We will prove that $G, \mathcal{T} \not\models \widehat{Q}$ is equivalent to the condition in the statement of the proposition.

Suppose that $G, \mathcal{T} \not\models \widehat{Q}$ and let H be a witnessing counter-model. Let $\widehat{G}$ be the graph obtained from G by adding to each node v all labels v has in H. As $\widehat{G}$ maps homomorphically into H, we have $\widehat{G} \not\models \widehat{Q}$ and $\widehat{G} \models \mathcal{T}_\forall$. Moreover, $\tau, \mathcal{T} \not\models \widehat{Q}$ for each maximal τ over $\Gamma_{\mathcal{T}} \cup \Gamma_Q$ realized in $\widehat{G}$, because H is a witnessing counter-model.

Conversely, let $\widehat{G}$ be a graph like in the statement of the proposition. Then, each maximal type τ over $\Gamma_\mathcal{T} \cup \Gamma_Q$ realized in $\widehat{G}$, is also realized in a graph G_τ such that $G_\tau \models \mathcal{T}$ and $G_\tau \not\models \widehat{Q}$. We construct a star-like graph H as follows. For the central part we take $\widehat{G}$. Then, for each maximal type τ over $\Gamma_\mathcal{T} \cup \Gamma_Q$ realized in $\widehat{G}$ and each node v of type τ in $\widehat{G}$, we add as a peripheral part an isomorphic copy of G_τ with an arbitrary node of type τ replaced with v. Let us see that H is a counter-model for $G, \mathcal{T} \not\models \widehat{Q}$. Since $\widehat{Q}$ is factorized and no part of H satisfies $\widehat{Q}$, we have $H \not\models \widehat{Q}$. By construction, $G \subseteq \widehat{G} \subseteq H$. Moreover, every part of H satisfies $\mathcal{T}_\forall$ and each node in H belongs to some peripheral part, all of which satisfy $\mathcal{T}$. By Lemma 3, $H \models \mathcal{T}$.

For $\models_{fin}$ the argument is identical, except that G_τ can be chosen finite, so H is finite as well. □

Based on Proposition 2, we can decide whether $G, \mathcal{T} \models Q$, using the following algorithm:

1. construct query $\widehat{Q}$ using Theorem 2,
2. guess graph $\widehat{G}$ by adding labels from $\Gamma_\mathcal{T} \cup \Gamma_{\widehat{Q}}$ to graph G,
3. check that $\widehat{G} \not\models \widehat{Q}$ and $\widehat{G} \models \mathcal{T}_\forall$,
4. check that $\tau, \mathcal{T} \not\models Q$ for each maximal type τ over $\Gamma_\mathcal{T} \cup \Gamma_{\widehat{Q}}$ realized in $\widehat{G}$.

For $G, \mathcal{T} \models_{fin} Q$ the algorithm is the same, except that in step 4 we replace $\tau, \mathcal{T} \not\models Q$ with $\tau, \mathcal{T} \not\models_{fin} Q$. This shows that both unrestricted and finite entailment reduce to the variant with input type, as promised. Note that it is a *Turing reduction*: we need multiple instances of the latter problem to solve a single instance of the former problem. The rest of the paper deals with the variant with input type, first over unrestricted and then over finite graphs.

5 The Simplicity of Infinity: Unravelling and Fixpoints

Moving on with the plan, we now solve the unrestricted entailment problem for UCRPQs. Relying on the reduction from Sect. 4, we assume that the input involves a single node type, rather than an arbitrary finite graph. We use the familiar strategy: first show that it is enough to check for special counter-models and then show how to decide if a special counter-model exists. This time our special counter-models will be trees—possibly infinite, but finitely-branching.

Special Counter-Models: Trees of Bounded Arity

We begin with a simple but useful observation. Given a type τ, an $\mathcal{ALC}$ TBox $\mathcal{T}$, and a UCRPQ Q, a graph G is a counter-model iff so is the graph G' obtained from G by dropping all labels except from those used in τ, $\mathcal{T}$, and Q. Indeed, the presence of the removed labels is irrelevant for τ, $\mathcal{T}$, and Q. For $\Gamma_0 \subseteq \Gamma$ and $\Sigma_0 \subseteq \Sigma$, by a *graph over Γ_0 and Σ_0* we mean a graph that uses only node labels from Γ_0 and edge labels from Σ_0. By the observation above, when searching for counter-models it suffices to consider graphs over $\Gamma_\tau \cup \Gamma_\mathcal{T} \cup \Gamma_Q$ and $\Sigma_\tau \cup \Sigma_\mathcal{T} \cup \Sigma_Q$, where Γ_τ and Σ_τ are the sets of node and edge labels used in type τ.

Next, we bound the number of successors a node can have. By the *out-degree* of a node in a graph G we mean the number of outgoing edges (including parallel edges). The out-degree of G is the maximum out-degree of its nodes.

Proposition 3 (bounded-degree counter-model property). *For every type τ, $\mathcal{ALC}$ TBox $\mathcal{T}$, and UCRPQ Q, $\tau, \mathcal{T} \not\models Q$ iff some graph of out-degree at most $|\mathcal{T}|$ is a counter-model, and similarly for $\models_{fin}$.*

Proof. Take any counter-model H. For each participation constraint $A \sqsubseteq \exists r.B$ in $\mathcal{T}$ and each node v with label A, pick an r-edge from v to a node with label B, and paint it red. Let H' be obtained from H by keeping all nodes but only red edges. H has out-degree at most $|\mathcal{T}|$ and it is a counter-model because:

- $H' \to H$, so $H' \models \mathcal{T}_\forall$ and $H' \not\models Q$ by Lemma 2;
- by construction, H' satisfies all participation constraints in $\mathcal{T}$;
- H' has the same nodes as H, with the same labels, so H' realizes type τ.

Note that if H is finite, so is H', which proves the claim for $\models_{fin}$. □

With Proposition 3 at hand, we easily prove the following.

Proposition 4 (tree counter-model property). *For every type τ, $\mathcal{ALC}$ TBox $\mathcal{T}$, and UCRPQ Q, $\tau, \mathcal{T} \not\models Q$ iff some $|\mathcal{T}|$-ary tree over $\Gamma_\tau \cup \Gamma_\mathcal{T} \cup \Gamma_Q$ and $\Sigma_\tau \cup \Sigma_\mathcal{T} \cup \Sigma_Q$ is a counter-model.*

Proof. We apply the classical construction of unravelling. Given a graph G and node v_0, the *unravelling of G from v_0* is a tree G_{v_0} such that

- nodes of G_{v_0} are directed paths in G (also non-simple) that start in v_0;
- node $v_0 \xrightarrow{r_1} v_1 \xrightarrow{r_2} \cdots \xrightarrow{r_{k-1}} v_{k-1} \xrightarrow{r_k} v_k$ has labels inherited from v_k and an incoming r_k-edge from $v_0 \xrightarrow{r_1} v_1 \xrightarrow{r_2} \cdots \xrightarrow{r_{k-1}} v_{k-1}$.

The function η defined as $\eta\bigl(v_0 \xrightarrow{r_1} v_1 \xrightarrow{r_2} \cdots \xrightarrow{r_k} v_k\bigr) = v_k$ is a homomorphism from G_{v_0} to G. Moreover, η preserves the out-degree and the types of successors:

- the out-degree of a node v' in G_{v_0} is equal to the out-degree of $\eta(v')$ in G.
- a node v' in G_{v_0} has an r-successor of type τ in G_{v_0} iff $\eta(v')$ has an r-successor of type τ in G.

To establish the lemma, let H be a counter-model for $\tau, \mathcal{T} \models Q$. By Proposition 3, we can assume that H has out-degree bounded by $|\mathcal{T}|$. By the initial observation we can also assume that H uses only labels mentioned in τ, $\mathcal{T}$, and Q. Pick a node v_0 of type τ in H and let $S = H_{v_0}$. Then, S is a tree over $\Gamma_\tau \cup \Gamma_\mathcal{T} \cup \Gamma_Q$ and $\Sigma_\tau \cup \Sigma_\mathcal{T} \cup \Sigma_Q$, and by the first property of η its out-degree is bounded by $|\mathcal{T}|$. S realizes type τ, because v_0 has type τ. As $H_{v_0} \to H$, we also know that $S \models \mathcal{T}_\forall$ and $S \not\models Q$, by Lemma 2. By the second property of η, S satisfies all participation constraints satisfied in H. Hence, $S \models \mathcal{T}$. □

The construction in the proof of Proposition 4 typically produces an infinite tree even if it starts from a finite counter-model. This cannot be avoided, as there is no tree counter-model property for finite entailment. Indeed, in Example 2, we saw that every non-empty finite model of the TBox {Person $\sqsubseteq \exists$ childOf. Person} contains a cycle.

Finding Tree-Shaped Counter-Models

As trees are very simple structures, there are many ways of finding tree-shaped counter-models. We use a variant of type elimination [12,14], which is particularly simple and elegant for factorized queries. We begin by reformulating the conditions a tree-shaped counter-model must satisfy in terms of local properties of small pieces of the counter-model.

By a *pointed graph* we mean a graph with a distinguished node. Two pointed graphs are considered isomorphic if they are isomorphic as graphs and the isomorphism preserves the distinguished node. Given a tree S and a node v in S, let G_v be the pointed graph obtained by restricting S to v and all v's children, with v as the distinguished node. We refer to graphs G_v as the *connectors* of S.

Lemma 6. *For a factorized UCRPQ Q, a tree S is a counter-model for $\tau, \mathcal{T} \models Q$ iff the following conditions hold*

(1) for some connector G_v in S, the distinguished node has type τ;
(2) for each connector G_v in S, $G_v \models \mathcal{T}_\forall$ and the distinguished node satisfies $\mathcal{T}_\exists$;
(3) for each connector G_v in S, $G_v \not\models Q$.

Proof. The connectors form a connected acyclic bubble cover of S. As each node v in S is the distinguished node of some connector in S (namely, G_v), it follows that tree S realizes type τ iff condition (1) holds. It also follows that each node in S satisfies $\mathcal{T}_\exists$ in some bubble iff the distinguished node of each connector satisfies $\mathcal{T}_\exists$. Hence, by Lemma 3, $S \models \mathcal{T}$ iff condition (2) holds. Finally, because Q is factorized, by Lemma 4, $S \not\models Q$ iff condition (3) holds. □

Given Lemma 6, it is easy to check if a tree-shaped counter-model exists.

Lemma 7. *Given a type τ, an $\mathcal{ALC}$ TBox $\mathcal{T}$, and a factorized UCRPQ Q, one can decide if some $|\mathcal{T}|$-ary tree is a counter-model for $\tau, \mathcal{T} \models Q$.*

Proof. Up to isomorphism, there are only finitely many possible connectors in $|\mathcal{T}|$-ary trees over $\Gamma_\tau \cup \Gamma_\mathcal{T} \cup \Gamma_Q$ and $\Sigma_\tau \cup \Sigma_\mathcal{T} \cup \Sigma_Q$. For every connector we can check easily if it satisfies conditions (2) and (3) in Lemma 6. Iterating over all possible connectors with nodes taken from a fixed finite set $\{v_0, v_1, \ldots, v_{|\mathcal{T}|}\}$ we can filter out those that do not satisfy conditions (2) and (3). This leaves us with the set Ψ of *legal* connectors. The question now is if we can build from them a tree that realizes type τ.

Consider the following greatest fixed point algorithm:

1. Let $\Psi_0 = \Psi$

2. Iteratively remove from Ψ_0 connectors that contain a child for which there is no connector with the distinguished node of the same type, until the set stabilizes.
3. ACCEPT iff the resulting set contains a connector with the distinguished node of type τ.

Note that when the algorithm terminates, for every connector in the computed set Ψ_0 and every child in this connector, there is another connector in Ψ whose distinguished element has the same type.

Suppose that the algorithm accepts. Then, we can define a counter-model as follows. We start from the connector in Ψ_0 whose distinguished element has type τ. Then, for each child, we attach an isomorphic copy of a connector from Ψ_0 whose distinguished element has the same type. Then we do the same for all children of each attached connector, and so on. We repeat this as long as there are nodes without corresponding connectors. If the procedure terminates in a finite number of steps (which happens if at some point all newly attached connectors have no children), we obtain a finite counter-model. Otherwise, the counter-model is infinite.

Conversely, suppose there is a $|\mathcal{T}|$-ary tree S that is a counter-model for $\tau, \mathcal{T} \models Q$. Let Ψ_S be the set of connectors with nodes from $\{v_0, v_1, \ldots, v_{|\mathcal{T}|}\}$ that are isomorphic to some connector of S. Then, $\Psi_S \subseteq \Psi$, and in each iteration of the algorithm, no element of Ψ_S is removed from Ψ_0. It follows that when the algorithm terminates, $\Psi_S \subseteq \Psi_0$. Since some node v in S has type τ and Ψ_0 contains a connector isomorphic to G_v, the algorithm will accept. □

Wrapping Up

It remains to put all the pieces together.

Proposition 5. *Given a type τ, an $\mathcal{ALC}$ TBox $\mathcal{T}$, and a UCRPQ Q, one can decide if $\tau, \mathcal{T} \models Q$.*

Proof. By Theorem 2 we can compute a factorized UCRPQ $\widehat{Q}$ that is almost equivalent to Q. Without loss of generality w can assume that he additional node labels introduced in $\widehat{Q}$ are not used in τ and $\mathcal{T}$. By Lemma 5, $\tau, \mathcal{T} \models Q$ iff $\tau, \mathcal{T} \models \widehat{Q}$. Hence, by Proposition 4, it suffices to check if there is a $|\mathcal{T}|$-ary tree that is a counter-model for $\tau, \mathcal{T} \models \widehat{Q}$. By Lemma 7, this is decidable. □

As an immediate corollary from Proposition 5 and the reduction described in Sect. 4, we achieve our stage goal.

Theorem 3. *The entailment problem for UCRPQs and $\mathcal{ALC}$ is decidable.*

6 Into the Finite: Coloured Blocking

Having dealt with the unrestricted case in one fell swoop, we move on to the finite case. We start small, but with style: we show that for unions of conjunctive queries, finite and unrestricted entailment coincide. This phenomenon is traditionally known as *finite controllability*. We present a proof based on *coloured blocking*, which is a general method of turning infinite graphs into finite ones, without satisfying any additional conjunctive queries of a given size.

For a node v in graph G, the *n-neighbourhood* $N_n^G(v)$ *of* v is a pointed graph obtained by restricting G to nodes within distance n from v, and taking v for the distinguished node. A graph G is *n-diverse* if for each v, every two nodes in $N_n^G(v)$ have different sets of labels.

Theorem 4 ([8,13]). *Let G be an n-diverse graph and let G' be obtained from G by redirecting some edges such that the old target and the new target have isomorphic n-neighbourhoods in G. Then, for each CQ q with at most n binary atoms, if $G \not\models q$, then $G' \not\models q$.*

Before applying Theorem 4 we need to ensure that the graph is n-diverse for a sufficiently large n. This is easy, as long as the graph has bounded degree.

Lemma 8. *If graph G has bounded degree, then for each $n \geq 0$ one can turn G into an n-diverse graph by labelling the nodes using finitely many fresh labels.*

Proof. Let $n \geq 0$. Because G has bounded degree, $2n$-neighbourhoods in G have size bounded by some m. We use m fresh labels, and give each node exactly one of them. We think about this as colouring nodes of G with one of m colours.

We colour nodes of G greedily, one by one. Pick an uncoloured node v. At most $m-1$ colours are already used in $N_{2n}^G(v)$. Assign to v any colour that is not yet used in $N_{2n}^G(v)$. Repeating this ad infinitum we colour all nodes of G.

The resulting graph is n-diverse, because for each v, all nodes in $N_n^G(v)$ have different colours. Indeed, consider two nodes u, u' from $N_n^G(v)$. Without loss of generality we can assume that u was coloured before u'. Because u belongs to $N_{2n}^G(u')$, when colouring u' we avoided the colour assigned to u. □

We are now ready to make the main step towards finite controllability.

Proposition 6. *For every finite type τ, $\mathcal{ALC}$ TBox $\mathcal{T}$, and UCQ Q,*

$$\tau, \mathcal{T} \models_{fin} Q \quad \textit{iff} \quad \tau, \mathcal{T} \models Q.$$

Proof. It suffices to prove the left-to-right implication. By contraposition, suppose that $\tau, \mathcal{T} \not\models Q$. We cannot work with an arbitrary counter-model, because we need bounded degree. However, Proposition 4 ensures that some $|\mathcal{T}|$-ary tree H is a counter-model. Crucially, the degree of H is at most $|\mathcal{T}|+1$. By passing to a suitable subtree, we can assume that the root of H has type τ. Dropping all labels except those used in τ, $\mathcal{T}$, or Q, we can assume that H uses only finitely many different labels. By Lemma 8, we can assume that H is n-diverse. As H has bounded degree and uses only finitely many different labels, there are only finitely many isomorphism types of n-neighbourhoods in H, say m. On each branch of H select the first node v such that for some ancestor v' of v, neighbourhoods $N_n^H(v)$ and $N_n^H(v')$ are isomorphic. Note that the depth of v

is at most m. Redirect the edge incoming to v so that its new target is v' and remove the subtree of H rooted at v from the graph. The resulting graph H' is finite, because only nodes of depth at most m were kept. It contains the root of H, because only nodes that have an ancestor have been removed. Hence, H' realizes type τ. The construction ensures that $H' \models \mathcal{T}$. Indeed, labels in H' are inherited from H, so CIs of the form $K \sqsubseteq L$ are not affected. For the remaining CIs, we observe that a node in H' has an r-successor with label B iff it has such a successor in H. Finally, by Theorem 4, $H' \not\models Q$. Hence, H' is a finite counter-model and $\tau, \mathcal{T} \not\models_{fin} Q$. □

We obtain finite controllability by combining Propositions 6 and 2.

Proposition 7. *For every finite graph G, $\mathcal{ALC}$ TBox $\mathcal{T}$, and UCQ Q,*

$$G, \mathcal{T} \models_{fin} Q \quad \text{iff} \quad G, \mathcal{T} \models Q.$$

Proof. We apply Proposition 2 twice. Suppose $G, \mathcal{T} \not\models Q$. By Proposition 2 for $\models$, this is equivalent to there being a graph $\widehat{G}$ obtained from G by adding labels such that

- $\widehat{G} \not\models \widehat{Q}, \widehat{G} \models \widehat{\mathcal{T}}_\forall$, and
- $\tau, \mathcal{T} \not\models \widehat{Q}$ for each maximal type τ over $\Gamma_\mathcal{T} \cup \Gamma_{\widehat{Q}}$ realized in $\widehat{G}$.

By Proposition 6, we can replace the second item with

- $\tau, \mathcal{T} \not\models_{fin} \widehat{Q}$ for each maximal type τ over $\Gamma_\mathcal{T} \cup \Gamma_{\widehat{Q}}$ realized in $\widehat{G}$.

By Proposition 2 for $\models_{fin}$, the resulting condition is equivalent to $G, \mathcal{T} \not\models_{fin} Q$ and we are done. □

7 Beyond Conjunctive Queries: Frames and the Coil

We are now leaving the safe waters of finite controllability to explore a relatively basic class of queries for which the notions of entailment and finite entailment diverge: simple UCRPQs.

Recall that a simple UCRPQ uses only regular expressions of the forms

$$r \quad \text{and} \quad (r_1 + r_2 + \cdots + r_k)^*$$

where $r, r_1, r_2, \ldots, r_k \in \Sigma$. We refer to atoms of the latter form as *reachability atoms*, or $\{r_1, r_2, \ldots, r_k\}$-*reachability atoms* if we want to specify the set of edge labels, and write R^* for $R = \{r_1, r_2, \ldots, r_k\} \subseteq \Sigma$ instead of $(r_1 + r_2 + \cdots + r_k)^*$ whenever convenient. The query $\exists x\, \text{childOf}^+(x, x)$ from Example 2 can be written equivalently as $\exists x\, \exists y\, \text{childOf}(x, y) \wedge \text{childOf}^*(y, x)$, which is a simple UCRPQ. Thus, Example 2 shows that simple UCRPQs do not enjoy finite controllability. Our stage goal for this section is the following result.

Theorem 5. *The finite entailment problem for simple CRPQs and $\mathcal{ALC}$ is decidable.*

By Theorem 2 and Lemma 5 we can restrict our attention to factorized simple UCRPQs. By the reduction described in Sect. 4, we can work with the variant of the problem where instead of a graph to extend we are given a type to realize. Our strategy is to show that it suffices to look for counter-models that can be built from simpler components whose existence reduces to simpler instances of finite entailment. A number of such simplifications will take us back to the case of UCQs, which we already know how to solve. As a first step, we introduce a general way of combining components into larger graphs.

Assembling Counter-Models

A *frame* is a finite graph without self-loops whose nodes represent disjoint components of a graph and edges represent edges between these components. More precisely, each frame node f is labelled with a pointed graph G_f with distinguished node v_f, and each edge originating in a frame node f is labelled with a pair (v, r) where $v \in dom(G_f)$ and $r \in \Sigma$. We assume that $dom(G_f)$ are pairwise disjoint for all f and parallel edges cannot have labels (u, r) and (v, s) with $u = v$.

For every frame node f and node $v \in dom(G_f)$ we define $G_{f,v}$ as the pointed graph obtained as follows. For the distinguished node we take v with labels inherited from G_f. For each edge from f to e with label (v, r) we add to $G_{f,v}$ the distinguished element v_e of G_e (with labels inherited from G_e) and an r-edge from v to v_e.

We call graphs G_f the *components* of the frame and $G_{f,v}$ the *connectors* of the frame. While components are arbitrary pointed graphs, connectors are depth-one trees with the distinguished node in the root.

Every frame F *represents* a graph G_F, obtained by taking the union of all its components and connectors.

Next, we show how to factorize TBoxes and queries over graphs represented by frames. To factorize an $\mathcal{ALC}$ TBox $\mathcal{T}$, we introduce a fresh label $\mathsf{Need}_{r,B}$ for each $r \in \Sigma_\mathcal{T}$ and $B \in \Gamma_\mathcal{T}$ and define two auxiliary TBoxes:

$$\mathcal{T}_{\mathrm{comp}} = \mathcal{T}_\forall \cup \{ A \sqsubseteq \mathsf{Need}_{r,B} \sqcup \exists r.B \mid A \sqsubseteq \exists r.B \in \mathcal{T} \},$$
$$\mathcal{T}_{\mathrm{conn}} = \mathcal{T}_\forall \cup \{ \mathsf{Need}_{r,B} \sqsubseteq \exists r.B \mid r \in \Sigma_\mathcal{T}, B \in \Gamma_\mathcal{T} \}.$$

Lemma 9. *For every frame F and $\mathcal{ALC}$ TBox $\mathcal{T}$, $G_F \models \mathcal{T}$ iff one can place labels $\mathsf{Need}_{r,B}$ in F in such a way that each component satisfies $\mathcal{T}_{\mathrm{comp}}$ and in each connector the distinguished node satisfies $\mathcal{T}_{\mathrm{conn}}$.*

Proof. Suppose that $G_F \models \mathcal{T}$. Let us first remove all labels of the form $\mathsf{Need}_{r,B}$ from all nodes in the components of F. This does not affect $\mathcal{T}$, because $\mathcal{T}$ does not mention these labels. Then, for each component G_f and each participation constraint $A \sqsubseteq \exists r.B \in \mathcal{T}$, add label $\mathsf{Need}_{r,B}$ in all nodes of G_f with label A that have no r-successors with label B in G_f. Because $G_F \models \mathcal{T}$, it follows that after this relabelling each component satisfies $\mathcal{T}_{\mathrm{comp}}$ and in each connector the distinguished node satisfies $\mathcal{T}_{\mathrm{conn}}$.

Conversely, suppose that after rearranging labels of the from $\mathsf{Need}_{r,B}$, each component in F satisfies $\mathcal{T}_{\text{comp}}$ and in each connector the distinguished node satisfies $\mathcal{T}_{\text{conn}}$. The connectors and components of F form a bubble cover of G_F. Each bubble satisfies $\mathcal{T}_\forall$. Moreover, a node v from G_f satisfies participation constraint $A \sqsubseteq \exists r.B$ from $\mathcal{T}$ either in $G_{f,v}$ or in G_f, depending on whether v has label $\mathsf{Need}_{r,B}$ or not. Applying Lemma 3 we conclude that $G_F \models \mathcal{T}$. □

Dealing with queries is again harder. We begin with a special case of tree-shaped frames, which we can get for free.

Lemma 10. *Let Q be a factorized UCRPQ. For every frame F that is a tree, $G_F \models Q$ iff some component or some connector of F satisfies Q.*

Proof. Because F is a tree, the connectors and components of F form a connected acyclic bubble cover of G_F. The claim follows by Lemma 4. □

For general frames Lemma 10 does not hold, but a weaker property can be shown: under certain assumptions, we can ensure that the represented graph does not satisfy the query by adjusting the frame carefully. We call two frames *locally isomorphic* if for each component of one frame there is an isomorphic component of the other, and similarly for connectors. Every path in graph G_F induces a path in frame F. For an RPQ φ, the *span of φ in F* is the maximum length of a path induced in F by a path witnessing φ in G_F.

Theorem 6 ([9]). *Consider a factorized UCRPQ Q and a finite frame F such that no component or connector of F satisfies Q and the span in F of each RPQ in Q is bounded. Then, there is a finite frame F' locally isomorphic to F such that $G_{F'} \not\models Q$.*

The idea is to unravel a given frame sufficiently, without making it infinite. This can be achieved using a construction dubbed the *coil*, which can be seen as a bounded-recall (or sliding-window) unravelling of the frame. We sketch the construction below.

For a graph F and $n \geq 0$, let $\text{Paths}(F, n)$ be the set of paths of length at most n in F, including paths of length 0 consisting of a single node. By the *n-suffix of a path π* we mean the suffix of length n of π if π has length at least n, and the whole path π otherwise. For a graph F and $n > 0$, $\text{Coil}(F, n)$ is the graph with nodes $\text{Paths}(F, n) \times \{0, \dots, n\}$ and an edge $((\pi, \ell), (\pi', \ell'))$ whenever $\ell' \equiv \ell + 1 \pmod{(n+1)}$ and π' is the n-suffix of an extension of π by one edge. The label of a node (π, ℓ) in $\text{Coil}(F, n)$ is inherited from the last node of π, and the label of an edge $((\pi, \ell), (\pi', \ell'))$ is inherited from the last edge of the path π'. For a frame F and $n > 1$, let F_n be obtained from $\text{Coil}(F, n)$ by relabelling to ensure that all components have disjoint domains: for each node e in $\text{Coil}(F, n)$ with label G_e, change its label to a fresh isomorphic copy $\tilde{G}_e$ of G_e, and change labels in all outgoing edges from (v, r) to $(\tilde{v}, r)$, where $\tilde{v}$ is the copy of v in $\tilde{G}_e$. For F' we take F_{km+1}, where k is the maximal span in F of an RPQ in Q and m is the maximal size of a CRPQ in Q.

Simple Counter-Model Property

As usually, we begin with a purely structural property.

Lemma 11. *For a type τ, $\mathcal{ALC}$ TBox $\mathcal{T}$, and UCRPQ Q, we have $\tau, \mathcal{T} \not\models_{\mathit{fin}} Q$ iff there is a frame F such that F is a finite tree and only uses edge labels from $\Sigma_{\mathcal{T}}$, all connectors are $|\mathcal{T}|$-ary trees, all components are finite and strongly connected, some component's distinguished node has type τ, and G_F is a counter-model.*

Proof. Suppose that $\tau, \mathcal{T} \not\models_{\mathit{fin}} Q$. By Proposition 3, there is a finite counter-model G of out-degree at most $|\mathcal{T}|$. Without loss of generality we can assume that it only uses edge labels from $\Sigma_{\mathcal{T}}$. For each node v in G let G_v be a pointed graph obtained by taking a fresh copy of the strongly connected component of G that contains v, with v as the distinguished node. Consider a graph F_0 with a node f_v labelled with G_v for each node v in G. Whenever there is an r-edge from node u to node v in a different strongly connected component, add an edge from f_w to f_v with label (u_w, r) for every w whose SCC in G contains u, with u_w being the copy of u in G_w. Graph F_0 need not be a tree. In fact, it may not even be a frame, because it may contain parallel edges that share the first component of the label. However, because F_0 is acyclic, we can turn it into a tree by unravelling it from any component whose distinguished node is of type τ (acyclicity ensures that the unravelling is finite), and adjusting the labels so that all components are disjoint. The resulting graph F is a concrete frame and a tree. Clearly, all components of F are finite and strongly connected. Mapping every node in G_F to its original in G we get a homomorphism $\eta : G_F \to G$. By Lemma 2, $G_F \models \mathcal{T}_\forall$ and $G_F \not\models Q$. Also, by construction, for every node v in G_F, η gives a bijection between r-successors of v in G_F and r-successors of $\eta(v)$ in G. It follows that each connector in F is a $|\mathcal{T}|$-ary tree, and that each node in G_F satisfies all participation constraints from $\mathcal{T}$. Hence, $G_F \models \mathcal{T}$. Finally, G_F realizes type τ because the distinguished node of the root of F has type τ. □

The next step is to reformulate the conditions on F in Lemma 11 entirely in terms of local properties of connectors and components of F. This time the reformulation is not equivalent for each frame, but it does ensure that there is a counter-model iff there is a frame satisfying the reformulated conditions.

Lemma 12. *Consider a type τ, an $\mathcal{ALC}$ TBox $\mathcal{T}$, and a factorized simple UCRPQ Q, and assume that they do not use labels $\mathsf{Need}_{r,B}$ for $r \in \Sigma_{\mathcal{T}}$ and $B \in \Gamma_{\mathcal{T}}$. Then $\tau, \mathcal{T} \not\models_{\mathit{fin}} Q$ iff there is a frame F such that F is a finite tree and*

- *each component is finite, satisfies $\mathcal{T}_{\mathrm{comp}}$, and does not satisfy $Q \bmod \Sigma_{\mathcal{T}}^*$, obtained from Q by dropping all Σ_0-reachability atoms with $\Sigma_{\mathcal{T}} \subseteq \Sigma_0$;*
- *each connector is a $|\mathcal{T}|$-ary tree, does not satisfy Q, and its distinguished node satisfies $\mathcal{T}_{\mathrm{conn}}$; and*
- *some component's distinguished node has type τ.*

Proof. Let F be a frame as described in the statement of the lemma. Let us see that G_F is a finite counter-model. Clearly, G_F is finite and realizes type τ. By Lemma 9, $G_F \models \mathcal{T}$. Because Q implies $Q \bmod \Sigma_\mathcal{T}^*$, no bubble satisfies Q. As Q is factorized, by Lemma 10, $G_F \not\models Q$.

Conversely, if $\tau, \mathcal{T} \not\models_{fin} Q$, then by Lemma 11 there is a frame F such that F is a finite tree and only uses edge labels from $\Sigma_\mathcal{T}$, all connectors are $|\mathcal{T}|$-ary trees, all components are finite and strongly connected, some component's distinguished node has type τ, and G_F is a counter-model. We can assume that G_F does not use labels $\mathsf{Need}_{r,B}$. By Lemma 10, no component or connector of F satisfies Q. Because each component is strongly connected and only uses edge labels from $\Sigma_\mathcal{T}$, all Σ_0-reachability atoms with $\Sigma_\mathcal{T} \subseteq \Sigma_0$ hold trivially for all pairs of nodes within the same component. Hence, in fact, no component satisfies $Q \bmod \Sigma_\mathcal{T}^*$. By Lemma 9, we can add labels $\mathsf{Need}_{r,B}$ in F in such a way that each component satisfies $\mathcal{T}_{\mathrm{comp}}$ and in each connector the distinguished node satisfies $\mathcal{T}_{\mathrm{conn}}$. □

Finding Simple Counter-Models

It remains to decide if there exists a frame F such that F is a finite tree, each of its components and connectors is *legal*, as specified in Lemma 12, and some component's distinguished node has type τ. If we had access to the set Φ of legal components and the set Ψ of legal connectors, we could use the following least fixpoint algorithm to test if a suitable frame F exists.

1. Start from the empty set of legal components $\Phi_0 = \emptyset$ and the set Ψ_0 of legal connectors that have no children.
2. Iteratively
   – add to Φ_0 all legal components that realize only types realized in the distinguished nodes of connectors from Ψ_0,
   – add to Ψ_0 all legal connectors that realize in non-distinguished nodes only types realized in the distinguished nodes of components from Φ_0,
   until the set stabilizes.
3. Accept iff the resulting set Φ_0 contains a component with distinguished node of type τ.

Note that in contrast to Sect. 5 we are using the least fixed point because F is supposed to be a *finite* tree.

As in Sect. 5, up to isomorphism there are only finitely many legal connectors and they can be easily computed. But there are infinitely many components, even up to isomorphism! How do we represent and compute the legal ones? The first key observation is that the fixpoint algorithm only cares about

– the type σ of the distinguished node of the component,
– the set Θ of types realized in the component.

Indeed, for nodes of the same type in a component we can use isomorphic connectors. In consequence, any two components with distinguished nodes of the same type and identical sets of realized types, are mutually replaceable in the algorithm. Hence, for the purpose of the fixpoint algorithm we can represent components abstractly as pairs of the form (σ, Θ).

How do we check if a pair (σ, Θ) represents a legal component? This is simply an instance of the finite entailment problem: a legal component with distinguished node of type σ and nodes of types from Θ exists iff

$$\sigma, \mathcal{T}_{\mathrm{comp}} \cup \mathcal{T}_\Theta \not\models_{\mathrm{fin}} Q \bmod \Sigma_\mathcal{T}^* \quad \text{where} \quad \mathcal{T}_\Theta = \left\{ \top \sqsubseteq \bigsqcup_{\theta \in \Theta} \bigsqcap_{A \in \theta} A \right\}.$$

If Q uses only $\Sigma_\mathcal{T}$-reachability atoms and r-atoms for $r \in \Sigma$, then $Q \bmod \Sigma_\mathcal{T}^*$ is a UCQ and we can use Propositions 5 and 6. If not, we know only that $|\Sigma_\mathcal{T}| \geq 2$ and $Q \bmod \Sigma_\mathcal{T}^*$ contains no Σ_0-reachability atoms with $\Sigma_\mathcal{T} \subseteq \Sigma_0$. That is, none of its reachability atoms can traverse all edges with all labels mentioned in $\mathcal{T}$. We deal with such queries next. Note that we can still assume that the queries are factorized simple UCRPQs. It can be shown that $Q \bmod \Sigma_\mathcal{T}^*$ is factorized, but we can also simply apply Theorem 2 and Lemma 5 to $Q \bmod \Sigma_\mathcal{T}^*$.

Queries with Restricted Reachability Atoms

Following the familiar strategy, we identify special counter-models that are sufficient to solve the finite entailment problem for simple UCRPQs using only reachability atoms that cannot traverse all edges with labels mentioned in the TBox.

In a frame F, a component or a connector is r-*free* if it contains no r-edges, and it is r-*only* if it contains only r-edges. For $\Sigma_0 = \{r_0, r_1, \ldots, r_{k-1}\} \subseteq \Sigma$ with $k \geq 2$, a frame F is Σ_0-*alternating* if the set of nodes of F can be split into disjoint sets $N_0, N_1, \ldots, N_{k-1}$ such that for each $i \in \{0, 1, \ldots, k-1\}$,

- all edges originating in N_i lead to $N_{(i+1) \bmod k}$;
- for all $f \in N_i$, component G_f is r_i-free; and
- for all $f \in N_i$ and $v \in G_f$, connector $G_{f,v}$ is r_i-only.

Lemma 13. *For a type τ, $\mathcal{ALC}$ TBox $\mathcal{T}$ with $|\Sigma_\mathcal{T}| \geq 2$, and UCRPQ Q, $\tau, \mathcal{T} \not\models_{\mathrm{fin}} Q$ iff there is a finite $\Sigma_\mathcal{T}$-alternating frame F such that all connectors are $|\mathcal{T}|$-ary trees, all components are finite, some component's distinguished node has type τ, and G_F is a counter-model.*

Proof. Suppose that $\tau, \mathcal{T} \not\models_{\mathrm{fin}} Q$. By Proposition 3, there is a finite counter-model G of out-degree at most $|\mathcal{T}|$. Without loss of generality we can assume that G only uses edge labels from $\Sigma_\mathcal{T}$. Let $\Sigma_\mathcal{T} = \{r_0, r_1, \ldots, r_{k-1}\}$. Because $k \geq 2$, $r_i \neq r_{(i+1) \bmod k}$. For each node v in G and each r_i, let G_{v,r_i} be a pointed graph obtained by taking a fresh copy of G with all r_i-edges removed and v chosen for the distinguished node. Consider a graph F with a node f_{v,r_i} labelled with G_{v,r_i} for each node v in G and each r_i. Whenever there is an r_i-edge from u to v, for every node w in G add an edge from f_{w,r_i} to $f_{v,r_{i+1}}$ with label (u_{w,r_i}, r_i), where u_{w,r_i} is the copy of u in G_{w,r_i}. Because $r_i \neq r_{(i+1) \bmod k}$, graph F contains no self-loops. By construction, F does not contain parallel edges with the same first component in the label. Hence, F is a frame. Moreover, F is $\Sigma_{\mathcal{T}}$-alternating, all its components are finite, some component's distinguished node has type τ (because some node of G has type τ), all connectors in F are $|\mathcal{T}|$-ary trees, and mapping every node in G_F to its original in G we get a surjective homomorphism $\eta : G_F \to G$. By Lemma 2, $G_F \models \mathcal{T}_\forall$ and $G_F \not\models Q$. By construction, for every node v in G_F, mapping η gives a bijection between r-successors of v in G_F and r-successors of $\eta(v)$ in G. It follows that each node in G_F satisfies all participation constraints from $\mathcal{T}$. Hence, $G_F \models \mathcal{T}$. □

As usual, the next step is to reformulate the conditions imposed on the frame in Lemma 13 in terms of local properties of connectors and components. This is where we use Theorem 6.

Lemma 14. *Consider a type τ, an $\mathcal{ALC}$ TBox $\mathcal{T}$ with $|\Sigma_{\mathcal{T}}| \geq 2$, and a factorized simple UCRPQ Q that contains no Σ_0-reachability atoms with $\Sigma_{\mathcal{T}} \subseteq \Sigma_0$, and assume that they do not use labels $\mathsf{Need}_{r,B}$ for $r \in \Sigma_{\mathcal{T}}$ and $B \in \Gamma_{\mathcal{T}}$. We have $\tau, \mathcal{T} \not\models_{\mathit{fin}} Q$ iff there is a finite $\Sigma_{\mathcal{T}}$-alternating frame F such that*

- *each component is finite, satisfies $\mathcal{T}_{\mathrm{comp}}$, and does not satisfy Q;*
- *each connector is a $|\mathcal{T}|$-ary tree, does not satisfy Q, and its distinguished node satisfies $\mathcal{T}_{\mathrm{conn}}$;*
- *some component's distinguished node has type τ.*

Proof. For the left-to-right implication, suppose that $\tau, \mathcal{T} \not\models_{\mathit{fin}} Q$. By Lemma 13, there is a finite $\Sigma_{\mathcal{T}}$-alternating frame F such that all connectors are $|\mathcal{T}|$-ary trees, all components are finite, some component's distinguished node has type τ, and G_F is a counter-model. Without loss of generality we can assume that F only uses labels from τ, $\mathcal{T}$, and Q. Because $G_F \not\models Q$, by Lemma 2, no graph that maps homomorphically into G_F satisfies Q. This includes all components and connectors of G_F. By Lemma 9, we can place labels $\mathsf{Need}_{r,B}$ in F in such a way that each component satisfies $\mathcal{T}_{\mathrm{comp}}$ and in each connector the distinguished node satisfies $\mathcal{T}_{\mathrm{conn}}$. This does not affect τ and Q. The resulting frame has all the properties the lemma promises.

For the right-to-left implication, take such a frame F. Because F is $\Sigma_{\mathcal{T}}$-alternating and Q contains no Σ_0-reachability atoms with $\Sigma_{\mathcal{T}} \subseteq \Sigma_0$, each RPQ in Q can only traverse at most $k-1$ connectors. That is, the span of each RPQ in Q is at most $k-1$. By Theorem 6, there is a finite frame F' locally isomorphic to F such that $G_{F'} \not\models Q$. Because F' is locally isomorphic to F, each component of F' is finite and satisfies $\mathcal{T}_{\mathrm{comp}}$, in each connector the distinguished node satisfies $\mathcal{T}_{\mathrm{conn}}$, and in some component, the distinguished node has type τ. Hence, $G_{F'}$ is finite, contains a node of type τ, and $G_{F'} \models \mathcal{T}$ by Lemma 9. That is, $G_{F'}$ is a finite counter-model, which means that $\tau, \mathcal{T} \not\models_{\mathit{fin}} Q$. □

It remains to decide if there is a frame with properties specified in Lemma 14. This time we use the greatest fixed point again.

1. Start from the set Φ_0 of all legal components and the set Ψ_0 of all legal connectors.

2. Iteratively, for each $r \in \Sigma_\mathcal{T}$,
   - remove from Φ_0 all r-free components realizing a type not realized in the distinguished node of any r-only connector in Ψ_0,
   - remove from Ψ_0 all r-only connectors realizing in a non-distinguished node a type not realized in the distinguished node of any r-free component in Φ_0,

   until the set stabilizes.
3. Accept iff the resulting set Φ_0 contains a component with the distinguished node of type τ.

Like before, we represent components abstractly, but because we are looking for a $\Sigma_\mathcal{T}$-alternating frame, we additionally indicate the forbidden edge label. Thus, an r-free component is represented as a triple of the form (σ, Θ, r), where σ is a type, Θ is a set of types, and $r \in \Sigma_\mathcal{T}$. Note that an r-free component satisfies $\mathcal{T}_{\text{comp}}$ iff it satisfies $\mathcal{T}_{\text{comp}} - r$ defined as $\mathcal{T}_{\text{comp}}$ with all concept inclusions $A \sqsubseteq \text{Need}_{r,B} \sqcup \exists r.B$ replaced with $A \sqsubseteq \text{Need}_{r,B}$. Consequently, there is a finite r-free component with the distinguished node of type σ, realizing only types from Θ, iff $\sigma, \mathcal{T} - r \not\models_{fin} Q$.

This way we have reduced the existence of a frame satisfying conditions specified in Lemma 14 to multiple instances of finite entailment for TBoxes using fewer edge labels. As the first reduction described in this section (passing from arbitrary simple UCRPQs to ones with restricted reachability atoms) does not introduce new edge labels, the two reductions together decrease the number of edge labels in the TBox by one, for any simple UCRPQ in the input. Repeating this as many times as needed we can ensure that only one edge label is used in the TBox. Then, the first reduction will yield instances of finite entailment of UCQs, which we already know how to solve. This completes the proof of Theorem 5.

8 Regular Reachability Conditions: Tape Construction

The final step of our plan is to solve finite entailment of general UCRPQs by reduction to finite entailment of simple UCRPQs. This time a single instance of the simpler problem is sufficient. Indeed, we show the following theorem.

Theorem 7. *Given a type τ, an $\mathcal{ALC}$ TBox $\mathcal{T}$, and a UCRPQ Q, one can compute an $\mathcal{ALC}$ TBox $\mathcal{T}'$ and a simple UCRPQ Q' such that $\tau, \mathcal{T} \models_{fin} Q$ iff $\tau, \mathcal{T}' \models_{fin} Q'$.*

By Theorem 5 and the reduction described in Sect. 4, this immediately implies Theorem 1.

Setting the Stage

Following [10], we work with UCRPQs represented by means of a (nondeterministic) *semiautomaton* [5] $\mathcal{A} = (S, \Delta, \delta)$ where S is a finite set of states,

$\Delta \subseteq \Gamma^{\pm} \cup \Sigma$ is a finite alphabet, and $\delta \subseteq S \times \Delta \times S$ is the transition relation. A semiautomaton is essentially a nondeterministic finite automaton without initial and final states; a run of a semiautomaton $\mathcal{A}$ over a word w is defined just like for a nondeterministic finite automaton, except that it can begin in any state and there is no notion of accepting runs. Under this representation, RPQs are atoms of the form $\mathcal{A}_{s,s'}(t,t')$ where $s, s' \in S$ are states of $\mathcal{A}$. In the definition of a match we rephrase item 3 as

3'. some run of $\mathcal{A}$ over $\ell_1 \ldots \ell_n$ begins in s and ends in s'.

Each UCRPQ Q can be effectively rewritten as a UCRPQ Q' expressed by means of a (nondeterministic) semiautomaton $\mathcal{A}$ of size linear in the total size of regular expressions in Q, by replacing each regular expression in Q with $\mathcal{A}_{s,s'}$ for some states s, s' of $\mathcal{A}$. Hence, without loss of generality we can assume that the input UCRPQ is represented by means of a semiautomaton.

Before proceeding with main construction, we simplify our task by reducing to the case of test-free UCRPQs. For UCRPQs represented by means of a semiautomaton, being test-free means that the alphabet of the semiautomaton contains only edge labels.

Lemma 15. *Given a type τ, an $\mathcal{ALC}$ TBox $\mathcal{T}$, and a UCRPQ Q, one can compute an $\mathcal{ALC}$ TBox $\mathcal{T}'$ and a test-free UCRPQ Q' represented by means of a semiautomaton over $\Sigma_{\mathcal{T}'}$ such that $\tau, \mathcal{T} \models_{\mathit{fin}} Q$ iff $\tau, \mathcal{T}' \models_{\mathit{fin}} Q'$.*

Proof. The idea is to record the type of each node in the labels of all outgoing edges. This will make the type available to test-free queries. Let Γ_0 be the set of node labels used in the semi-automaton underlying the input query. For every maximal type τ over Γ_0 and edge label $r \in \Sigma_{\mathcal{T}}$, we fix a fresh role name $\langle \tau, r \rangle$.

Let $\mathcal{T}'$ be obtained from $\mathcal{T}$ by replacing CIs of the forms $A \sqsubseteq \exists r.B$ and $A \sqsubseteq \forall r.B$ with sets of CIs

$$A \sqcap \bigsqcap_{C \in \tau} C \sqsubseteq \exists \langle \tau, r \rangle.B \quad \text{and} \quad A \sqcap \bigsqcap_{C \in \tau} C \sqsubseteq \forall \langle \tau, r \rangle.B,$$

respectively, where τ ranges over maximal types over Γ_0, and adding CI

$$\bigsqcap_{C \in \tau} C \sqsubseteq \forall \langle \tau', r \rangle.\bot$$

for each pair of different maximal types τ, τ' over Γ_0. Note that $\mathcal{T}'$ is not in the normal form, but it can be normalized as any other TBox.

To adjust the query, we first replace the underlying semiautomaton. The new one has the same set of states, and, for every maximal type τ over Γ_0, whenever in the original semiautomaton there is a run from state s to state s' that uses only transitions over labels from τ and there is a transition from s' to s'' over $r \in \Sigma_{\mathcal{T}}$, the new automaton has a transition from s to s'' over $\langle \tau, r \rangle$. It remains to take care of the node labels visited at the end of the runs of the original automaton. To this end, we take the query Q' defined as the union of all CRPQs

that can be obtained from a CRPQ $q \in Q$ by replacing each atom $\mathcal{A}_{s,s'}(x,y)$ in the query with
$$\mathcal{A}_{s,t}(x,y) \wedge \bigwedge_{A \in \tau} A(y)$$
for a state t and a type τ over Γ_0 such that in the original semiautomaton there is a run from state t to state s' that uses only transitions over labels from τ. It is straightforward to check that $\tau, \mathcal{T} \models_{fin} Q$ iff $\tau, \mathcal{T}' \models_{fin} Q'$. □

Thus, from now on we can assume without loss of generality that the alphabet of the semiautomaton underlying the input UCRPQ Q is the set $\Sigma_{\mathcal{T}}$ of edge labels used in the input TBox $\mathcal{T}$.

Expansion

In order to handle UCRPQs expressed by means of a semiautomaton $\mathcal{A}$ we need to be able to trace runs of $\mathcal{A}$ that begin in all possible states, on all infixes of the input word. We achieve this using the following construction.

Let us fix an arbitrary linear order on the set S of states of $\mathcal{A}$. The *expansion* of $\mathcal{A}$ is a semiautomaton $\widehat{\mathcal{A}}$ whose set of states is the set $\widehat{S}$ of all permutations of S. Thus, an element of $\widehat{S}$ can be seen as a tuple $\mathbf{p} = (p_1, p_2, \ldots, p_n)$ such that p_i is the image of the ith state of $\mathcal{A}$ under the respective permutation. We refer to the positions in this tuple as *levels*. In particular, the *level of state* $s \in S$ in $\mathbf{p}$ is the unique i such that $s = p_i$. Assuming $\delta : S \times \Sigma_{\mathcal{T}} \to S$ is the transition function of $\mathcal{A}$, we define the transition function
$$\widehat{\delta} : \widehat{S} \times \Sigma_{\mathcal{T}} \to \widehat{S}$$
of $\widehat{\mathcal{A}}$ by letting $\widehat{\delta}(\mathbf{p}, r)$ be the permutation $\mathbf{p}'$ obtained by listing all states appearing in the sequence
$$\delta(\mathbf{p}, r) = \big(\delta(p_1, r), \delta(p_2, r), \ldots, \delta(p_n, r)\big)$$
in the order of their first appearances, followed by all remaining states of $\mathcal{A}$ ordered as in S. For example, if the states in S are $s_1 < s_2 < s_3 < s_4$ and $\delta(\mathbf{p}, r) = (s_3, s_3, s_1, s_1)$, then $\widehat{\delta}(\mathbf{p}, r) = (s_3, s_1, s_2, s_4)$. Note that the level of $\delta(p_i, r)$ in $\widehat{\delta}(\mathbf{p}, r)$ is at most i. Consider the set $J \subseteq \{1, 2, \ldots, n\}$ of levels i such that the level of $\delta(p_i, r)$ in $\widehat{\delta}(\mathbf{p}, r)$ is equal to i. It follows from the definition of $\widehat{\delta}(\mathbf{p}, r)$ that $J = \{1, 2, \ldots, \ell\}$ for some $\ell \in \{1, 2, \ldots, n\}$. We call this number ℓ the *level of transition* $\mathbf{p} \xrightarrow{r} \mathbf{p}'$.

From each run of $\widehat{\mathcal{A}}$ on a word w we can reconstruct all runs of $\mathcal{A}$ on w. Let $\mathbf{p}_0, \mathbf{p}_1, \ldots, \mathbf{p}_m$ be a run of $\widehat{\mathcal{A}}$ on w. Consider a run $s_0, s_1, \ldots, s_m$ of $\mathcal{A}$ on w. For $i = 0, 1, \ldots, m$, let ℓ_i be the level of s_i in $\mathbf{p}_i$. Any sequence $\ell_0, \ell_1, \ldots, \ell_m$ associated like this with a run of $\mathcal{A}$ will be called a *thread* in the run of $\widehat{\mathcal{A}}$ (see Fig. 1). Notice that two threads that begin at different levels can meet at the same level somewhere along the run; if this happens they remain equal until the end of the run. Also, threads can be born in the middle of a run of $\widehat{\mathcal{A}}$, but they never disappear. A crucial property of threads is that they are non-increasing sequences: the level of s_{i+1} in $\mathbf{p}_{i+1}$ is bounded by the level of s_i in $\mathbf{p}_i$.

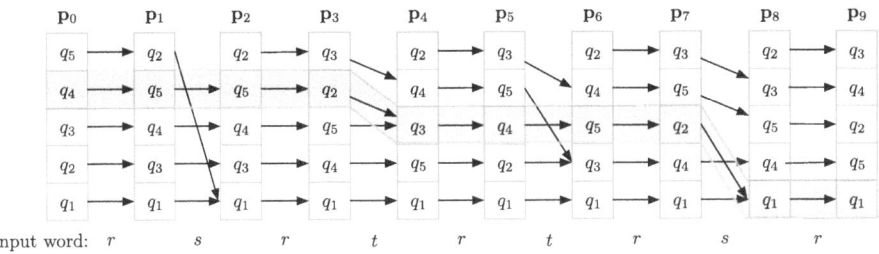

Fig. 1. A thread in a run of the expansion of a semiautomaton.

Lemma 16. *Let $\mathbf{p}_0, \mathbf{p}_1, \ldots, \mathbf{p}_m$ be a run of $\widehat{\mathcal{A}}$ on w, and let s, s' be states of $\mathcal{A}$. There is a run of $\mathcal{A}$ on w from s to s' iff there are positions $0 \leq j_1 < j_2 < \cdots < j_k = m$, levels $n \geq \ell_1 > \ell_2 > \cdots > \ell_k \geq 1$, and states $s_0, s_1, \ldots, s_k$ with $1 \leq k \leq n$ such that $s_0 = s$, $s_k = s'$, and*

- *the level of s_0 in $\mathbf{p}_0$ is ℓ_1 and the level of s_k in $\mathbf{p}_m$ is ℓ_k;*
- *for all $i \in \{1, 2, \ldots, k-1\}$, the level of s_i in $\mathbf{p}_{j_i}$ is ℓ_i and the level of $\delta(s_i, w[j_i+1])$ in $\mathbf{p}_{j_i+1}$ is ℓ_{i+1};*
- *for all $i \in \{1, 2, \ldots, k\}$, each transition taken in the segment of the run from $\mathbf{p}_{j_{i-1}+1}$ (or $\mathbf{p}_0$ for $i = 1$) to $\mathbf{p}_{j_i}$ has level at least ℓ_i.*

Example 4. As an illustration of Lemma 16, consider the run of the expanded semiautomaton shown in Fig. 1. Tracing the run of the original semiautomaton on the same word, starting in state q_4, we discover the positions $j_1 = 3$ and $j_2 = 7$ where the corresponding thread drops to a lower level. Between these positions, the thread stays at the same level, beginning with $\ell_1 = 4$ (taking transitions of levels $5, 4, 5 \geq \ell_1$), followed by $\ell_2 = 3$ (taking transitions of levels $5, 3, 5 \geq \ell_2$), and $\ell_3 = 1$ (taking a transition of level $5 \geq \ell_3$).

Reduction

We are now ready to describe the reduction. The idea is to ingrain the computation of $\widehat{\mathcal{A}}$ into counter-models. Towards this end we introduce a fresh node label $\langle \mathbf{p} \rangle$ for each state $\mathbf{p}$ of $\widehat{\mathcal{A}}$, and a fresh edge label $\langle \mathbf{p}, r, \mathbf{q} \rangle$ for each transition $\mathbf{p} \xrightarrow{r} \mathbf{q}$ of $\widehat{\mathcal{A}}$. We define $\mathcal{T}'$ as follows. To ensure that nodes and edges are consistently labelled with states and transitions of $\widehat{\mathcal{A}}$, we add to $\mathcal{T}'$ concept inclusions

$$\top \sqsubseteq \bigsqcup_{\mathbf{p}} \langle \mathbf{p} \rangle, \quad \bigsqcup_{\mathbf{p} \neq \mathbf{q}} \langle \mathbf{q} \rangle \sqcap \langle \mathbf{q} \rangle \sqsubseteq \bot, \quad \top \sqsubseteq \forall \langle \mathbf{p}, r, \mathbf{q} \rangle.\langle \mathbf{q} \rangle, \quad \text{and} \quad \exists \langle \mathbf{p}, r, \mathbf{q} \rangle.\top \sqsubseteq \langle \mathbf{p} \rangle$$

for all transitions $\mathbf{p} \xrightarrow{r} \mathbf{q}$ of $\widehat{\mathcal{A}}$. Then, for all $K \sqsubseteq L$, $A \sqsubseteq \forall r.B$, and $A \sqsubseteq \exists r.B$ in $\mathcal{T}$, we add to $\mathcal{T}'$ concept inclusions

$$K \sqsubseteq L, \quad A \sqsubseteq \bigsqcap_{\mathbf{p},\mathbf{q}:\ \mathbf{p} \xrightarrow{r} \mathbf{q}} \forall \langle \mathbf{p}, r, \mathbf{q} \rangle.B, \quad \text{and} \quad A \sqsubseteq \bigsqcup_{\mathbf{p},\mathbf{q}:\ \mathbf{p} \xrightarrow{r} \mathbf{q}} \exists \langle \mathbf{p}, r, \mathbf{q} \rangle.B,$$

respectively.

To define Q' we shall decompose RPQs in Q into segments corresponding to different levels, as was done for the runs of $\widehat{\mathcal{A}}$ in Lemma 16. By a *stratified path query* we mean a simple CRPQ of the form

$$\langle \mathbf{p}_1 \rangle(x_1) \wedge T^*_{\ell_1}(x_1, y_1) \wedge \langle \mathbf{q}_1, r_1, \mathbf{p}_2 \rangle(y_1, x_2) \wedge$$
$$\wedge T^*_{\ell_2}(x_2, y_2) \wedge \langle \mathbf{q}_2, r_2, \mathbf{p}_3 \rangle(y_2, x_3) \wedge$$
$$\vdots$$
$$\wedge T^*_{\ell_k}(x_k, y_k) \wedge \langle \mathbf{q}_k \rangle(y_k)$$

for $1 \leq k \leq n$, where

- $n \geq \ell_1 > \ell_2 > \cdots > \ell_{k-1} > \ell_k \geq 1$;
- for each $i \in \{1, 2, \ldots, k\}$, $T^*_{\ell_i}(x_i, y_i)$ is the T_{ℓ_i}-reachability atom with variables x_i, y_i, where T_ℓ is the set of edge labels $\langle \mathbf{p}, r, \mathbf{q} \rangle$ such that transition $\mathbf{p} \xrightarrow{r} \mathbf{q}$ has level at least ℓ;
- for each $i \in \{1, 2, \ldots, k-1\}$, if s_i is the state at level ℓ_i in $\mathbf{q}_i$ then $\delta(s_i, r_i)$ has level ℓ_{i+1} in $\mathbf{p}_{i+1}$.

Up to renaming variables, there are only finitely many stratified path queries for a fixed $\mathcal{A}$. A *stratification of an RPQ* $\mathcal{A}_{s,s'}(x, x')$ is a stratified path query of the form described above such that

- $x_1 = x$, $y_k = x'$, and the remaining variables are fresh;
- the level of s in $\mathbf{p}_1$ is ℓ_1, and the level of s' in $\mathbf{q}_k$ is ℓ_k.

A *stratification of a CRPQ* q is any CRPQ that can be obtained from q by replacing each RPQ atom with one of its stratifications (using disjoint sets of fresh variables). We define Q' as the union of all stratifications of CRPQs in Q.

We claim that
$$\tau, \mathcal{T} \models_{fin} Q \quad \text{iff} \quad \tau, \mathcal{T}' \models_{fin} Q'.$$

(The equivalence holds for unrestricted entailment as well, but it is of no consequence to us.)

Suppose that a graph G is a counter-model for $\tau, \mathcal{T} \models_{fin} Q$. Without loss of generality we can assume that G only uses edge labels from $\Sigma_{\mathcal{T}}$. Let G' be defined as follows:

- $dom(G') = dom(G) \times \widehat{S}$,
- $A^{G'} = A^G \times \widehat{S}$ for all $A \in \Gamma_{\mathcal{T}}$,
- $\langle \mathbf{p} \rangle^{G'} = dom(G) \times \{\mathbf{p}\}$ for all $\mathbf{p} \in \widehat{S}$,
- $\langle \mathbf{p}, r, \mathbf{q} \rangle^{G'} = \{((u, \mathbf{p}), (v, \mathbf{q})) : (u, v) \in r^G\}$ for all transitions $\mathbf{p} \xrightarrow{r} \mathbf{q}$ in $\widehat{\mathcal{A}}$.

It is routine to check that G' realizes type τ and satisfies TBox $\mathcal{T}'$. It remains to see that $G' \not\models Q'$. Towards this end, consider a path ρ in G'. Let w be the word over the alphabet $\Sigma_{\mathcal{T}}$ obtained by reading off the original edge labels from ρ. From Lemma 16 it follows that ρ is a witnessing path for some stratification of an RPQ $\mathcal{A}_{s,s'}(x,x')$ iff there is a run of $\mathcal{A}$ over w from state s to state s'. Let h map each node $(u,\mathbf{p})$ in G' to u. The mapping h would be a homomorphism from G' to G if we dropped the first and last component in each edge label in G'. By the initial observation about witnessing paths for RPQs, it follows easily that by composing a match of a stratification of $q \in Q$ in graph G' with the mapping h, we get a match of q in graph G. This means that $G' \not\models Q'$.

Conversely, suppose G' is a counter-model for the $\tau, \mathcal{T}' \models_{fin} Q'$. Without loss of generality we can assume that it only uses edge labels from $\Sigma_{\mathcal{T}'}$. Let G be the graph obtained from G' by dropping the first and the last component in each edge label. An argument similar to the one above shows that G is a counter-model for $\tau, \mathcal{T} \models_{fin} Q$.

This completes the proof of the claim and of Theorem 7.

9 Outlook

Table 1. Popular extensions of $\mathcal{ALC}$

Acronym	Feature	Syntax
$\mathcal{O}$	use constants as singleton concepts $\{a\}$	$A \sqsubseteq \exists r.\{a\}$
$\mathcal{I}$	use inverse roles r^- anywhere	$A \sqsubseteq \exists r^-.B$
$\mathcal{F}$	declare role r to be a partial function	$\mathsf{fun}(r)$
$\mathcal{Q}$	use counting quantifiers $\exists^{\leq n}, \exists^{\geq n}$	$A \sqsubseteq \exists^{\leq 5} r.B$
$\mathcal{S}$	declare role r to be transitive	$\mathsf{tra}(r)$
$\mathcal{H}$	declare role r to be contained in role s	$r \sqsubseteq s$

Thus we have reached the end of our journey. Along the way we have learned to use multiple tools and methods: query and TBox factorization, unravelling, type elimination, coloured blocking, frames, the coil, and the tape construction. And all this to solve a single problem: finite entailment for UCRPQs and $\mathcal{ALC}$. Was all of this necessary? Can any of this be useful elsewhere?

The answer to the first question is: not really. It is not hard to make the proof of Theorem 5 self-contained (modulo the elimination of the input graph described in Sect. 4). Indeed, alternating the two reductions described in Sect. 7 we ultimately arrive at the case where only one edge label is used in the TBox, and the query is a UCQ. We can solve this case by applying the greatest fixed point algorithm from Sect. 5 directly to finite entailment and using the coil construction to show correctness, in the spirit of Lemma 14 (dropping the condition that the frame is $\Sigma_{\mathcal{T}}$-alternating, but adding the condition that each component is actually a single isolated node). This way we could avoid unravelling and coloured blocking.

The answer to the second question is: yes. Throughout the paper we worked with the most basic description logic, $\mathcal{ALC}$. This logic can be extended with multiple features, such as constants, inverses, counting, or transitivity. Table 1 shows a selection of features that have been considered in the past. Added features are indicated by concatenating suitable letters to the name of the basic logic, resulting in acronyms such as $\mathcal{ALCHOIF}$ or $\mathcal{SOQ}$ ($\mathcal{S}$ is a traditional shorthand for $\mathcal{ALCS}$). This spawns a zoo of finite entailment problems. Some of these have been solved, many using the methods discussed in this paper. Indeed, each discussed method has been used in at least one of the results reviewed below. Many other problems are still open, leaving ample opportunities for reusing the discussed methods in combination with new ideas that will surely be needed.

Most existing work on finite entailment concerns UCQs. The problem is known to be decidable for $\mathcal{SIF}$ [8], $\mathcal{SOQ}$ [7], and $\mathcal{SHOI}$ [4], as well as for some classical fragments of first order logic, such as the guarded fragment $\mathcal{GF}$ [2] or the two-variable guarded fragment with counting $\mathcal{GC}^2$ [15]; it is also known to be undecidable for $\mathcal{SHOIF}$ [16]. For $\mathcal{ALCOIF}$ it is a hard open problem. Indeed, $\mathcal{ALCOIF}$ is rather notorious because even in the unrestricted case we do not know everything: the problem is known to be decidable [17], but there is no complexity upper bound, as decidability is obtained by showing that both the problem and its complement are recursively enumerable.

For UCRPQs, the problem known to be decidable for $\mathcal{ALCI}$ and $\mathcal{ALCQ}$ [9]. A natural next step would be to extend this to $\mathcal{ALCOI}$ and $\mathcal{ALCOQ}$.

Apart from extending the logic, one can also extend the query language. A common and practical extension is to allow traversing edges in the opposite direction, which leads to *two-way* UCRPQs (UC2RPQs). For such queries we know that finite entailment is undecidable for $\mathcal{ALCOIF}$ [16], but even for the basic logic $\mathcal{ALC}$ the status of decidability is open.

References

1. Baader, F., Horrocks, I., Lutz, C., Sattler, U.: An Introduction to Description Logic. Cambridge University Press (2017)
2. Bárány, V., Gottlob, G., Otto, M.: Querying the guarded fragment. Log. Methods Comput. Sci. **10**(2) (2014)
3. Bonifati, A., Fletcher, G.H.L., Voigt, H., Yakovets, N.: Querying Graphs. Morgan & Claypool Publishers, Synthesis Lectures on Data Management (2018)
4. Danielski, D., Kieroński, E.: Finite satisfiability of unary negation fragment with transitivity. In: Proceedings of the MFCS 2019. LIPIcs, vol. 138, pp. 17:1–17:15 (2019)
5. Ginzburg, A.: Algebraic Theory of Automata. Academic Press (1968)
6. Gogacz, T., Gutiérrez-Basulto, V., Gutowski, A., Ibáñez-García, Y., Murlak, F.: On finite entailment of non-local queries in description logics. In: Proceedings of the KR 2020. IJCAI Organization (2020)
7. Gogacz, T., Gutiérrez-Basulto, V., Ibáñez-García, Y., Jung, J.C., Murlak, F.: On finite and unrestricted query entailment beyond SQ with number restrictions on transitive roles. In: Proceedings of the IJCAI 2019, pp. 1719–1725. ijcai.org (2019)
8. Gogacz, T., Ibáñez-García, Y.A., Murlak, F.: Finite query answering in expressive description logics with transitive roles. In: Proceedings of the KR 2018, pp. 369–378. AAAI Press (2018)

9. Gutiérrez-Basulto, V., Gutowski, A., Ibáñez García, Y.A., Murlak, F.: Containment of graph queries modulo schema. Proc. ACM Manag. Data **2**(2) (2024)
10. Gutiérrez-Basulto, V., Gutowski, A., Ibáñez-García, Y., Murlak, F.: Finite entailment of UCRPQs over ALC ontologies. In: Proceedings of the KR 2022. IJCAI Organization (2022)
11. Gutiérrez-Basulto, V., Ibáñez-García, Y., Jung, J.C., Murlak, F.: Answering regular path queries mediated by unrestricted SQ ontologies. Artif. Intell. **314** (2023)
12. Harel, D., Tiuryn, J., Kozen, D.: Dynamic Logic. MIT Press, Cambridge, MA, USA (2000)
13. Kuklis, J.: Data complexity of finite query entailment in description logics with transitive roles. In: Proceedings of the DL 2020. CEUR-WS.org (2020)
14. Pratt, V.R.: Models of program logics. In: Proceedings of the FOCS 1979, pp. 115–122. IEEE Computer Society (1979)
15. Pratt-Hartmann, I.: Data-complexity of the two-variable fragment with counting quantifiers. Inf. Comput. **207**(8), 867–888 (2009)
16. Rudolph, S.: Undecidability results for database-inspired reasoning problems in very expressive description logics. In: Proceedings of the KR 2016, pp. 247–257. AAAI Press (2016)
17. Rudolph, S., Glimm, B.: Nominals, inverses, counting, and conjunctive queries or: why infinity is your friend! J. Artif. Intell. Res. **39**, 429–481 (2010)

Controlled Query Evaluation in Description Logic Ontologies

Gianluca Cima[1], Domenico Lembo[1], Lorenzo Marconi[1], Riccardo Rosati[1(✉)], and Domenico Fabio Savo[2]

[1] Dipartimento di Ingegneria informatica, automatica e gestionale,
Sapienza Università di Roma, Rome, Italy
{cima,lembo,marconi,rosati}@diag.uniroma1.it
[2] Università degli Studi di Bergamo, Bergamo, Italy
domenicofabio.savo@unibg.it

1 Introduction

In this paper we present some of our recent results on query answering in Description Logics (DLs) obtained in the context of *Controlled Query Evaluation (CQE)*, a confidentiality-preserving query answering method studied both for databases [7,10,22] and for ontologies [11,19].

CQE is a *declarative* approach, in which a data protection *policy* is specified in terms of logical formulas, and the enforcement of the policy is formalized through the notion of *censor*. Such a notion models the behaviour of a query answering system that guarantees the satisfaction of the policy. Essentially, a censor defines a subset of formulas in a given language, called the *censor language*, that are logical consequences of the ontology and do not violate the data protection policy. Then, the notion of *optimal censor* is defined as a maximal set of formulas of the above form: such a notion models the behaviour of a system that maximizes query answers while still ensuring that the policy is not violated.

Example 1. Consider a scenario in which a pharmacy discloses part of the data it collects but wants to keep secret some personal information about the health of its customers, as the fact that someone purchased both medicines m_A and m_B. Suppose that the pharmacy's ground knowledge consists solely of the set of facts $\{\mathsf{buy}(\mathsf{mary}, m_A), \mathsf{buy}(\mathsf{mary}, m_B)\}$, and that everyone who buys something is inferred to be a customer (modeled via the unary predicate customer). If the censor language is the set of all the ground atoms, then exactly two optimal censors exist: $\{\mathsf{buy}(\mathsf{mary}, m_A), \mathsf{customer}(\mathsf{mary})\}$ and $\{\mathsf{buy}(\mathsf{mary}, m_B), \mathsf{customer}(\mathsf{mary})\}$. Any subset of these sets would also be a censor, though not necessarily optimal.

As shown by the previous example, given a censor language, *multiple* optimal censors may exist for the same ontology and protection policy. As a consequence, different notions of confidentiality-preserving query entailment can actually be defined, depending on the choice of the censor language and the way in which the presence of multiple optimal censors is managed at the semantic level.

We now formally introduce the CQE framework for DL ontologies. We consider a fixed first-order signature Σ of unary and binary predicates (called atomic concepts and atomic roles, respectively) and constants (also known as individuals). A *CQE instance* is a triple $\langle \mathcal{T}, \mathcal{A}, \mathcal{P} \rangle$, where $\mathcal{T}$ is a DL TBox (that is, a finite set of intensional DL axioms [3]), $\mathcal{A}$ is an atomic DL ABox (that is, a finite set of ground atoms over atomic concepts or atomic roles), and $\mathcal{P}$, called the *policy*, is a set of denial assertions of the form $\forall \boldsymbol{x} \, (\bigwedge_i \alpha_i \to \bot)$, where each α_i is a predicate atom and $\boldsymbol{x}$ are the free variables of such atoms. E.g., the data protection policy used in Example 1 is formalized by the following denial assertion:

$$\forall x \, (\mathsf{buy}(x, \mathsf{m_A}) \wedge \mathsf{buy}(x, \mathsf{m_B}) \to \bot)$$

Let $\mathcal{L}$ be the language of function-free first-order (FO) sentences over Σ and let $\mathcal{L}_c \subseteq \mathcal{L}$. An $\mathcal{L}_c$-*censor* for a CQE instance $\mathcal{E}$ is a subset $\mathcal{C}$ of $\mathcal{L}_c$ such that $\mathcal{T} \cup \mathcal{A} \models \mathcal{C}$ and $\mathcal{T} \cup \mathcal{C} \cup \mathcal{P}$ is consistent. An *optimal* $\mathcal{L}_c$-*censor* for $\mathcal{E}$ is an $\mathcal{L}_c$-censor $\mathcal{C}$ for $\mathcal{E}$ such that there exists no $\mathcal{L}_c$-censor $\mathcal{C}'$ for $\mathcal{E}$ such that $\mathcal{C} \subset \mathcal{C}'$. We denote by $OptCens(\mathcal{E}, \mathcal{L}_c)$ the set of optimal $\mathcal{L}_c$-censors for $\mathcal{E}$.

We will present results for two censor languages $\mathcal{L}_c$:

- the language of ground atoms, denoted by **GA**;
- the language of Boolean Conjunctive Queries (BCQs), denoted by **CQ**.

2 Problems and Results

In this section we discuss three approaches to CQE: (i) randomly construct an optimal censor and use it for query answering; (ii) reason skeptically over all possible optimal censors; (iii) use the intersection of all optimal censors for query answering. For each approach, we specify the censor language(s) and the DL language(s) we consider and recall some computational results.

2.1 Computing an Optimal Censor

We begin our investigation by focusing on the problem of computing an (arbitrarily chosen) optimal censor. Since, in general, CQ censors do not possess a finite representation, we focus on the computation of censors in **GA**, i.e., censors expressed as sets of ground atoms.

Inspired by the idea from [8,18], which involves arbitrarily selecting a single optimal censor and using it to filter query answers, paper [17] proposes the algorithm computeOptGA, which, for any DL-Lite$_\mathcal{R}$ CQE instance $\mathcal{E} = \langle \mathcal{T}, \mathcal{A}, \mathcal{P} \rangle$, returns an ABox $\mathcal{A}_\mathcal{C}$ that serves as an optimal GA censor for $\mathcal{E}$. The algorithm operates by first computing the set $\mathcal{A}_\mathcal{T}$ of ground atoms entailed by $\mathcal{T} \cup \mathcal{A}$. It then iteratively selects a ground atom α from $\mathcal{A}_\mathcal{T}$ in lexicographic order, adding α to the current ABox $\mathcal{A}'$ if $\mathcal{T} \cup \mathcal{A}' \cup \{\alpha\}$ does not violate the policy $\mathcal{P}$. This algorithm runs in polynomial time w.r.t. to the size of $\mathcal{A}$, as stated in the following theorem, which also establishes the algorithm's correctness.

Theorem 1 (Cima et al. IJCAI 2020). *Let $\mathcal{E} = \langle \mathcal{T}, \mathcal{A}, \mathcal{P} \rangle$ be a DL-Lite$_\mathcal{R}$ CQE instance. (i) There exists an optimal GA censor $\mathcal{C}$ for $\mathcal{E}$ such that computeOptGA($\mathcal{E}$) returns $\mathcal{C}$; (ii) computeOptGA($\mathcal{E}$) runs in polynomial time in the size of $\mathcal{A}$.*

From the above theorem and the fact that query entailment in DL-Lite$_\mathcal{R}$ is in AC^0 in data complexity, it directly follows that, given a DL-Lite$_\mathcal{R}$ CQE instance $\mathcal{E} = \langle \mathcal{T}, \mathcal{A}, \mathcal{P} \rangle$ and a BCQ q, it is possible to check in polynomial time (w.r.t. the size of $\mathcal{A}$) whether $\mathcal{T} \cup \mathcal{C} \models q$, where $\mathcal{C}$ is the optimal GA censor for $\mathcal{E}$ returned by computeOptGA($\mathcal{E}$).

2.2 Skeptical Entailment Over Optimal Censors

In general, selecting one single optimal censor to enforce data confidentiality according to the policy might be an arbitrary choice, especially if there is no other information (meta-data) to prefer a censor over the others. Based on this observation, an alternative approach has been proposed [13,20], in which CQE is defined as a form of skeptical reasoning over all possible censors. This approach is also inspired by work on consistent query answering [1,4,5], where processing queries amounts to reasoning over all optimal repairs. In the context of DL ontologies, optimal repairs are maximal subsets of the ABox that are consistent with the TBox, just as optimal $\mathcal{L}_c$-censors are maximal subsets of the set of sentences in $\mathcal{L}_c$ entailed by the ABox and TBox and that are consistent with the TBox and the policy. The entailment problem defined in [13,20] is as follows.

Definition 1. *Given a CQE instance $\mathcal{E}$, a FO sentence q, and a language $\mathcal{L}_c$, we say that q is $\mathcal{L}_c$-entailed by $\mathcal{E}$, denoted by $\mathcal{E} \models^{cqe}_{\mathcal{L}_c} q$, if $\mathcal{T} \cup \mathcal{C} \models q$, for every $\mathcal{C} \in OptCens(\mathcal{E}, \mathcal{L}_c)$.*

Then, we denote by $\mathcal{L}_c\text{-}Ent_{\mathcal{L}_t}(\mathcal{Q})$ the following decision problem: given a CQE instance $\mathcal{E} = \langle \mathcal{T}, \mathcal{A}, \mathcal{P} \rangle$, where $\mathcal{T}$ is a TBox expressed in $\mathcal{L}_t$, a set of FO sentences $\mathcal{Q} \subseteq \mathcal{L}$, and a sentence $q \in \mathcal{Q}$, decide whether $\mathcal{E} \models^{cqe}_{\mathcal{L}_c} q$.

The above decision problem has been investigated in [13,20] for the case when $\mathcal{L}_c = \mathbf{GA}$ or $\mathcal{L}_c = \mathbf{CQ}$, $\mathcal{Q} = \mathbf{GA}$ or $\mathcal{Q} = \mathbf{CQ}$, the TBox is specified either in DL-Lite$_\mathcal{R}$ [12] or in $\mathcal{EL}_\bot$ [2], two popular lightweight ontology languages, which are at the basis of two OWL tractable profiles[1]. Data complexity results established in [13] for such decision problems are given in Fig. 1. We recall that when $\mathcal{Q} = \mathbf{GA}$ the entailment problem is called instance checking.

Results in Fig. 1 show that there are practically relevant cases for which CQE as a form of skeptical reasoning is tractable. In particular, for all the problems with an AC^0 upper bound, it is possible to show that the problem is *FO-rewritable*, i.e. given a TBox $\mathcal{T}$, a policy $\mathcal{P}$, and a query $q \in \mathcal{Q}$, we can effectively compute a FO query q_r such that, for every ABox $\mathcal{A}$, we have that $\langle \mathcal{T}, \mathcal{A}, \mathcal{P} \rangle \models^{cqe}_{\mathcal{L}_c} q$ if and only if the evaluation of q_r over the ABox $\mathcal{A}$ (seen

---

[1] https://www.w3.org/TR/owl2-profiles/.

	Instance Checking $\mathcal{Q} = \mathbf{GA}$	BCQ Entailment $\mathcal{Q} = \mathbf{CQ}$
GA-$Ent_{\text{DL-Lite}_{\mathcal{R}}}(\mathcal{Q})$	$\leq \text{AC}^0$	$= \text{coNP}$
CQ-$Ent_{\text{DL-Lite}_{\mathcal{R}}}(\mathcal{Q})$	$\leq \text{AC}^0$	$\leq \text{AC}^0$
GA-$Ent_{\mathcal{EL}_\bot}(\mathcal{Q})$	$= \text{coNP}$	$= \text{coNP}$
CQ-$Ent_{\mathcal{EL}_\bot}(\mathcal{Q})$	$\leq \text{coNP}$ $\geq \text{PTime}$	$\leq \text{coNP}$ $\geq \text{PTime}$

Fig. 1. Data complexity of $\mathcal{L}_c$-$Ent_{\mathcal{L}_t}(\mathcal{Q})$ for $\mathcal{L}_c, \mathcal{Q} \in \{\mathbf{GA}, \mathbf{CQ}\}$ and $\mathcal{L}_t \in \{\text{DL-Lite}_\mathcal{R}, \mathcal{EL}_\bot\}$

as an interpretation) is true. This result is clearly relevant for practical implementations of CQE based on SQL rewritings and the use of standard relational database systems.

2.3 Intersection-Based Query Entailment

We now analyze a different well-founded semantics for CQE based on the notion of the *intersection of all the optimal censors*, thus avoiding arbitrary choice by always being unique. This new semantics soundly approximates the skeptical reasoning approach for CQE but it turns out to be tractable also for the case of **GA** as censor language.

Given a CQE instance $\mathcal{E} = \langle \mathcal{T}, \mathcal{A}, \mathcal{P} \rangle$ and a censor language $\mathcal{L}_c$, we let $\mathcal{C}^\cap_{\mathcal{E}, \mathcal{L}_c}$ be the *intersection-based $\mathcal{L}_c$-censor for $\mathcal{E}$*, i.e.:

$$\mathcal{C}^\cap_{\mathcal{E}, \mathcal{L}_c} = \bigcap_{\mathcal{C} \in OptCens(\mathcal{E}, \mathcal{L}_c)} \mathcal{C}$$

Furthermore, given a FO sentence q, we denote by $\mathcal{E} \models^{\cap, cqe}_{\mathcal{L}_c} q$ the fact that $\mathcal{T} \cup \mathcal{C}^\cap_{\mathcal{E}, \mathcal{L}_c} \models q$. By definition, one can easily see that the following properties hold: (*i*) $\mathcal{C}^\cap_{\mathcal{E}, \mathcal{L}_c}$ exists and is unique, (*ii*) $\mathcal{C}^\cap_{\mathcal{E}, \mathcal{L}_c}$ is an $\mathcal{L}_c$-censor for $\mathcal{E}$, (*iii*) if $\mathcal{E} \models^{\cap, cqe}_{\mathcal{L}_c} q$, then $\mathcal{E} \models^{cqe}_{\mathcal{L}_c} q$ as well (i.e. the intersection-based query entailment is always a sound approximation of the skeptical query entailment semantics), and (*iv*) if $\mathcal{E} \models^{cqe}_{\mathcal{L}_c} q$ and $q \in \mathcal{L}_c$, then q must belong to each optimal $\mathcal{L}_c$-censor for $\mathcal{E}$, and so $\mathcal{E} \models^{\cap, cqe}_{\mathcal{L}_c} q$ as well (i.e. the other way around holds whenever $q \in \mathcal{L}_c$).

We now introduce the decision problem concerning the entailment of queries under intersection-based semantics, which has been mainly studied when $\mathcal{L}_c = \mathbf{GA}$ or $\mathcal{L}_c = \mathbf{CQ}$ and when the TBox is specified in DL-Lite$_\mathcal{R}$.

Definition 2. $\mathcal{L}_c$-*IntEnt*($\mathcal{Q}$): *Given a CQE instance $\mathcal{E} = \langle \mathcal{T}, \mathcal{A}, \mathcal{P} \rangle$, where $\mathcal{T}$ is a TBox expressed in DL-Lite$_\mathcal{R}$, and a sentence $q \in \mathcal{Q}$, decide whether $\mathcal{E} \models^{\cap, cqe}_{\mathcal{L}_c} q$.*

Note that, by combining the observations (*iii*) and (*iv*) done above with the results of the previous section, we can immediately derive that **GA**-*IntEnt*(**GA**) and **CQ**-*IntEnt*(**CQ**) are both in AC^0 in data complexity.

It thus remains to address the case of entailment of BCQs when $\mathcal{L}_c = \mathbf{GA}$ (i.e. $\mathbf{GA}$-*IntEnt*($\mathbf{CQ}$)). Interestingly, while for this case skeptical reasoning is intractable (coNP-complete in data complexity, see previous section), it turns out to be tractable when we consider the intersection-based semantics.

Theorem 2 (Cima et al. IJCAI 2020). $\mathbf{GA}$-*IntEnt*($\mathbf{CQ}$) *is in AC^0 in data complexity.*

3 Conclusions

In this article, we provided an introduction to CQE in the context of DL ontologies. Depending on the specific reasoning task, the techniques suitable for solving the problems presented may vary according to several parameters, including the chosen DL, the query language and the censor language. Actually, all the results mentioned in the present paper are given (or can easily be extended to) the case in which the query is a *union of BCQs*.

In some applications, reasoning skeptically over multiple censors may show limitations regarding the amount of information disclosed through query answering. In order to improve this aspect, [15] studies an extension of the CQE framework that exploits a priority relation between ontology predicates. Such a priority relation can be used for reducing the set of censors that are used for entailment and, hence, increasing the number of query answers under both the skeptical and the intersection-based semantics.

The analysis conducted in [15] indicates that such an approach has in general a high computational cost, as already shown e.g. in [6] in a different scenario. However, the above paper presented a CQE semantics exploiting priorities under which answering BCQs over DL-Lite$_\mathcal{R}$ ontologies is still in AC^0 data complexity and it collapses to the intersection-based semantics in the absence of preferences. Consequently, such an approach to CQE is potentially able to increase non-confidential answers to queries while remaining feasible in practice.

The CQE framework has also been extended in other directions. For example, reference [9] describes how to progressively reduce the set of censors according to the history of user queries, which allows for revealing more information (as for the prioritized case). At the same time, this approach guarantees a *maximal cooperativity* property that, intuitively, consists in answering the user truthfully for as long as it is possible.

Furthermore, the paper [16] studied a policy language whose expressive power goes significantly beyond denials. A distinctive feature of this language is the usage of an epistemic operator K.

Finally, [14] described a practical approach to CQE based on the Ontology-based Data Access (OBDA) methodology [21], also providing an implementation that we used for conducting experiments.

Acknowledgements. This work was partially supported by: projects FAIR (PE0000013) and SERICS (PE00000014) under the MUR National Recovery and Resilience Plan funded by the EU - NextGenerationEU; GLACIATION project funded by the EU (N. 101070141); ANTHEM (AdvaNced Technologies for Human-centrEd Medicine) project (CUP B53C22006700001) funded by the National Plan for NRRP Complementary Investments; the MUR PRIN 2022LA8XBH project Polar (POLicy specificAtion and enfoRcement for privacy-enhanced data management); and by the EU under the H2020-EU.2.1.1 project TAILOR (grant id. 952215).

References

1. Arenas, M., Bertossi, L.E., Chomicki, J.: Consistent query answers in inconsistent databases. In: Proceedings of the 18th ACM SIGMOD SIGACT SIGART Symposium on Principles of Database Systems (PODS), pp. 68–79 (1999)
2. Baader, F., Brandt, S., Lutz, C.: Pushing the $\mathcal{EL}$ envelope. In: Proceedings of the 19th International Joint Conference on Artificial Intelligence (IJCAI), pp. 364–369 (2005)
3. Baader, F., Calvanese, D., McGuinness,D., Nardi, D., Patel-Schneider, P.F. (eds.): The Description Logic Handbook: Theory, Implementation and Applications. Cambridge University Press, 2nd edition (2007)
4. Bertossi, L.E.: Database Repairing and Consistent Query Answering. Synthesis Lectures on Data Management. Morgan & Claypool Publishers (2011)
5. Bienvenu, M., Bourgaux, C.: Inconsistency-tolerant querying of description logic knowledge bases. In: Reasoning Web: Logical Foundation of Knowledge Graph Construction and Query Answering – 12th International Summer School Tutorial Lectures (RW), volume 9885 of Lecture Notes in Computer Science, pp. 156–202. Springer (2016)
6. Bienvenu, M., Bourgaux, C.: Querying and repairing inconsistent prioritized knowledge bases: Complexity analysis and links with abstract argumentation. In: Proceedings of the 17th International Conference on Principles of Knowledge Representation and Reasoning (KR), pp. 141–151 (2020)
7. Biskup, J.: For unknown secrecies refusal is better than lying. Data Knowl. Eng. **33**(1), 1–23 (2000)
8. Biskup, J., Bonatti, P.A.: Controlled query evaluation with open queries for a decidable relational submodel. Ann. of Math. Artif. Intell. **50**(1–2), 39–77 (2007)
9. Bonatti, P., et al.: Controlled query evaluation in OWL 2 QL: a "longest honeymoon" approach. In: Proceedings of the 21st International Semantic Web Conference (ISWC), volume 12922 of Lecture Notes in Computer Science, pp. 428–444. Springer (2022)
10. Bonatti, P.A., Kraus, S., Subrahmanian, V.S.: Foundations of secure deductive databases. IEEE Trans. Knowl. Data Eng. 7(3), 406–422 (1995)
11. Bonatti, P.A., Sauro, L.: A confidentiality model for ontologies. In: Proceedings of the 12th International Semantic Web Conference (ISWC), pp. 17–32 (2013)
12. Calvanese, D., De Giacomo, G., Lembo, D., Lenzerini, M., Rosati, R.: Tractable reasoning and efficient query answering in description logics: the DL-Lite family. J. Autom. Reasoning **39**(3), 385–429 (2007)
13. Cima, G., Lembo, D., Rosati, R., Savo, D.F.: Controlled query evaluation in description logics through consistent query answering. Artif. Intell. **334**, 104176 (2024)
14. Cima, G., Lembo, D., Marconi, L., Rosati, R., Savo, D.F.: Controlled query evaluation in ontology-based data access. In: Proceedings of the 19th International Semantic Web Conference (ISWC), volume 12506 of Lecture Notes in Computer Science, pp. 128–146. Springer (2020)

15. Cima, G., Lembo, D., Marconi, L., Rosati, R., Savo, D.F.: Controlled query evaluation over prioritized ontologies with expressive data protection policies. In: Proceedings of the 20th International Semantic Web Conference (ISWC), volume 12922 of Lecture Notes in Computer Science, pp. 374–391. Springer (2021)
16. Cima, G., Lembo, D., Marconi, L., Rosati, R., Savo, D.F.: Enhancing controlled query evaluation through epistemic policies. In: Proceedings of the 33rd International Joint Conference on Artificial Intelligence (IJCAI) (2024). To appear
17. Cima, G., Lembo, D., Marconi, L., Rosati, R., Savo, D.F.: Controlled query evaluation in description logics through instance indistinguishability. In: Proceedings of the 29th International Joint Conference on Artificial Intelligence (IJCAI), pp. 1791–1797 (2020)
18. Cuenca Grau, B., Kharlamov, E., Kostylev, E.V., Zheleznyakov, D.: Controlled query evaluation over OWL 2 RL ontologies. In: Proceedings of the 12th International Semantic Web Conference (ISWC), pp. 49–65 (2013)
19. Cuenca Grau, B., Kharlamov, E., Kostylev, E.V., Zheleznyakov, D.: Controlled query evaluation for datalog and OWL 2 profile ontologies. In: Proceedings of the 24th International Joint Conference on Artificial Intelligence (IJCAI), pp. 2883–2889 (2015)
20. Lembo, D., Rosati, R., Savo, D.F.: Revisiting controlled query evaluation in description logics. In: Proceedings of the 28th International Joint Conference on Artificial Intelligence (IJCAI), pp. 1786–1792 (2019)
21. Poggi, A., Lembo, D., Calvanese, D., De Giacomo, G., Lenzerini, M., Rosati, R.: Linking data to ontologies. J. Data Semant. **x**, 133–173 (2008)
22. Sicherman, G.L., de Jonge, W., van de Riet, R.P.: Answering queries without revealing secrets. ACM Trans. Database Syst. **8**(1), 41–59 (1983)

Actively Learning from Machine Learning Models with Queries and Counterexamples

Ana Ozaki[✉][iD]

University of Oslo and University of Bergen, Bergen, Norway
`anaoz@uio.no`

Abstract. We provide an overview of recent approaches to extract simpler abstractions of complex neural networks using Angluin's exact learning framework with queries and counterexamples. These simpler models approximate parts of the original model by focusing on a relevant collection of inputs/outputs. The aim of constructing such abstractions is to obtain high level information about machine learning models, which can be useful to detect harmful biases and other issues. We focus on concept classes applied for actively learning from machine learning models within Angluin's framework, namely, automata and Horn logic. We also discuss approaches from the literature to extract decision trees from neural networks. We highlight the benefits and drawbacks of these approaches. Finally, we discuss promising possible next steps and applications of these approaches for extracting high level information from machine learning models.

Keywords: Active Learning · Exact Learning · PAC Learning · Explanations

1 Introduction

Complex machine learning (ML) models are currently applied to various tasks such as predicting medical interventions based on records of patient cohorts, facilitating the work of designers by generating images according to a given description, helping programmers to create code when provided with a higher level specification of a program, among many others. In many of these applications, ML models are used as black-boxes and there is no simple way of replacing such models with alternatives where users can understand why the results are in a given way—the well-known explainability issue in artificial intelligence (AI).

To deal with this challenge, the field of Explainable AI has emerged, with multiple approaches attempting to extract high level information from the models which could be useful for finding plausible explanations. The format of an explanation can vary according to the task at hand and what the user would

---

Supported by the Norwegian Research Council, project number 316022.

© The Author(s), under exclusive license to Springer Nature Switzerland AG 2025
M. Console and B. Konev (Eds.): Reasoning Web. Declarative Artificial Intelligence: Knowledge, Rules, Logic, LNCS 15400, pp. 61–77, 2025.
https://doi.org/10.1007/978-3-031-80283-6_4

like to understand. One can either focus on attempting to explain the output of the model given a particular input or the general behaviour of the model (independent of particular input/output). In the former case, a popular strategy consists of computing the so-called shapley values, which provide useful information regarding which feature values in the input are most relevant for the output (see e.g. [4]). Here we consider recent approaches to tackle the latter case. In particular, we consider recent approaches to extract abstractions that approximate of complex neural networks using Angluin's exact learning framework [2]. Such approximations can be understood as simpler abstractions of the original model, providing support to plausible explanations of the overall behaviour of a model, in particular, giving high level information such as biases.

In Angluin's exact learning framework, a learner attempts to learn a target concept from an oracle by posing questions. The idea of re-purposing the framework in the context of explanations is to probe a black-box model as if it was the oracle in Angluin's framework. One of the benefits of this approach is that one can explore out-of-distribution inputs/outputs [17] and systematically investigate the behaviour of the model [35]. The most studied communication protocol between the learner and the oracle has two kinds of queries: membership and equivalence queries. A membership query can be simulated by probing a black-box model (that is, sending an input and receiving the output of the model). Equivalence queries are more intricate since in this case the learner hypothesizes the target and sends it to the oracle, expecting either a confirmation of being correct or receiving some information—called a *counterexample*—which exemplifies incorrectness. A general approach to deal with this is to simulate equivalence queries with a collection of membership queries, resulting in a batch of classified examples where the learner either finds a counterexample or terminates with a probabilistic guarantee regarding the correctness of the hypothesis. This theoretical guarantee is based on the probably approximately correct (PAC) learning framework.

We formally introduce the exact and PAC frameworks and then focus on two classical concept classes applied for extracting abstractions within these frameworks, namely, automata and logic, in particular, Horn logic. We also discuss approaches from the literature to extract decision trees from machine learning models. We highlight benefits and drawbacks of these approaches. Finally, we present promising possible next steps in this line of research, namely, to consider more expressive formalisms which can also express uncertainty within the explanation given to the users.

2 Basic Definitions

We provide basic definitions for the exact and the PAC learning frameworks and for the two concept classes we focus in these lecture notes, namely, the class of automata and the class of Horn expressions. The case of decision trees is explored in Sect. 5.

2.1 Exact and PAC Learning Frameworks

A *concept class* $\mathbb{C}$ is a triple $(\mathcal{E}, C, \mu)$ where $\mathcal{E}$ is a set of *examples*, C is a set of *concept representations*, and $\mu : C \to 2^{\mathcal{E}}$ is a function mapping each concept representation $c \in C$ to a set of examples in $\mathcal{E}$ that c represents. Given a concept $c \in C$, examples in $\mu(c)$ are called *positive examples*, while examples in $\mathcal{E} \setminus \mu(c)$ are *negative examples*. A *membership query* is a call to a *membership oracle*, defined as follows. Given a concept class $\mathbb{C} = (\mathcal{E}, C, \mu)$ and a concept $c \in C$, a membership oracle (for $\mathbb{C}$ and c) is a function, denoted $\mathsf{MQ}_{\mathbb{C},c}$, that takes as input an example $e \in \mathcal{E}$ and returns 'yes' if $e \in \mu(c)$ and 'no' otherwise. An *equivalence query* is a call to an *equivalence oracle*, defined as follows. Given a concept class $\mathbb{C} = (\mathcal{E}, C, \mu)$ and a concept $c \in C$, an equivalence oracle (for $\mathbb{C}$ and c) is a procedure that takes as input a concept $h \in C$—the *hypothesis*—and returns 'yes' if $\mu(c) = \mu(h)$ and 'no' plus some *counterexample* $e \in \mu(c) \oplus \mu(h)$ otherwise, where $\oplus$ denotes symmetric set difference. There may be multiple counterexamples that an equivalence oracle can return. Such procedure of selecting counterexamples is non-deterministic and write $\mathsf{EQ}_{\mathbb{C},c}(h)$ to refer to an equivalence oracle for a concept class $\mathbb{C} = (\mathcal{E}, C, \mu)$ and a concept $c \in C$.

Definition 1 (Exact Learning). *A concept class exact $\mathbb{C}$ is exactly learnable if*

- *there is a deterministic algorithm such that, for every $c \in C$, it eventually halts and outputs some $h \in C$ with $\mu(h) = \mu(c)$. Such algorithm is allowed to call the oracles $\mathsf{MQ}_{\mathbb{C},c}$ and $\mathsf{EQ}_{\mathbb{C},c}$.*

If the number of computation steps used by the algorithm is bounded by a polynomial $p(|c|, |e|)$, where $c \in C$ is the target and $e \in E$ is the largest counterexample seen so far, then $\mathbb{C}$ is exactly learnable in polynomial time.

A *sample query* is a call to a *sample oracle*, defined as follows. Given a concept class $\mathbb{C} = (\mathcal{E}, C, \mu)$ and a concept $c \in C$, a sample oracle (for $\mathbb{C}$ and c) is a procedure that takes nothing as input and outputs a pair (e, l) where $e \in \mathcal{E}$ and $l = +$ if $e \in \mu(c)$, otherwise $l = -$. Classified examples are selected according to a probability distribution. We write $\mathsf{EX}_{\mathbb{C},c}^{\mathcal{D}}$ to refer to a sample oracle for a concept class $\mathbb{C} = (\mathcal{E}, C, \mu)$, a probability distribution $\mathcal{D}$, and a concept $c \in C$.

Definition 2 (PAC Learning). *A concept class $\mathbb{C}$ is PAC learnable if*

- *there is a function $f : (0,1)^2 \to \mathbb{N}$ and a deterministic algorithm such that, for every $\epsilon, \delta \in (0,1) \subset \mathbb{R}$, every probability distribution $\mathcal{D}$ on $\mathcal{E}$, and every target $t \in C$, given a sample of size $m \geq f(\epsilon, \delta)$ generated by $\mathsf{EX}_{\mathbb{C},t}^{\mathcal{D}}$, the algorithm always halts and outputs $h \in C$ such that with probability at least $(1-\delta)$ over the choice of m examples in $\mathcal{E}$, we have that $\mathcal{D}(\mu(h) \oplus \mu(t)) \leq \epsilon$.*

If the number of computation steps used by the algorithm is bounded by a polynomial function $p(|t|, |e|, 1/\epsilon, 1/\delta)$, where e is the largest example in the sample generated by $\mathsf{EX}^{\mathcal{D}}_{\mathbb{C},t}$, then $\mathbb{C}$ is PAC learnable in polynomial time. If the algorithm is allowed to perform membership queries then we say that the concept class is PAC learnable (or PAC learnable in polynomial time) with membership queries.

The next theorem establishes that equivalence queries can be simulated. The idea is to sample a number of classified examples and either find a counterexample or stop providing a high probabilistic guarantee of low error on the resulting hypothesis (depending on the size of the sample).

Theorem 1 ([2]). *If a concept class $\mathbb{C}$ is exactly learnable then $\mathbb{C}$ is PAC learnable with membership queries. Moreover, if $\mathbb{C}$ is exactly learnable in polynomial time and deciding whether an example is positive is in PTime then $\mathbb{C}$ is PAC learnable in polynomial time with membership queries.*

Other learning frameworks between the exact and the PAC learning models have also been investigated [10].

2.2 Concept Classes: Automata and Horn Expressions

We provide basic notions about automata and Horn logic, useful for the definition of their respective concept classes and the algorithms presented in the next section (for more information about these basic notions see e.g. [31]).

Automata. A finite automaton is a computational model that abstracts the notion of a computer with limited memory [31]. Many electric mechanical devices can be represented using the notion of an automaton, as Example 1.

Example 1. To illustrate, consider the case of an electric gate with a front pad and a rear pad. There are four possible configurations, as depicted in Fig. 2. In the first configuration, the gate is closed and there is no one standing on the pads. In the second, a person is on the front pad, which triggers the opening of the gate. In the third, a person stands on the rear pad, which causes the gate to remain open. Finally, there is the state in which a person stands on the front pad but in this scenario the gate does not open to avoid clashing with another person on the rear pad.

The configurations in Fig. 1 are represented by the automaton in Fig. 1. Formally, an automaton is a tuple $(Q, \Sigma, \delta, F, q^i)$ where Q is a finite set of states, Σ is a finite set of *alphabet symbols*, $\delta : Q \times \Sigma \to Q$ is a relation that maps states and alphabet symbols to (next) states, $F \subseteq Q$ is the set of final states, and q^i is the initial state. We call such relation the *transition relation* and say that an automaton is *deterministic* if the transition relation is a function. Given a finite set of alphabet symbols Σ, we denote by Σ^* the set of all finite sequences of symbols in Σ. Such finite sequences are *words* in Σ^*. An automaton $(Q, \Sigma, \delta, F, q^i)$ *accepts* a word $w = a_1 \ldots a_n$ in Σ^* if there is a sequence of states $q_0 \ldots q_n$ with $q_0 = q^i$, $q_n \in F$, and $\delta(q_j, a_{j+1}) = q_{j+1}$ for all $0 \leq j \leq n$. We instantiate these notions in Example 2. An automaton *recognizes* a (regular) language L iff it accepts exactly those words in L.

Example 2. The automaton illustrated in Fig. 2 is the tuple $\mathcal{A} = (Q, \Sigma, \delta, F, q_i)$, where $Q = \{\text{closed, open}\}$, $\Sigma = \{R, B, N, F\}$, $F = \{\text{closed}\}$, $q_i = \text{open}$, and δ is the transition function given by the arrows in the figure (e.g., $\delta(\text{closed}, F) = \text{open}$). We have that $\mathcal{A}$ accepts, e.g., 'NFRN' and 'N' but it does not accept, e.g., 'FRRB'.

Fig. 1. Four Gate Configurations

The Class of Automata. We denote by $\mathbb{C}(\mathbf{A}) = (\mathcal{E}, C, \mu)$ the class of automata, where $\mathcal{E}$ is the set of all words in Σ^*, C is the set of all automata that can recognize a regular language in Σ^*, and μ is a function that maps each automaton to the set of words in Σ^* that it accepts.

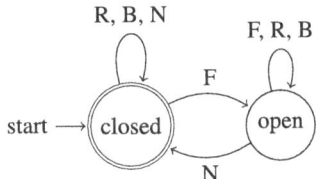

Fig. 2. Automaton for the Gate: 'R' stands for '*only* rear pad', 'F' stands for '*only* front pad', 'B' stands for 'both pads', and 'N' stands for 'neither of the pads'

Horn Expressions. Let $\mathcal{V}$ be a finite set of propositional symbols, also called propositional variables. A *literal* is a propositional variable v in $\mathcal{V}$ or its negation, denoted $\neg v$. Literals with negation are called *negative literals* and literals without negation are referred to as *positive literals*. A *clause* is a (finite) *disjunction of literals*, in symbols, $l_1 \vee \ldots \vee l_n$. If a clause has at most one positive literal then it is called a *Horn clause*. We often write Horn clauses in the format of an implication. Horn clauses with one positive literal $\neg l_1 \vee \ldots \vee \neg l_n \vee l$, called *definite clauses*, are written as $(l_1 \wedge \ldots \wedge l_n) \to l$ (or $\top \to l$ if the clause has only one positive literal l) and Horn clauses with only negative literals $\neg l_1 \vee \ldots \vee \neg l_n$ are written as $(l_1 \wedge \ldots \wedge l_n) \to \bot$. A *Horn expression* is a conjunction of Horn clauses. An alternative way to define Horn expressions is to define it as a set of Horn clauses. We may treat sets and the conjunction of their elements interchangeably.

In our formulas, we represent the logical constant 'true' with $\top$ and the logical constant 'false' with $\bot$.

The semantics of Horn expressions is given by *interpretations*. An interpretation over a set of propositional variables $\mathcal{V}$ is a function that maps $\top$ to 1 ('true'), $\bot$ to 0 ('false'), and each symbol in $\mathcal{V}$ to either 1 ('true') or 0 ('false'). An alternative way to define interpretations is as a subset of $\mathcal{V}$ union $\{\top\}$, where variables in the subset correspond to those assigned to 'true' in the definition of interpretation as a function. An interpretation $\mathcal{I}$ *satisfies* a positive literal if the corresponding variable is assigned to 1 in $\mathcal{I}$. It satisfies a negative literal if the variable occurring in it is assigned to 0 in $\mathcal{I}$. It satisfies a *clause* iff at least one of its literals are satisfied. Finally, an interpretation $\mathcal{I}$ satisfies a Horn expression Φ, in symbols $\mathcal{I} \models \Phi$, iff all (Horn) clauses in it are satisfied.

Example 3. Let $\mathcal{V} = \{a, b, c, d\}$ and $\Phi = \{(b \wedge c \wedge d) \rightarrow a, (a \wedge d) \rightarrow c\}$. Then, for $\mathcal{I} = \{a, d, c, \top\}$ we have that $\mathcal{I} \models \Phi$ and $\mathcal{J} = \{b, d, c, \top\}$ we have that $\mathcal{J} \not\models \Phi$.

The Class of Horn Expressions. We denote by $\mathbb{C}(\mathbf{H}) = (\mathcal{E}, C, \mu)$ the class of Horn expressions, where $\mathcal{E}$ is the set of all interpretations over $\mathcal{V}$, C is the set of all Horn expressions with symbols in $\mathcal{V}$, and μ is a function that maps each Horn expression $c \in C$ to the subset of $\mathcal{E}$ that corresponds to the interpretations that satisfy c. In symbols, for $c \in C$ we have that: $\mu(c) = \{e \in \mathcal{E} \mid e \models c\}$.

3 Extracting Automata from Machine Learning Models

In this section, we first describe the classical L* algorithm proposed by Dana Angluin [1] (Sect. 3.1). Then, we discuss how one can employ L* to extract high level (and global) information from a machine learning model [33,34] (Sect. 3.2).

3.1 The L* Algorithm

In this section we describe Anlguin's classical L* algorithm [1]. To describe the algorithm, we use the notion of prefix- and suffix-closed sets, defined as follows. A set is *prefix-closed* iff every prefix of every member of the set is also a member of the set. Similarly, a set is *suffix-closed* iff every suffix of every member of the set is also a member of the set. For instance, $\{1, 10\}$ and $\{1, 10, 100, 101\}$ are prefix-closed while $\{0, 10\}$ and $\{1, 01, 101, 001\}$ are suffix-closed. The L* algorithm keeps an observation table. This table records whether strings are accepted by the target automaton. The observation table has three components:

1. A non-empty finite prefix-closed set S of words.
2. A non-empty finite suffix-closed set E of words.
3. A function T mapping $(S \cup S.\Sigma).E$ to $\{1, 0\}$ (true or false).

Algorithm 1, we write λ to denote the empty string (Line 1). We denote by $row(s)$ the finite function f from $e \in E$ to $\{0, 1\}$ defined by $f(e) = T(s.e)$. Angluin's algorithm requires that the observation table satisfies two properties (see Lines 2 and 6).

1. The table is *closed*: for each t in $S.\Sigma$, there is s in S such that $row(t) = row(s)$.
2. The table is *consistent*: for all s_1, s_2 in S, if $row(s_1) = row(s_2)$ then, for all a in Σ, $row(s_1.a) = row(s_2.a)$.

Membership queries are used to keep the properties. Whenever the table is not closed, we add t to S. Whenever the table is not consistent, we add a to E.

Algorithm 1: The L* Algorithm [1]

input: $\mathsf{MQ}_{\mathcal{C}(\mathbf{A}),L}$ and $\mathsf{EQ}_{\mathcal{C}(\mathbf{A}),L}$ oracles.
output: An automaton $\mathcal{A}$ such that $\mathcal{A}$ recognizes the target regular language L.

1. Create initial T with $S = E = \{\lambda\}$
2. Ensure T is closed and consistent (membership queries)
3. Create a hypothesis $\mathcal{A}$ based on T
4. **while** $\mathsf{EQ}_{\mathcal{C}(\mathbf{A}),L}(\mathcal{A}) = (no, e)$ **do**
5. $\quad$ Extend T with the counterexample e returned (add e to S)
6. $\quad$ Ensure T is closed and consistent (membership queries)
7. $\quad$ Create a hypothesis $\mathcal{A}$ based on T
8. **return** $(\mathcal{A})$

Given an observation table (S, E, T), the L^* algorithm defines a hypothesis in the format of an automaton $(Q, \Sigma, \delta, F, q^i)$ as follows (Lines 3 and 7):

- $Q = \{row(s) \mid s \in S\}$;
- Σ is the alphabet of the automaton as well;
- $\delta(row(s), a) = row(s.a)$;
- $q^i = row(\lambda)$; and
- $F = \{row(s) \mid s \in S \text{ and } T(s) = 1\}$.

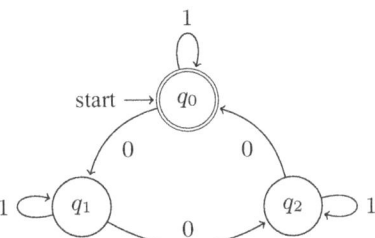

Fig. 3. Automaton for $L = \{w \mid \text{number of 0's is } 3 \cdot n \text{ and } n \text{ is a natural number}\}$

An Example Run. Suppose the target automaton is the one in Fig. 3, which recognizes the language $L = \{w \mid $ number of 0's is $3 \cdot n$ and n is a natural number$\}$. The algorithm creates Table 1a with $S = E = \{\lambda\}$. Since this table is not closed, the algorithm adds 0 to S, resulting in Table 1b, which now is closed and consistent. In Line 3, Algorithm 1 creates the automaton in Fig. 4a based on Table 1b. In Line 2, the algorithm makes an equivalence query. As the automaton in Fig. 4a is not equivalent to the automaton in Fig. 4a (that is, does not recognize the same regular language), the answer is 'no' together with a counterexample. Suppose the counterexample is 000. Algorithm 1 adds 000 to S and completes the table by posing membership queries, resulting in Table 1c. This table is closed but not consistent. To make it consistent, the algorithm adds a new column labelled 0 and completes the table by posing membership queries, resulting in Table 1d (the 'yes/no' values in the column 0 correspond to the answer of the membership oracle given the string in E concatenated with 0 as input). Since Table 1d is closed and consistent, Algorithm 1 creates in Line 7 the automaton in Fig. 4b based on Table 1d. In Line 2, the algorithm makes again an equivalence query, which this time returns 'yes'. So the algorithm ends the 'while-loop' and returns the automaton in Fig. 4b, as required.

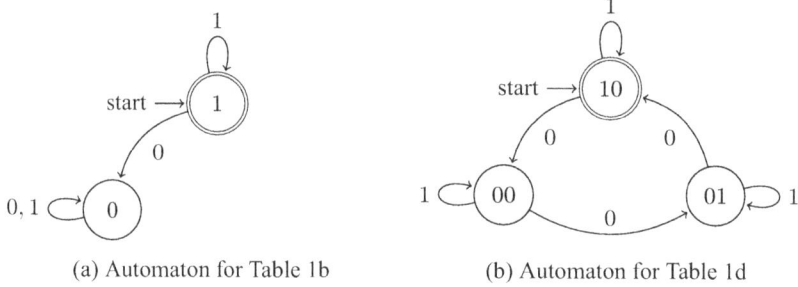

Fig. 4. Hypotheses generated by the tables in the example run of Algorithm 1

Theorem 2 ([1]). *The class $\mathbb{C}(\mathbf{A})$ of automata is exactly learnable in polynomial time.*

3.2 Extracting Automata from RNNs

Weiss et al. [33,34] investigate the extraction of automata from recurrent neural networks using Angluin's L* algorithm. One of the challenges that the authors point out is that the machine learning model can be tailored to answer membership queries (such queries would correspond to asking the model to classify an example), however, it cannot answer *equivalence queries* (as mentioned in the Introduction). The authors solve this issue by creating a sample randomly and using the neural network to classify it. If a counterexample is found in the sample, the algorithm can continue as if the answer to an equivalence query was 'no'

Table 1. Observation table at different stages of the algorithm. First, we have the initial table in (a) with $S = E = \{\lambda\}$ and in (b) after adding 0 to S. Then (c) is the table after receiving the counterexample 000 and (d) is after making it consistent.

(a) T is consistent but not closed

		T
		E \; λ
S	λ	yes
$S.\Sigma$	0	no
	1	yes

(b) T is closed and consistent

		T
		E \; λ
S	λ	yes
	0	no
$S.\Sigma$	0	no
	1	yes
	00	no
	01	no

(c) T is closed but not consistent

		T
		E \; λ
S	λ	yes
	0	no
	00	no
	000	yes
$S.\Sigma$	0	no
	1	yes
	00	no
	01	no
	000	yes
	001	no
	0000	no
	0001	yes

(d) T is closed and consistent

		T	
		E \; λ	0
S	λ	yes	no
	0	no	no
	00	no	yes
	000	yes	no
$S.\Sigma$	0	no	no
	1	yes	no
	00	no	yes
	01	no	no
	000	yes	no
	001	no	yes
	0000	no	no
	0001	yes	no

and the mentioned counterexample is the one returned by the oracle. Though, if no counterexample is found then the algorithm proceeds as if an equivalence query had 'yes' as answer (although in this case equivalence cannot be guaranteed because the search for a counterexample is just performed on a sample). The idea for this strategy stems from the proof of Theorem 1.

The authors also present an alternative approach to sampling, which had moderate the results when compared to sampling. The paper leaves open some theoretical questions. In particular, regarding the size of such samples and whether they can be used for providing a PAC guarantee in the sense of Definition 2. Another open question left by the authors is that Angluin's proof of polynomial time exact learnability assumes that the target is representing a regular language, while this may not be the case for the underlying language of the recurrent neural network. Indeed, even if trained on a dataset that corresponds to a regular language, this does not mean that the machine learning model will respond as the L* algorithm expects since the model will generalize the training data and, therefore, it may not represent a regular language.

Balanced Parenthesis. The work by Weiss et al. [33,34] produced interesting results in various problem settings. One of their settings involved the extraction of automata from a recurrent neural network trained for deciding whether an expression has balanced parenthesis or not (considering a fixed maximum nesting of parenthesis). We illustrate in Fig. 5 examples of automata extracted from such neural network. For instance, the sequence of characters "good (morning)" would be a positive example, and the sequence "good ((morning)" would be a negative example. In fact the latter would be a negative counterexample for the automaton on the left of Fig. 5 and the target but not a negative counterexample for the automaton on the right of Fig. 5 and the target, since it is not accepted by the automaton on the right and it is not in the target language.

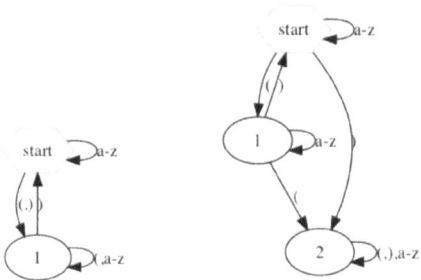

Fig. 5. Automata extracted from recurrent neural network trained for classifying whether an expression has balanced parenthesis [33]

4 Extracting Horn Expressions from Language Models

In this section, we first explain the classical Horn algorithm proposed by Angluin et al. [3] (Sect. 4.1) and then how it can be applied to extracting Horn expressions from complex ML models [6,24,25]. (Sect. 4.2).

4.1 The Horn Algorithm

The algorithm for exact learning Horn expressions in polynomial time is given by Algorithm 2. It maintains a sequence $\mathcal{J}$ of negative examples. In each iteration of the main loop, if the hypothesis $\mathcal{H}$ is not equivalent to the target Φ then the oracle $\mathsf{EQ}_{\mathcal{C}(\mathbf{H}),\Phi}$ provides the learner with an interpretation $\mathcal{I}$ that is a counterexample. If it is positive then Algorithm 2 removes all clauses in it that are violated by $\mathcal{I}$ and returns to the main loop asking the oracle if the modified hypothesis is equivalent to the target. Otherwise, the learner receives a negative counterexample which either is used to refine one element of $\mathfrak{J}$, or is added to the end of $\mathfrak{J}$. It then recomputes the hypothesis based on the modified list of negative examples and returns to the main loop asking whether the modified hypothesis is equivalent to the target. In order to learn all of the clauses in Φ, one would like the clauses induced by the (negative) examples in $\mathfrak{J}$ to approximate distinct clauses in Φ. This will happen if the examples in $\mathfrak{J}$ violate distinct clauses in Φ.

As explained in [3], overzealous refinement may result in several examples in $\mathfrak{J}$ violating the same clause of Φ. This is avoided in Algorithm 2 by refining at most one (the first) element of $\mathfrak{J}$ per iteration (whenever there are multiple elements in $\mathfrak{J}$ which can be refined by a counterexample).

Algorithm 2: The HORN Algorithm [3]

input: $\mathrm{MQ}_{\mathcal{C}(\mathbf{H}),\Phi}$ and $\mathrm{EQ}_{\mathcal{C}(\mathbf{H}),\Phi}$ oracles.
output: A Horn formula $\mathcal{H}$ such that $\mathcal{H} \equiv \Phi$.

1   $\mathcal{H} := \mathfrak{J} := \emptyset$
2   **while** $\mathrm{EQ}_{\mathcal{C}(\mathbf{H}),\Phi}(\mathcal{H}) = (\mathrm{no}, \mathcal{I})$ **do**
3   **if** $\mathcal{I} \not\models \mathcal{H}$ **then**
4   remove from $\mathcal{H}$ all $\phi \in \mathcal{H}$ such that $\mathcal{I} \not\models \phi$
5   **else**
6   **if** there is $\mathcal{I}_j \in \mathfrak{J}$ such that $\mathrm{MQ}_{\mathcal{C}(\mathbf{H}),\Phi}(\mathcal{I} \cap \mathcal{I}_j) = \mathrm{no}$ and $\mathcal{I} \cap \mathcal{I}_j \subset \mathcal{I}_j$ **then**
7   let $\mathcal{I}_i$ be the first such negative example
8   replace $\mathcal{I}_i \in \mathfrak{J}$ with $\mathcal{I} \cap \mathcal{I}_i$
9   **else**
10   append $\mathcal{I}$ to $\mathfrak{J}$
11         $\mathcal{H} := \bigcup_{\mathcal{I} \in \mathfrak{J}} \{\bigwedge_{v \in \mathcal{I}} v \to u \mid u \notin \mathcal{I}\} \cup \{\bigwedge_{v \in \mathcal{I}} v \to \bot\}$

12 **return** $(\mathcal{H})$

An Example Run. Let $\mathcal{V} = \{a, b, c, d\}$ and $\Phi = \{(b \wedge c \wedge d) \to a, (a \wedge d) \to c\}$. The hypothesis $\mathcal{H}$ is initially empty. In the first iteration assume that the oracle gives as counterexample (which can only be negative because the hypothesis is empty) the interpretation $\mathcal{I}_1 = \{a, b, d, \top\}$. Algorithm 2 then appends $\mathcal{I}_1$ to $\mathfrak{J}$ and computes

$$\mathcal{H} = \{(a \wedge b \wedge d) \to c\}.$$

Suppose that in the second iteration the oracle gives the negative counterexample $\mathcal{I}_2 = \{a, d, \top\}$. Then, as $(\mathcal{I}_1 \cap \mathcal{I}_2) \subset \mathcal{I}_1$ and $(\mathcal{I}_1 \cap \mathcal{I}_2) \not\models \Phi$, Algorithm 2 refines $\mathcal{I}_1$ with $(\mathcal{I}_1 \cap \mathcal{I}_2) = \{a, d, \top\}$ and computes

$$\mathcal{H} = \{(a \wedge d) \to b, (a \wedge d) \to c\}.$$

In the third iteration, the oracle gives $\mathcal{I}_3 = \{b, c, d, \top\}$. We have that $(\mathcal{I}_1 \cap \mathcal{I}_3) = \{d, \top\}$ and so $(\mathcal{I}_1 \cap \mathcal{I}_3) \subset \mathcal{I}_1$ but $(\mathcal{I}_1 \cap \mathcal{I}_3) \models \Phi$. Then, $\mathcal{I}_3$ is appended to $\mathfrak{J}$ and, then,
$$\mathcal{H} = \{(a \wedge d) \to b, (a \wedge d) \to c, (b \wedge c \wedge d) \to a\}.$$
Note that $\Phi \not\models (a \wedge d) \to b$. So, in the fourth iteration, the oracle can give the positive counterexample $\mathcal{I}_4 = \{a, c, d, \top\}$, which makes Algorithm 2 remove $(a \wedge d) \to b$ from $\mathcal{H}$. Finally, in the fifth equivalence query the oracle returns 'yes' and Algorithm 2 halts with $\mathcal{H} \equiv \Phi$, as required.

Theorem 3 ([3]). *The class $\mathbb{C}(\mathbf{H})$ of Horn expressions is exactly learnable in polynomial time.*

4.2 Extracting Horn Envelopes from BERT-Based Language Models

Here we discuss how one can employ Angluin's algorithm for extracting Horn expressions from ML models [6,24,25]. There are three main issues to be solved. The first is the fact that we do not have a way to answer an equivalence query. We have already mentioned this in Sect. 3.2 and we solve this issue in the same way, by creating a sample with classified examples and attempting to find a counterexample in the sample or terminating the algorithm if no counterexample is found. As it happens with the automata case, one cannot expect that the neural network will generalize to the format expected by an algorithm designed within the exact learning framework. In particular, one cannot expect that it will generalize to a Horn theory (which has the closure under intersection property). This results in another challenge since Angluin's Horn algorithm is not guaranteed to terminate when this assumption is lost [24].

The issue can be solved by limiting in the experiments the number of equivalence queries (therefore enforcing termination) or by adapting the algorithm to extract Horn envelopes from the machine learning model [6]. The last challenge to solve is that Angluin's algorithm expects binary vectors as input for membership queries and as counterexamples (the interpretations). When using tabular data, a naive but effective approach is to binarize the data and then use it to train the neural network [24,25]. If the machine learning model is a language model, one can create a look up table where different positions in a binary vector correspond to different words that can be added or not to a sentence [6].

Biases in Language Models. The work by Blum et al. [6] presents an experiment on BERT-based language models where features such as occupation, gender, location, and time period are binarized and the Horn algorithm is used to study the relationship between these features. The experiment creates sentences such as "[MASK] was born between 1892 and 1934 in Europe and is a nurse." and asks BERT-based models to complete the sentence by replacing [MASK] with a word. Because of the format of the sentence, the language model normally completes with either 'she' or 'he'. The completed sentences are mapped to binary vectors representing interpretations, as expected by the exact learning algorithm for learning Horn expressions. In the experiments, the algorithm extracted rules indicating occupation-based gender biases in these models. The authors extracted rules expressing e.g. that 'men cannot be nurses' and 'women cannot be bankers'. Although, it is not surprising that such biases exist in these models, the extraction of Horn expressions validate and extend results from the literature in a different way, as it does not require any kind of dataset for detecting harmful biases.

5 Extracting Decision Trees from Machine Learning Models

Decision trees are natural candidates for the format of global explanations. Even though there are also algorithms for extracting decision trees [9,11] within the exact learning framework and theoretical results linking PAC learning with decision trees [19], to the best of our knowledge, they have not yet been applied to the case in which the oracle is a neural network. In the context of neural network verification, Angluin's framework has been applied to extract decision diagrams [30]. Several decision tree algorithms, not designed within the exact and PAC frameworks, have been applied for extracting decision trees from neural networks [5,7,8,12–14,18,21,23,27,29,32].

We also point out the work by Persia et al. [24,25], which employed the Hoeffding Decision Tree algorithm [15] to extract decision trees from neural networks (Hoeffding was chosen over classical decision tree algorithms such as C4.5 [26] because it is an incremental algorithm, thus, it can naturally adjust according to the result of queries posed to the neural network). In the experiments, the authors compare the performance of the decision tree with the performance of Angluin's Horn algorithm (with a bound on the number of equivalence queries to avoid infinite loops, an issue formally solved more recently [6]). The estimated true error of the extracted decision tree is similar to the estimated true error of Horn expressions [24,25].

6 Discussion and Next Steps

Given the results of the mentioned works a natural question is: which formalism is the most adequate for being extracted? There is no simple solution to this question as it seems each approach has its benefits and shortcomings.

Automata, Horn Expressions, or Decision Trees? Automata are natural candidates because one can visualize the different states and the transition function can reveal information about the global behaviour of the model in a way that cannot be as easily visualized with a logic-based formalism. On the other hand, logic-based formalisms allow for deductive reasoning and Horn logic is a interesting candidate not only because of its tractable complexity of reasoning but also because in some cases rules can be easier to interpret (see literature on knowledge compilation [28]). Decision trees are also a natural and interesting formalism for extracting a high level view of a machine learning model, though, the more complex is the model the larger the tree tends to become, which in turn hinders interpretability (a similar issue also happens with automata, rules can also become long but they can be analysed separately).

Richer Formalisms and Dealing with Uncertainty. The benefit of using the formalisms mentioned above, namely, automata, Horn expressions, and decision trees, is that there are known exact learning algorithms with membership and equivalence queries with proven polynomial time complexity [1,3,11]. However, there is a trade-off between expressivity and fast computation. Since neural networks can be very complex, extracting information in a particular formalism can potentially limit the information extracted in a significant way. Recently, Yellin et al. [36] extended the work by Weiss et al. [33] to extract context-free grammars from recurrent neural networks, which are more powerful than the class of regular languages captured by (deterministic finite) automata. On the logic side, one could employ, e.g., the algorithm by Konev et al. [20] (see also [16]) to extract an $\mathcal{EL}$ ontology (or a fragment of it). First results on this direction have been recently presented [22]. $\mathcal{EL}$ ontologies have been extensively studied in the description logic community, the language corresponds to a fragment of first-order logic with tractable complexity for various reasoning tasks. Regarding uncertainty, in logic-based formalisms, a natural step forward in the search for rules (or ontologies) explaining neural networks is to consider formulas annotated with information about its confidence, e.g., using probabilistic or possibilistic logic [24].

Scalability. Providing theoretical guarantees for complex machine learning models in a feasible way can largely depend on the possibility of reducing the space of inputs/outputs under consideration. Within the exact and PAC learning frameworks, this can be achieved by restricting to a specific concept class of (automata, Horn logic, decision trees, among others) expressed within a vocabulary of interest (e.g. occupations in the Biases in Language Models study case [6]). Regarding the PAC framework, the sample complexity can be high even if the concept class and the vocabulary are restricted. One way of further reducing the search space meaningfully is to also restrict the problem to a family of probability distributions (instead of assuming it can be any distribution) if some information about the probability distribution of examples is known.

Other Settings. We should mention that the exact and PAC frameworks have been mostly studied for supervised learning settings, in particular, with binary classification, meaning that non-trivial extensions of algorithms designed within these frameworks may be needed to deal with multi-class classification settings and unsupervised learning. One possible way of dealing with the mismatch between the frameworks and machine learning models is to ask the model to respond in the format expected by the algorithm [22]. However, some machine learning models may return different outputs given the same input, with large language models designed for engaging in conversations being a typical example. This means that significant changes in the exact and PAC learning frameworks may be needed for analysing such systems in a formal sense.

Acknowledgements. Ozaki is supported by the Norwegian Research Council, grant 316022. This work was also supported by the Research Council of Norway, Integreat - Norwegian Centre for knowledge-driven machine learning, project number 332645.

References

1. Angluin, D.: Learning regular sets from queries and counterexamples. Inf. Comput. **75**(2), 87–106 (1987)
2. Angluin, D.: Queries and concept learning. Mach. Learn. **2**(4), 319–342 (1988)
3. Angluin, D., Frazier, M., Pitt, L.: Learning conjunctions of horn clauses. Mach. Learn. **9**, 147–164 (1992)
4. Arenas, M., Barceló, P., Bertossi, L.E., Monet, M.: On the complexity of shap-score-based explanations: tractability via knowledge compilation and non-approximability results. J. Mach. Learn. Res. **24**, 63:1–63:58 (2023). http://jmlr.org/papers/v24/21-0389.html
5. Awudu, K., Zhou, S.: X-trepan: a multi class regression and adapted extraction of comprehensible decision tree in artificial neural networks. arXiv arXiv:1508.07551 (2015). https://api.semanticscholar.org/CorpusID:15052370
6. Blum, S., Koudijs, R., Ozaki, A., Touileb, S.: Learning horn envelopes via queries from language models. Int. J. Approximate Reasoning **171**, 109026 (2023). https://doi.org/10.1016/j.ijar.2023.109026, https://www.sciencedirect.com/science/article/pii/S0888613X23001573
7. Bologna, G., Hayashi, Y.: A comparison study on rule extraction from neural network ensembles, boosted shallow trees, and svms. Appl. Comput. Intell. Soft Comput. **2018**, 4084850:1–4084850:20 (2018). https://doi.org/10.1155/2018/4084850
8. Boz, O.: Extracting decision trees from trained neural networks. In: Proceedings of the Eighth ACM SIGKDD International Conference on Knowledge Discovery and Data Mining, July 23–26, 2002, Edmonton, Alberta, Canada, pp. 456–461. ACM (2002). https://doi.org/10.1145/775047.775113
9. Bshouty, N.H., Haddad-Zaknoon, C.A.: Adaptive exact learning of decision trees from membership queries. In: Garivier, A., Kale, S. (eds.) ALT. Proceedings of Machine Learning Research, vol. 98, pp. 207–234. PMLR (2019)
10. Bshouty, N.H., Jackson, J.C., Tamon, C.: Exploring learnability between exact and PAC. J. Comput. Syst. Sci. **70**(4), 471–484 (2005)
11. Bshouty, N.: Exact learning via the monotone theory. In: Proceedings of 1993 IEEE 34th Annual Foundations of Computer Science, pp. 302–311 (1993). https://doi.org/10.1109/SFCS.1993.366857
12. Burkhardt, S., Brugger, J., Wagner, N., Ahmadi, Z., Kersting, K., Kramer, S.: Rule extraction from binary neural networks with convolutional rules for model validation. Frontiers Artif. Intell. **4**, 642263 (2021). https://doi.org/10.3389/FRAI.2021.642263
13. Craven, M.W., Shavlik, J.W.: Extracting tree-structured representations of trained networks. In: NIPS 1995, pp. 24–30. MIT Press (1995)

14. Dancey, D., McLean, D., Bandar, Z.: Decision tree extraction from trained neural networks. In: Barr, V., Markov, Z. (eds.) Proceedings of the Seventeenth International Florida Artificial Intelligence Research Society Conference, Miami Beach, Florida, USA, pp. 515–519. AAAI Press (2004). http://www.aaai.org/Library/FLAIRS/2004/flairs04-089.php
15. Domingos, P., Hulten, G.: Mining high-speed data streams. In: Proceedings of the Sixth ACM SIGKDD International Conference on Knowledge Discovery and Data Mining, pp. 71–80. KDD '00, Association for Computing Machinery, New York, NY, USA (2000). https://doi.org/10.1145/347090.347107
16. Duarte, M.R.C., Konev, B., Ozaki, A.: Exactlearner: a tool for exact learning of EL ontologies. In: KR, pp. 409–414 (2018)
17. Geirhos, R., et al.: Shortcut learning in deep neural networks. Nat. Mach. Intell. **2**(11), 665–673 (2020). https://doi.org/10.1038/s42256-020-00257-z
18. Young, W.A., et al.: An investigation of TREPAN utilising a continuous oracle model. Int. J. Data Anal. Tech. Strateg. **3**(4), 325–352 (2011). https://doi.org/10.1504/IJDATS.2011.042953
19. Kearns, M.J., Mansour, Y.: On the boosting ability of top-down decision tree learning algorithms. J. Comput. Syst. Sci. **58**(1), 109–128 (1999). https://doi.org/10.1006/jcss.1997.1543
20. Konev, B., Lutz, C., Ozaki, A., Wolter, F.: Exact learning of lightweight description logic ontologies. J. Mach. Learn. Res. **18**, 201:1–201:63 (2017)
21. Krishnan, R., Sivakumar, G., Bhattacharya, P.: Extracting decision trees from trained neural networks. Pattern Recogn. **32**(12), 1999–2009 (1999). https://doi.org/10.1016/S0031-3203(98)00181-2
22. Matteo Magnini, Ana Ozaki, R.S.: Actively learning ontologies from LLMs: first results (extended abstract). In: Laura Giordano, J.C.J., Ozaki, A. (eds.) DL. CEUR Workshop Proceedings, vol. 3739 (2024). https://ceur-ws.org/Vol-3739/abstract-18.pdf
23. Nanfack, G., Temple, P., Frénay, B.: Global explanations with decision rules: a co-learning approach. In: de Campos, C.P., Maathuis, M.H., Quaeghebeur, E. (eds.) UAI. Proceedings of Machine Learning Research, vol. 161, pp. 589–599. AUAI Press (2021). https://proceedings.mlr.press/v161/nanfack21a.html
24. Persia, C., Jøsang, J., Ozaki, A.: Extracting horn theories from neural networks with queries and counterexamples. In: International Workshop on Knowledge Representation for Hybrid intelligence (2022). https://sites.google.com/view/kr4hi/programme
25. Persia, C., Ozaki, A.: Extracting rules from neural networks with partial interpretations. In: Northern Lights Deep Learning Conference (2022). https://www.nldl.org/program2022
26. QUINLAN, J.R.: Chapter 2 - constructing decision trees. In: Quinlan, J.R. (ed.) C4.5, pp. 17–26. Morgan Kaufmann, San Francisco (CA) (1993). https://doi.org/10.1016/B978-0-08-050058-4.50007-3, https://www.sciencedirect.com/science/article/pii/B9780080500584500073
27. Schmitz, G.P.J., Aldrich, C., Gouws, F.S.: ANN-DT: an algorithm for extraction of decision trees from artificial neural networks. IEEE Trans. Neural Networks **10**(6), 1392–1401 (1999). https://doi.org/10.1109/72.809084
28. Selman, B., Kautz, H.: Knowledge compilation and theory approximation. J. ACM **43**(2), 193–224 (1996). https://doi.org/10.1145/226643.226644
29. Setiono, R., Liu, H.: Understanding neural networks via rule extraction. In: Proceedings of the Fourteenth International Joint Conference on Artificial Intelligence,

IJCAI 95, Montréal Québec, Canada, August 20–25 1995, 2 Volumes, pp. 480–487. Morgan Kaufmann (1995). http://ijcai.org/Proceedings/95-1/Papers/063.pdf
30. Shih, A., Darwiche, A., Choi, A.: Verifying binarized neural networks by angluin-style learning. In: Janota, M., Lynce, I. (eds.) Theory and Applications of Satisfiability Testing - SAT. Lecture Notes in Computer Science, vol. 11628, pp. 354–370. Springer (2019). https://doi.org/10.1007/978-3-030-24258-9_25
31. Sipser, M.: Introduction to the Theory of Computation. Thomson Course Technology, international edition of second edn. (2005)
32. Vasilev, N., Mincheva, Z., Nikolov, V.: Decision tree extraction using trained neural network. In: Klein, C., Helfert, M. (eds.) Proceedings of the 9th International Conference on Smart Cities and Green ICT Systems, SMARTGREENS 2020, Prague, Czech Republic, May 2–4, 2020. pp. 194–200. SCITEPRESS (2020). https://doi.org/10.5220/0009351801940200
33. Weiss, G., Goldberg, Y., Yahav, E.: Extracting automata from recurrent neural networks using queries and counterexamples. In: Dy, J.G., Krause, A. (eds.) ICML. Proceedings of Machine Learning Research, vol. 80, pp. 5244–5253. PMLR (2018). http://proceedings.mlr.press/v80/weiss18a.html
34. Weiss, G., Goldberg, Y., Yahav, E.: Learning deterministic weighted automata with queries and counterexamples. In: Wallach, H.M., Larochelle, H., Beygelzimer, A., d'Alché-Buc, F., Fox, E.B., Garnett, R. (eds.) NeurIPS, pp. 8558–8569 (2019). https://proceedings.neurips.cc/paper/2019/hash/d3f93e7766e8e1b7ef66dfdd9a8be93b-Abstract.html
35. Weiss, G., Goldberg, Y., Yahav, E.: Extracting automata from recurrent neural networks using queries and counterexamples (extended version). Mach. Learn. **113**(5), 2877–2919 (2024). https://doi.org/10.1007/S10994-022-06163-2
36. Yellin, D.M., Weiss, G.: Synthesizing context-free grammars from recurrent neural networks. In: Groote, J.F., Larsen, K.G. (eds.) TACAS. Lecture Notes in Computer Science, vol. 12651, pp. 351–369. Springer (2021). https://doi.org/10.1007/978-3-030-72016-2_19

A Tutorial in Proof-Theoretic Approaches to Logical Argumentation

Kees van Berkel[1(✉)] and Christian Straßer[2]

[1] Institute for Logic and Computation, TU Wien, Vienna, Austria
kees.van.berkel@tuwien.ac.at
[2] Institute for Philosophy II, Ruhr University Bochum, Bochum, Germany
christian.strasser@rub.de

Abstract. This article provides a tutorial in proof-theoretic approaches to logical argumentation. We first introduce and discuss defeasible reasoning and nonmonotonic logic. This naturally paves the way to formal argumentation. An argumentation framework structures a given knowledge base by tracking conflicts. Argumentation semantics offer ways of selecting arguments. Logical argumentation provides structure both to arguments and to attacks. By adopting a proof-theoretic perspective on logical argumentation, we generate arguments and derive new ones from those derived previously. We study some meta-theoretic properties of the resulting systems. Finally, we apply these formal methods to the problem of reasoning with norms and obligations with a special emphasis on explanations. In closing we, discuss an enhanced Argumentative Knowledge Representation and Reasoning pipeline, including the construction of explanations.

Keywords: defeasible reasoning · formal argumentation · logical argumentation · proof theory · nonmonotonic logic · deontic logic · explanation · sequent calculus

1 Defeasible Reasoning and Nonmonotonic Logic

Reasoning is making inferences.[1] It is the drawing of conclusions from assumptions and some given information (including previously drawn conclusions). We reason defeasibly when we retain the option to retract certain inferences upon acquiring new information. We typically do so when our available information is incomplete or uncertain. For instance, upon listening to the following beginning of a fantasy novel

> **Story 1** *It has been told that princess Charlotte killed the dragon Norbert...*

---

[1] Versions of this tutorial were given at the 19th Reasoning Web Summer School, Oslo, Sept. 2023 and at the 6th Summer School on Argumentation, Hagen, Sept. 2024.

we may infer that Norbert is a large creature. Or that Charlotte is a skilled fighter, since dragons are typically large and dangerous. Or that (at least in the story), Charlotte really did kill Norbert. While these inferences would serve us well in most fantasy novels, they are based on incomplete information. We jump to conclusions: after all, we were not told that Charlotte is a skilled fighter nor that Norbert is a large and dangerous creature. In fact, the story may very well continue as follows:

> **STORY 1 CONT. A** *The local dragon protection guild was outraged. Since years they have been lobbying at the king's court that baby dragons are not to be admitted to show fights with the royal offspring. "It is barbarous!"*

Given the new information, we clearly want to retract some of our previous inferences.

Moreover, the information in our story is uncertain: not everything that "has been told" is in fact true. Indeed, an alternative continuation of the story would be perfectly consistent (albeit rather unusual):

> **STORY 1 CONT. B** *The royal propagandists planted the story of the princess' brave killing in all the royal news outlets, while in reality poor Norbert died of old age in the loving arms of his dragon wife Draca.*

If this were the beginning of the second chapter of our novel, we would surely retract our previous inference that Charlotte killed Norbert.

Logics that allow for the retraction of conclusions when new information arises are called *"nonmonotonic logics"* (in short, NMLs). The majority of logics encountered in logic textbooks are different, though. They are of the "monotonic" type, with classical logic (CL) being the quintessential archetype. In CL, when the initial assumptions are true, any inference supported by CL ensures that the truth of the conclusion is absolutely warranted and holds without exception: CL preserves the truth throughout the inference process. This is why inferences in CL are never retracted, and conclusions accumulate as more assumptions are added. This property, known as "monotonicity," is highly valuable in domains of reasoning such as mathematics, where CL reigns (although there are influential alternatives, such as intuitionistic logic). Whereas deductive reasoning may be essential to scientific research and mathematics, most of our everyday reasoning is defeasible, depending on generalizations and uncertainties [46, 79].

NMLs are not mere curiosities. They provide means for reasoning with incomplete, uncertain, and possibly inconsistent information (such as knowledge bases) and take up a central role in Knowledge Representation and Reasoning, a subfield of (symbolic) Artificial Intelligence (AI). Going back as far as the 1970s, the class of NMLs is of a highly diverse kind.[2] An early and influential account is found in the work by Rescher [71]. It utilizes reasoning with maximal consistent subsets of given assumptions (see Sect. 4). An idea that has been picked up and generalized for instance in the work of Makinson and van der Torre [50, 52]. Reiter's work on default logic is more of a (rule-based) proof-theoretic type [69].

---

[2] See [77, 78] for a brief expedition through the NML landscape.

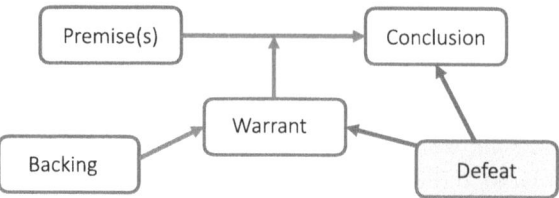

Fig. 1. Toulmin's [79] well-known argument scheme.

Autoepistemic logic investigates fixed-points of agents that use epistemic logic to reason about their own beliefs [58] (it is strongly related to logic programming [41]). Preferential semantics use selection functions on interpretations to filter out preferred interpretations: An idea that has roots in investigations into subjunctive conditionals [49,76] and deontic logic [43,80] and found its way to nonmonotonic logic with the works of Batens [15], Shoham [75], and the seminal "KLM" papers [47,48].

While many of these approaches originated in the 1980s, the conceptual grounds and motivation for NMLs has been prepared earlier. Hart [44] introduced the term "defeasibility" to philosophy when discussing legal contracts as a defeasible concept. Defeasible reasoning, applied to duties and their prima facie nature, can be traced back to Ross [72]. In fact, defeasible reasoning has been central to argumentation theory, with discussions as early as Aristotle's *Topics* [12]. What is more, the lack of an ability to deal with defeasible reasoning has been the basis of a rigorous attack on classical logic by Toulmin [79].

As a response to his criticism of classical inference, Toulmin [79] proposed the influential argument scheme depicted in Fig. 1. In this scheme, a warrant is an inference license to draw the given conclusion from the given premises. It can, for instance, take the form of a default, such as "birds fly." The backing further justifies the warrant, providing evidence for it (such as statistically relevant regularities, references to laws, etc.). Warrants (and their backings) are often assumed in the background and, as such, not explicitly stated. While arguments obtain their validity by being warranted, following Toulmin, this validity is by no means a guarantee. Even if the premises of an argument are true, there is a possibility that the conclusion of the argument is false since *defeaters* may exist (and even if the conclusion is true too, the asserted link between premises and conclusion may be problematic). In fact, most arguments outside of the realm of mathematics, are subject to potential defeat. Defeaters can be expressed by counter-arguments (see Sect. 2 for different types of argumentative defeats).

The idea of reasoning in terms of arguing with oneself and arguing with others is quite natural [54], and so it is not surprising that Toulmin's ideas left their footprint in NML under the name of *formal argumentation*. Two of the most influential accounts are by Pollock [63] and Dung [32]. Moreover, formal argumentation has proven to be a uniform framework for the representation of large classes of NMLs in AI.[3] We dig deeper into this topic in what follows.

The remainder of this tutorial is structured as follows: in Sect. 2, we discuss the basics of abstract argumentation, which include argumentation frameworks and the selection of jointly justifiable arguments. In Sect. 3, we introduce the reader to logical argumentation and how proof calculi may generate arguments with different kinds of attacks. Section 4 sees a discussion of the metatheory, it includes an overview of rationality postulates which are properties that argumentative inference relations ideally satisfy. Last, we apply the discussed formalism to the context of normative reasoning in Sect. 5. We provide a proof calculus for reasoning with normative knowledge bases and we discuss how to increase transparency on the level of logical argumentation and obtain explanations from the obtained argumentation frameworks. We conclude by discussing the tutorial in light of the new Argumentative Knowledge Representation and Reasoning pipeline, which includes explainability.

2 Formal Argumentation

Formal argumentation takes Toulmin's idea at face value: inferences are retracted as a consequence of argumentative defeat.[4] In what follows, we use $a, b, c, \ldots$ as argument labels. Now, take our previous example. The argument

- a. Norbert is a dragon. Therefore Norbert is a giant creature, since Dragons are usually giant creatures.

can be extracted from our STORY 1, and is defeated in the continuation A by

- b. Norbert is a baby dragon. So, Norbert is not a giant creature since baby dragons are not giant.

Things become more complicated when arguments mutually attack each other. Consider

STORY 2 *Norbert has a twin dragon, Albert. According to her sister, Charlotte killed Norbert but not Albert. However, according to her brother, he saw how Charlotte killed Albert, not Norbert.*

Without knowing who of Charlotte's siblings is more reliable, we cannot resolve the conflict between the mutually attacking arguments

- c. Charlotte killed Norbert, since her sister says so.

and

---

[3] See [7] for an overview of said representation results.
[4] Following Prakken [67], there are broadly two views on formal argumentation: argumentation as inference and argumentation as dialogue. This manuscript deals with the former. For models of dialogue, where agents debate the acceptability of an argument, see, e.g., [3,11,22,53,65].

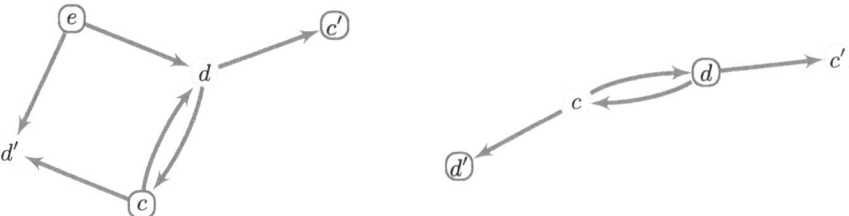

Fig. 2. Left: An abstract argumentation framework for STORY 2 CONT. Highlighted is its grounded extension $\{e, c', c\}$. In this case, it coincides with the unique stable and preferred extension. Right: The argumentation framework for STORY 2 with highlighted one of the two stable (resp. preferred) extensions $\{d, d'\}$ (the second stable set is $\{c, c'\}$).

- d. Charlotte killed Albert, since her brother saw her doing so.

Of course, more arguments can be extracted from our story, building on c and d. For instance, we can construct the arguments

- c'. Charlotte killed a dragon, since her sister claimed she killed Norbert and Norbert is a dragon.

and

- d'. Charlotte killed a dragon, since her brother saw her killing Albert and Albert is a dragon.

Looking at c' and d', the claim that Charlotte killed a dragon is a so-called *floating conclusion*: it is based on two conflicting arguments. We come back to this on page 14.

Consider the following continuation of STORY 2.

STORY 2 CONT. *The queen was so proud of her son, not even the dragon hunt could stop him from attending his weekly knitting class.*

- e. Charlotte's brother did not see her killing Albert, since he was not present at the dragon hunt.

Argument e defeats argument d and therefore liberates argument c from the defeat by d. In cases in which the defeater of an argument is itself defeated, the original argument is said to be *reinstated* (other things being equal).

As we can see, the more arguments are accumulated[5], the more complicated things become. Dung [32] developed the notion of a so-called *argumentation framework*, a useful tool for keeping an overview of arguments and their intricate relations. An argumentation framework is a directed graph ⟨Arg, Attack⟩ comprising a given set of arguments Arg and a relation that tracks argumentative attack Attack between those arguments.[6] For STORY 2 (and its continuation) the resulting graph is given in Fig. 2.

---

[5] For instance, through the course of a dialogue or the extension of a knowledge base.
[6] Another commonly studied relation between arguments is that of support [1]. We will not pursue alternatives here.

For a reasoner whose available information is represented by an argumentation framework, the question arises: what arguments to select and which conclusions to commit to in the reasoning process? Dung [32] defined several intuitive properties, referred to as *semantics*, for selecting sets of arguments called *extensions*. Let us recall some. Suppose a set of arguments $\mathcal{A} \subseteq \mathsf{Arg}$ in the context of the argumentation framework $\langle \mathsf{Arg}, \mathsf{Attack} \rangle$.

Conflict-freeness: $\mathcal{A}$ is conflict-free if no two arguments in $\mathcal{A}$ attack each other. Formally, for all $a, b \in \mathcal{A}$, $(a, b) \notin \mathsf{Attack}$.

Conflict-freeness is a good starting point for selecting arguments, but in no way a sufficient criterion for a rational selection. For instance, $\{d, d'\}$ is a conflict-free set in Fig. 2 (left), but clearly lacking since it cannot defend itself against the attack by e. We say that the set of arguments $\mathcal{A}$ *defends some* $b \in \mathsf{Arg}$ in case $\mathcal{A}$ reinstates b from every attack. Formally, if for all $(c, b) \in \mathsf{Attack}$ there is a $d \in \mathcal{A}$ such that $(d, c) \in \mathsf{Attack}$.

Admissibility: $\mathcal{A}$ is admissible if it is conflict-free and it defends all of its arguments.

Also admissibility is sub-optimal. For instance, $\emptyset$ is always admissible, but in our example we would like to at least choose e since it does not have any attackers. Improvements of admissibility are the following:

Completeness: $\mathcal{A}$ is complete if it is admissible and it contains all arguments that it defends.

Grounded: $\mathcal{A}$ is grounded if it is $\subseteq$-minimally complete.

Dung showed that the grounded extension always exists and it is unique (the smallest possible grounded extension being the empty-set). In our example (Fig. 2, left) it is given by $\{e, c, c'\}$.

Let us have a brief look at two other types of extensions defined by Dung:

Stable: $\mathcal{A}$ is stable if it is conflict-free and it attacks every arguments outside of it. Formally, for all $b \in \mathsf{Arg} \setminus \mathcal{A}$ there is a $c \in \mathcal{A}$ such that $(c, b) \in \mathsf{Attack}$.

Stability underlies an "opinionated" reasoning style: an agent making use of it either accepts an argument or attacks it.

Preferred: $\mathcal{A}$ is preferred if it is $\subseteq$-maximal admissible.

Dung also proved some interesting connections between these semantics, for instance: every stable extension is preferred and every preferred extension is complete. Furthermore, the grounded extension is the unique smallest complete extension a subset of all complete extensions. We refer to [13] for an overview of various semantics and their relations.[7]

---

[7] Other ways of characterizing semantic notions have been developed: for instance, *argument games* procedurally construct semantic extensions through interactive games between a proponent and an opponent of an argument [56]; *dialogue models* lift games to a dialogical exchange of arguments, in which more natural locutions are available to the involved interlocutors, e.g., [65]; and *argument labellings* provide procedures for labelling arguments 'in,' 'out,' and 'undecided,' where different labeling procedures yield different semantic extensions [56].

3 A Proof-Theoretic Approach to Formal Argumentation

So far, we only investigated formal methods to choose sets of arguments from an informal discourse represented by an argumentation framework, where each informal argument is *abstractly* represented (by a label $a, b, c, \ldots$). Abstract argumentation, as the name indicates, abstracts away from the content of arguments and studies their external relations. In contrast, *structured* argumentation explicates the content of arguments (e.g., claims, warrants, reasons, premises), which yield, for instance, various types of attack between arguments [33,57,64,82]. Logical argumentation, which is the central topic of this tutorial, considers structured arguments generated by an underlying base logic. In this section, we use proof-theory to generate arguments.

We, first, address how to represent arguments and attacks in a formally precise way, that is, in a formal language. Our method is symbolic, based on a formal language. In what follows, we will use a propositional language.

Propositional language: Let Atoms $= \{p, q, r, \ldots\}$ be a denumerable set of propositional atoms. The propositional language $\mathcal{L}$ is given by the following BNF grammar:

$$\varphi ::= p \mid \top \mid \bot \mid \neg\varphi \mid \varphi \vee \varphi \mid \varphi \wedge \varphi \mid \varphi \supset \varphi$$

where $p \in$ Atoms.

By taking all connectives as primitive, the formalism is modular with respect to a large class of propositional base logics (including but not limited to classical logic). For the sake of simplicity, we focus in this tutorial on classical logic (CL) (see, e.g., [8] and [9] for a more general account). We use $p, q, \ldots$ (possibly indexed) for propositional atoms, reserve $\varphi, \psi, \ldots$ (possibly indexed) for arbitrary formulas of $\mathcal{L}$, and use $\mathcal{S}, \mathcal{R}, \ldots$ and $\Gamma, \Delta, \ldots$ for arbitrary, respectively, finite sets of formulas of $\mathcal{L}$.

Reasoning, typically, is based on assumptions, some of which are taken to be certain (or, strict), others defeasible. A *knowledge base*

$$\mathbb{K} = \langle \mathcal{A}_s, \mathcal{A}_d \rangle$$

collects these assumptions, the strict ones in $\mathcal{A}_s \subseteq \mathcal{L}$ and the defeasible ones in $\mathcal{A}_d \subseteq \mathcal{L}$. We slightly abuse notation and write $\mathbb{K}$ for $\mathcal{A}_s \cup \mathcal{A}_d$. Furthermore, strict assumptions $\mathcal{A}_s$ are considered logically consistent (i.e., $\mathcal{A}_s \nvdash_{CL} \bot$, where $\vdash_{CL}$ denotes the logical consequence relation of classical logic). The question is, how to construct arguments on the bases of $\mathbb{K}$?

From a logical point of view, an *argument* is based on premises and offers a conclusion. Here, we represent arguments as premise-conclusion pairs, written as *sequents* [42]. Paradigmatically, an argument (sequent) has, then, the form $\Gamma \Rightarrow \varphi$ where $\Gamma \subseteq \mathcal{L}$ is a possibly empty, but always finite set of premises and $\varphi \in \mathcal{L}$ is a formula, the conclusion of the argument.[8] Often, we are particularly

---

[8] In the remainder, we use sequent and argument interchangeably to refer to $\Gamma \Rightarrow \varphi$.

interested in $\mathbb{K}$-based arguments, that is, arguments whose premises are assumptions in $\mathbb{K}$. More generally (and in the tradition of sequent-style calculi [42,59]), we allow for arguments of the form

$$\Gamma \Rightarrow \Delta$$

where Γ is as before and read conjunctively and Δ is a finite and possibly empty set of formulas that is read disjunctively: "given the premises in Γ, at least some formula in Δ holds." (If $\Delta = \emptyset$ this expresses that the assumptions in Γ form an inconsistent set.) Whenever Γ contains a defeasible assumption from the knowledge base $\mathbb{K}$, the argument is defeasible, namely, it allows for defeat (discussed below).

Now, given an argument $\Gamma \Rightarrow \varphi$, what justifies concluding φ from Γ? In the case of logical argumentation, a logic justifies this inference. In our illustrative case, this is classical logic. Classical logic comes with many proof calculi: e.g., Hilbert-style axiomatic systems, natural deduction, semantic tableaux [68]. We here focus on so-called sequent-calculi (originating with the work of Gentzen [42]). These proof systems allow us to generate arguments and derive new arguments from others. The rules of Gentzen's [42] well-known calculus LK for classical logic are listed in Fig. 3.

Sequent calculi are proof systems characterized by sets of *rules*. Such rules lay down the conditions under which sequents may be derived from other sequents. There are two types of rules: logical and structural rules. Roughly, logical rules equip logical connectives with meaning by manipulating logical formulas occurring in sequents, whereas structural rules manipulate the structure of sequents. The top sequents of a rule denote the rule's premises (or conditions). The bottom-sequent expresses the conclusion of a rule. By using these rules, sequent systems generate proofs as labelled trees: The leaves of a tree have an empty label, all other nodes are labelled by sequents, branches emerge as the result of rule applications, and the root of the tree is the proof's concluding sequent [59].[9]

To illustrate the use of LK, consider the following example derivation of a classical logic theorem $\varphi \supset (\varphi \vee \neg \psi)$:

$$\dfrac{\dfrac{\dfrac{\dfrac{\quad}{\varphi, \psi \Rightarrow \varphi} Ax}{\varphi \Rightarrow \varphi, \neg \psi} R\neg}{\varphi \Rightarrow (\varphi \vee \neg \psi)} R\vee}{\Rightarrow \varphi \supset (\varphi \vee \neg \psi)} R\supset$$

---

[9] Some sequent calculi have the property of *analyticity*, which expresses that any derivable sequent is derivable with a proof solely consisting of subformulas of the sequent in question. That is, one can construct proofs by merely decomposing the sequent to be proven, making it an effective tool for proof search (this is called root-first proof search). Analyticity is also useful for determining other properties, such as the consistency of a logic. Often, these results are obtained by showing that the sequent calculus enjoys certain structural properties such as invertibility of logical rules and admissibility of structural rules. The system LK enjoys these properties. See [59] for an extensive introduction to these terms.

$$\frac{}{\varphi, \Gamma \Rightarrow \Delta, \varphi} \, Ax \qquad \frac{}{\bot, \Gamma \Rightarrow \Delta} \, L\bot$$

$$\frac{\varphi, \psi, \Gamma \Rightarrow \Delta}{\varphi \wedge \psi, \Gamma \Rightarrow \Delta} \, L\wedge \qquad \frac{\Gamma \Rightarrow \Delta, \varphi \quad \Gamma \Rightarrow \Delta, \psi}{\Gamma \Rightarrow \Delta, \varphi \wedge \psi} \, R\wedge$$

$$\frac{\varphi, \Gamma \Rightarrow \Delta \quad \psi, \Gamma \Rightarrow \Delta}{\varphi \vee \psi, \Gamma \Rightarrow \Delta} \, L\vee \qquad \frac{\Gamma \Rightarrow \Delta, \varphi, \psi}{\Gamma \Rightarrow \Delta, \varphi \vee \psi} \, R\vee$$

$$\frac{\Gamma \Rightarrow \Delta, \varphi \quad \psi, \Gamma \Rightarrow \Delta}{\varphi \supset \psi, \Gamma \Rightarrow \Delta} \, L\supset \qquad \frac{\varphi, \Gamma \Rightarrow \Delta, \psi}{\Gamma \Rightarrow \Delta, \varphi \supset \psi} \, R\supset$$

$$\frac{\Gamma \Rightarrow \Delta, \varphi}{\Gamma, \neg \varphi \Rightarrow \Delta} \, L\neg \qquad \frac{\varphi, \Gamma \Rightarrow \Delta}{\Gamma \Rightarrow \Delta, \neg \varphi} \, R\neg$$

$$\frac{\Gamma \Rightarrow \Delta}{\varphi, \Gamma \Rightarrow \Delta} \, LW \qquad \frac{\Gamma \Rightarrow \Delta}{\Gamma \Rightarrow \Delta, \varphi} \, RW \qquad \frac{\varphi, \varphi, \Gamma \Rightarrow \Delta}{\varphi, \Gamma \Rightarrow \Delta} \, LC \qquad \frac{\Gamma \Rightarrow \Delta, \varphi, \varphi}{\Gamma \Rightarrow \Delta, \varphi} \, RC$$

$$\frac{\Gamma \Rightarrow \Delta, \varphi \quad \varphi, \Gamma' \Rightarrow \Delta'}{\Gamma, \Gamma' \Rightarrow \Delta, \Delta'} \, Cut$$

Fig. 3. Sequent Calculus LK [42]: sound and complete for classical logic. The top half contains logical rules of LK and the bottom half structural rules. The rules Ax and $L\bot$ are initial rules, introducing sequents in a proof. The labels LW, RW, LC, and RC stand for left weakening, right weakening, left contraction, respectively right contraction.

An argument based on a knowledge base $\mathbb{K}$ is a sequent $\Gamma \Rightarrow \varphi$ derivable by the underlying proof calculus (in our case, LK) for which $\Gamma \subseteq \mathbb{K}$. Clearly, we are not interested in arguments that make use of assumptions that are not listed in our knowledge base. We let $\mathsf{Arg}(\mathbb{K})$ be the set that collects all derivable arguments based on $\mathbb{K}$.

Consider again our narrative from Sect. 2. When modeling specific reasoning scenarios the language may be enriched, e.g., with labels, modal or other operators. We will see an example in the context of normative reasoning in Sect. 5. For modeling our STORY, we add two parametrized propositional operators ◁$_{\mathsf{agent}}$ and ⊚$_{\mathsf{agent}}$ that indicate that agent stated resp. saw something. Our individuals in STORY 2 CONT. are

$$\mathsf{Agents} = \{\mathsf{bro}, \mathsf{sis}, \mathsf{Nor}, \mathsf{Alb}, \mathsf{Cha}\}.$$

Our defeasible assumptions express that when an individual states or sees something, it is usually the case:

$$\mathcal{A}_d = \{ \circledcirc_{\mathsf{agent}} \varphi \supset \varphi \mid \varphi \in \mathcal{L}, \mathsf{agent} \in \mathsf{Agents} \}$$
$$\cup \{ \triangleleft_{\mathsf{agent}} \varphi \supset \varphi \mid \varphi \in \mathcal{L}, \mathsf{agent} \in \mathsf{Agents} \}.$$

In the following, we abbreviate $\odot_{\mathsf{agent}} A \supset A$ [resp. $\bowtie_{\mathsf{agent}} A \supset A$] with $\odot^{\mathsf{rel}}_{\mathsf{agent}} A$ [resp. $\bowtie^{\mathsf{rel}}_{\mathsf{agent}} A$], where the superscript rel stands for *reliable*. For every $\varphi \in \mathcal{L}$ the following sequents are derivable in LK:

$$\odot_{\mathsf{agent}}\varphi, \odot^{\mathsf{rel}}_{\mathsf{agent}}\varphi \Rightarrow \varphi \tag{1}$$

$$\bowtie_{\mathsf{agent}}\varphi, \bowtie^{\mathsf{rel}}_{\mathsf{agent}}\varphi \Rightarrow \varphi \tag{2}$$

What we see here is an application of Modus Ponens, since (1) is an abbreviation of: $\odot_{\mathsf{agent}}\varphi, \odot_{\mathsf{agent}}\varphi \supset \varphi \Rightarrow \varphi$ (and similar for (2)). Here is the simple LK-proof of (1):

$$\frac{\overline{\odot_{\mathsf{agent}}\varphi \Rightarrow \odot_{\mathsf{agent}}\varphi}\; Ax \quad \overline{\varphi \Rightarrow \varphi}\; Ax}{\odot_{\mathsf{agent}}\varphi, \odot_{\mathsf{agent}}\varphi \supset \varphi \Rightarrow \varphi}\; L\supset$$

For instance (2) can be interpreted as:

"If agent reliably states φ, then φ."

We can now model our STORY 2 CONT. (omitting some details) with the knowledge base $\mathbb{K}_2 = \langle \mathcal{A}_s, \mathcal{A}_d \rangle$.

$$\mathcal{A}_s = \{\bowtie_{\mathsf{sis}} n,$$
$$\bowtie_{\mathsf{bro}} \odot_{\mathsf{bro}} a,$$
$$\texttt{knitting(bro)},$$
$$\neg(\texttt{knitting(bro)} \wedge \odot_{\mathsf{bro}} a)\},$$

where $n := (\texttt{killed(Cha, Nor)} \wedge \neg\texttt{killed(Cha, Alb)})$
$a := (\texttt{killed(Cha, Alb)} \wedge \neg\texttt{killed(Cha, Nor)})$

Applying LK, we can derive, for instance, the following argument (see (2)):

$$c_0: \quad \bowtie_{\mathsf{sis}} n, \bowtie^{\mathsf{rel}}_{\mathsf{sis}} n \Rightarrow n$$

Since the arguments $n \Rightarrow \texttt{killed(Cha, Nor)}$ and $n \Rightarrow \neg\texttt{killed(Cha, Alb)}$ are LK-derivable, we can also derive the following arguments applying *Cut*:

$$c_1: \quad \bowtie_{\mathsf{sis}} n, \bowtie^{\mathsf{rel}}_{\mathsf{sis}} n \Rightarrow \texttt{killed(Cha, Nor)}$$
$$c_2: \quad \bowtie_{\mathsf{sis}} n, \bowtie^{\mathsf{rel}}_{\mathsf{sis}} n \Rightarrow \neg\texttt{killed(Cha, Alb)}$$

Here is the simple derivation of c_1:

$$\frac{\vdots \qquad \dfrac{\dfrac{\overline{\texttt{killed(Cha, Nor)} \Rightarrow \texttt{killed(Cha, Nor)}}\; Ax}{\dfrac{\texttt{killed(Cha, Nor)}, \neg\texttt{killed(Cha, Alb)} \Rightarrow \texttt{killed(Cha, Nor)}}{n \Rightarrow \texttt{killed(Cha, Nor)}}\; L\wedge}\; LW}{c_0: \bowtie_{\mathsf{sis}} n, \bowtie^{\mathsf{rel}}_{\mathsf{sis}} n \Rightarrow n \qquad}}{c_1: \bowtie_{\mathsf{sis}} n, \bowtie^{\mathsf{rel}}_{\mathsf{sis}} n \Rightarrow \texttt{killed(Cha, Nor)}}\; Cut$$

The following arguments are derived analogously:

$d_0: K_{bro} O_{bro} a, K^{rel}_{bro} O_{bro} a \Rightarrow O_{bro} a$

$d_1: K_{bro} O_{bro} a, K^{rel}_{bro} O_{bro} a, O^{rel}_{bro} a \Rightarrow a$

$d_2: K_{bro} O_{bro} a, K^{rel}_{bro} O_{bro} a, O^{rel}_{bro} a \Rightarrow \texttt{killed(Cha, Alb)}$

$d_3: K_{bro} O_{bro} a, K^{rel}_{bro} O_{bro} a, O^{rel}_{bro} a \Rightarrow \neg\texttt{killed(Cha, Nor)}$

Argument e below expresses that the brother could not have seen Charlotte killing Albert since he was at the knitting course at the time. Therefore, the default assumption that what he states is reliably true cannot hold (f).

$e: \texttt{knitting(bro)}, \neg(\texttt{knitting(bro)} \wedge O_{bro} a) \Rightarrow \neg O_{bro} a$

$f: \texttt{knitting(bro)}, \neg(\texttt{knitting(bro)} \wedge O_{bro} a), K_{bro} O_{bro} a \Rightarrow \neg K^{rel}_{bro} O_{bro} a$

Clearly, what the sister and what the brother state conflicts. If we assume that what the sister states is true, then either the brother states something false, or he is mistaken for what he saw (g). If, on the other hand, we believe the brother, then what the sister states cannot hold (h).

$g: K_{sis} n, K^{rel}_{sis} n, K_{bro} O_{bro} a \Rightarrow \neg(K^{rel}_{bro} O_{bro} a \wedge O^{rel}_{bro} a)$

$h: K_{bro} O_{bro} a, K^{rel}_{bro} O_{bro} a, O^{rel}_{bro} a, K_{sis} n \Rightarrow \neg K^{rel}_{sis} n$

Finally, we cannot consistently assume that both, sister and brother, state the truth (x_0). Note that anything follows from an inconsistency in classical logic, and so we may conclude, e.g., $\neg K^{rel}_{sis} n$ (x_1).

$x_0: K_{sis} n, K^{rel}_{sis} n, K_{bro} O_{bro} a, K^{rel}_{bro} O_{bro} a, O^{rel}_{bro} a \Rightarrow$

$x_1: K_{sis} n, K^{rel}_{sis} n, K_{bro} O_{bro} a, K^{rel}_{bro} O_{bro} a, O^{rel}_{bro} a \Rightarrow \neg K^{rel}_{sis} n$

However, by three applications of $R\neg$ to x_0 and some basic LK-reasoning, we can derive y, which states the inconsistency of our three defeasible assumptions. Observe that argument y only makes use of strict assumptions in $\mathbb{K}$.

$y: K_{sis} n, K_{bro} O_{bro} a \Rightarrow \neg(K^{rel}_{sis} n \wedge K^{rel}_{bro} O_{bro} a \wedge O^{rel}_{bro} a)$

Now that we have seen how sequent calculi are employed to generate arguments, let us consider the idea of argumentative attack. In logical argumentation, several attack types have been considered.[10]

---

[10] In this paper, we use 'attack' and 'defeat' interchangeably. However, sometimes the two are differentiated where 'defeat' is reserved for a successful attack (e.g., after evaluating argument preferences [2]). For an overview of attack definitions see [7]. We here consider those from [8].

Rebut (Reb): $\Gamma_1 \Rightarrow \varphi$ rebuts $\Gamma_2 \Rightarrow -\varphi$ if $\Gamma_2 \cap \mathcal{A}_d \neq \emptyset$, and where $-\varphi = \psi$ if $\varphi = \neg\psi$ and $-\varphi = \neg\varphi$ otherwise.

A rebut challenges the conclusion of an argument. For instance, c_2 rebuts d_2 and vice versa.

Defeat (Def): $\Gamma_1 \Rightarrow \neg \bigwedge \Gamma_2$ defeats $\Gamma_2, \Gamma_2' \Rightarrow \psi$, if $\emptyset \neq \Gamma_2 \subseteq \mathcal{A}_d$.

Direct Defeat (DirDef): $\Gamma_1 \Rightarrow \varphi$ defeats $\Gamma_2, -\varphi \Rightarrow \psi$, if $\varphi \in \mathcal{A}_d$ and where $-\varphi = \psi$ if $\varphi = \neg\psi$ and $-\varphi = \neg\varphi$ otherwise.

A defeat is an attack that challenges some defeasible assumptions of another argument. A direct defeat is a defeat that targets exactly one defeasible assumption. For instance, f directly defeats arguments based on the assumption $\triangleleft_{\text{bro}}^{\text{rel}} \odot_{\text{bro}} a$, such as $d_0, \ldots, d_3$. The argument g defeats $d_1, \ldots, d_3$, but does not directly defeat them.

Consistency Defeat (ConDef): $\Gamma_1 \Rightarrow \neg \bigwedge \Gamma_2$ consistency defeats $\Gamma_2, \Gamma_2' \Rightarrow \psi$, if $\Gamma_1 \subseteq \mathcal{A}_s$ and $\Gamma_2 \subseteq \mathcal{A}_d$.

A consistency defeat is a defeat performed by an argument that is based on strict assumptions only. Such an argument can therefore not be attacked. For instance, y consistency defeats x_0 and x_1. We note that direct and consistency defeats are special cases of defeat.

Let in the following AttAll = {Def, DirDef, Reb, ConDef}, AttDir = {DirDef}, AttDef = {Def}, and AttDirCon = {DirDef, ConDef}.

Choosing a collection of attack types $\emptyset \neq \text{Att} \subseteq \text{AttAll}$, we obtain an argumentation framework $\text{AF}_{\text{Att}}(\mathbb{K}) = \langle \text{Arg}(\mathbb{K}), \text{Att}\rangle$ for a given knowledge base $\mathbb{K}$. That is, for AF_{Att} the attack types in Att determine which arguments in $\text{Arg}(\mathbb{K})$ attack others. Accordingly, we may apply the argumentative semantics from Sect. 2 to the resulting framework. In Fig. 4 we see an excerpt of the argumentation framework $\text{AF}_{\text{AttAll}}(\mathbb{K}_2)$ based on STORY 2 CONT.

Fixing an argumentation semantics sem $\in$ {grounded, stable, preferred}, we obtain extensions of arguments from an argumentation framework $\text{AF}_{\text{Att}}(\mathbb{K})$. These extensions are supposed to represent argumentative commitments of rational participants in the debate based on $\mathbb{K}$. Using these extensions, argumentation semantics allow us to define various nonmonotonic consequence relations[11] (e.g., see [66]):

Skeptical, shared arguments: $\mathbb{K} \mathrel{|\!\sim}_{\cap\text{arg}}^{\text{Att,sem}} \varphi$ iff there is an argument a with conclusions φ that is contained in every sem-extension of $\text{AF}_{\text{Att}}(\mathbb{K})$.

Skeptical, shared conclusions: $\mathbb{K} \mathrel{|\!\sim}_{\cap\text{con}}^{\text{Att,sem}} \varphi$ iff in every sem-extension $\mathcal{S}$ of $\text{AF}_{\text{Att}}(\mathbb{K})$ there is an argument a with conclusion φ.

Credulous: $\mathbb{K} \mathrel{|\!\sim}_{\cup}^{\text{Att,sem}} \varphi$ iff there is a sem-extension in which there is an argument a with conclusion φ.

---

[11] In this paper, we use the terms 'inference' and 'consequence' interchangeably.

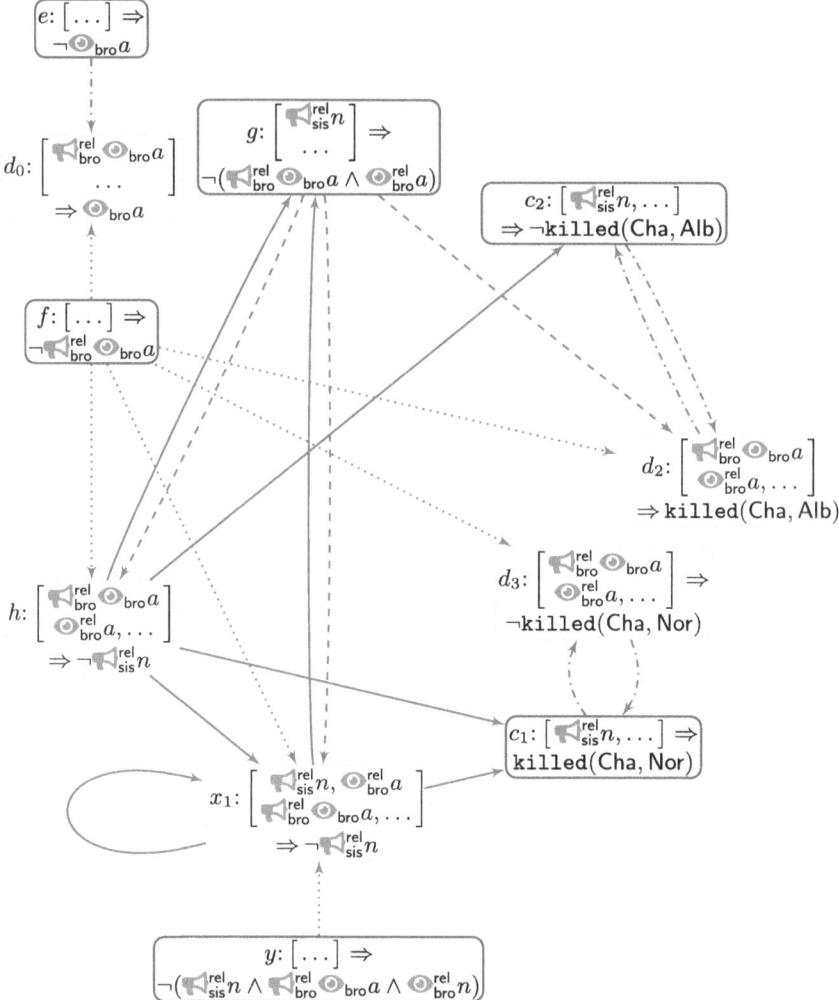

Fig. 4. Excerpt of the argumentation framework for STORY 2. We omit strict assumptions in the arguments (denoted by [...]). Direct defeats are represented by solid arrows, consistency defeats by dotted arrows (arrows stemming from f are also direct defeats), (other) defeats by dashed arrows, rebuts by dash-dot arrows. The grounded extension is highlighted and shaded (green). (Color figure online)

The use of formal argumentation introduces nuances in nonmonotonic inference. This is reflected in the two distinct notions of skeptical inference: the consequence relation $\mathrel{|\!\!\sim}_{\cap\mathrm{con}}^{\mathrm{Att,sem}}$ denotes a conclusion shared by all extensions, whereas $\mathrel{|\!\!\sim}_{\cap\mathrm{arg}}^{\mathrm{Att,sem}}$ denotes a shared argument by all extensions, that is, shared justification for φ. Last, $\mathrel{|\!\!\sim}_{\cup}^{\mathrm{Att,sem}}$ denotes the existence of an argument (justification) in favor of a conclusion φ with respect to some extension, thus constituting a defensible stance for φ. Although both skeptical and credulous inference play an important role in NMLs, in the remainder we focus on skeptical inference.

In the context of $\mathsf{AF}_{\mathsf{AttAll}}(\mathbb{K}_2)$ all consequence relations coincide under any semantics $\mathsf{sem} \in \{\mathsf{stable}, \mathsf{preferred}, \mathsf{grounded}\}$ and where $\star \in \{\cap\mathsf{arg}, \cap\mathsf{con}, \cup\}$. For instance, we have:

$$\mathbb{K}_2 \mathrel|\joinrel\sim_\star^{\mathsf{AttAll},\mathsf{sem}} \texttt{killed}(\texttt{Cha},\texttt{Nor}) \qquad (3)$$

$$\mathbb{K}_2 \not\mathrel|\joinrel\sim_\star^{\mathsf{AttAll},\mathsf{sem}} \texttt{killed}(\texttt{Cha},\texttt{Alb}) \qquad (4)$$

The reason is that the information that the brother attended the knitting class unambiguously resolves the conflict between the testimony of the sister and the brother in favor of the former. Note that the argument c_1 concluding $\texttt{killed}(\texttt{Cha},\texttt{Nor})$ is contained in the grounded extension, and therefore also in every stable and preferred extension. Indeed, for $\mathsf{AF}_{\mathsf{AttAll}}(\mathbb{K}_2)$ the grounded extensions is also the only stable and the only preferred extension. Hence, in this particular case, the three inference relations coincide for these three semantics.

We can use this example also to highlight the nonmonotonicity of the argumentative consequence relations. Assume for this the knowledge base $\mathbb{K}_{\mathsf{bro}} = \langle \{\rhd_{\mathsf{bro}} \odot_{\mathsf{bro}} a\}, \mathcal{A}_d \rangle$. According to this knowledge base, we only have the testimony of the brother, not of the sister. This knowledge base is a subset of $\mathbb{K}_2$ for which

$$\mathbb{K}_{\mathsf{bro}} \mathrel|\joinrel\sim_\star^{\mathsf{AttAll},\mathsf{sem}} \texttt{killed}(\texttt{Cha},\texttt{Alb}) \qquad (5)$$

for the simple reason that argument $d_2 \in \mathsf{Arg}(\mathbb{K}_{\mathsf{bro}})$ remains unchallenged. In view of (4) and (5) (and similar for non-empty subsets of attack rules from AttAll) we have the general result:

Proposition 1. *Where* $\mathsf{sem} \in \{\mathsf{stable}, \mathsf{preferred}, \mathsf{grounded}\}$, $\star \in \{\cap\mathsf{arg}, \cap\mathsf{con}, \cup\}$ *and* $\emptyset \neq \mathsf{Att} \subseteq \mathsf{AttAll}$, $\mathrel|\joinrel\sim_\star^{\mathsf{Att},\mathsf{sem}}$ *is nonmonotonic.*

Let us now introduce some argumentative tensions that cannot be so easily resolved as those based on $\mathbb{K}_2$. We do this by removing the information about the brother's knitting class. It will also facilitate highlighting the usefulness of various other kinds of semantics, such as the stable semantics. So, let us for now omit the information given in STORY 2 CONT. and only consider STORY 2. We also add the strict assumptions expressing that killing a dragon renders Charlotte a brave warrior. We let $\mathbb{K}'_2 = \langle \mathcal{A}'_s, \mathcal{A}_d \rangle$, where

$$\mathcal{A}'_s = \{\rhd_{\mathsf{sis}} n, \rhd_{\mathsf{bro}} \odot_{\mathsf{bro}} a,$$
$$\texttt{killed}(\texttt{Cha},\texttt{Nor}) \supset \texttt{brave}(\texttt{Cha}),$$
$$\texttt{killed}(\texttt{Cha},\texttt{Alb}) \supset \texttt{brave}(\texttt{Cha})\}$$

We can derive some new arguments, for instance:

$$o_1 : \rhd_{\mathsf{sis}} n, \rhd_{\mathsf{sis}}^{\mathsf{rel}} n \Rightarrow \texttt{brave}(\texttt{Cha})$$
$$o_2 : \rhd_{\mathsf{bro}} \odot_{\mathsf{bro}} a, \rhd_{\mathsf{bro}}^{\mathsf{rel}} \odot_{\mathsf{bro}} a, \odot_{\mathsf{bro}}^{\mathsf{rel}} a \Rightarrow \texttt{brave}(\texttt{Cha})$$

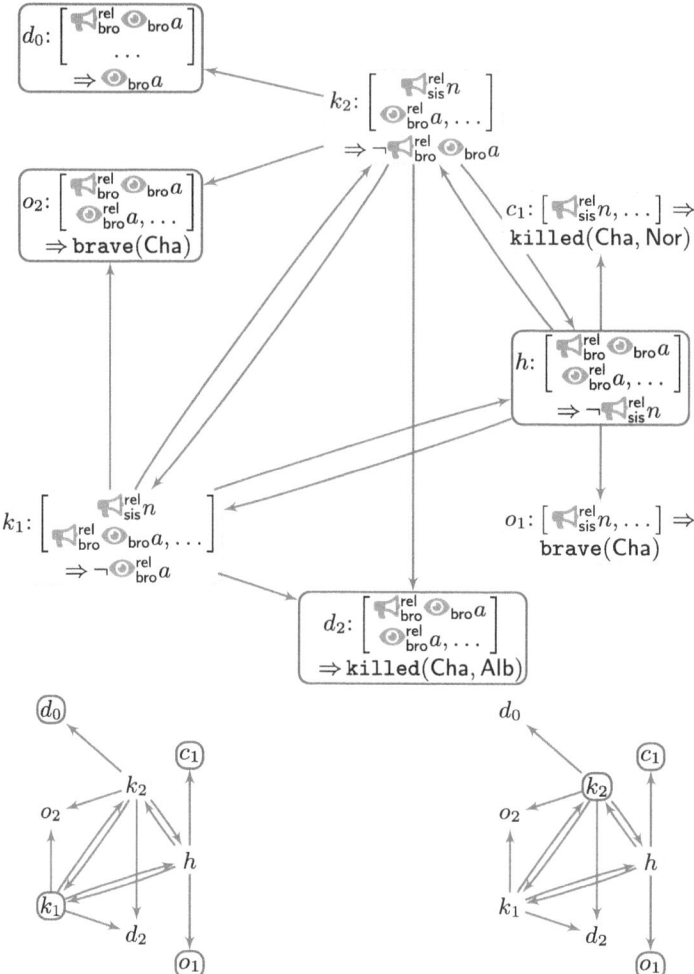

Fig. 5. Excerpt of the argumentation framework for STORY 2 with direct defeats. Highlighted are the three stable extensions. We omit strict assumptions in the arguments (denote by '[...]'). Top: the stable extension relies on the brother's account. Bottom: the two stable extensions rely on the sister's account.

The conclusion brave(Cha) is a so-called *floating conclusion*: it follows from two arguments which conflict. The premises of o_1 and o_2 are incompatible in the context of $\mathbb{K}'_2$, as witnessed by the mutual attacks between h and g, which make use of the same defeasible assumptions as o_1 and o_2, respectively.

In Fig. 5, we see an excerpt of the argumentation framework $\mathsf{AF}_{\mathsf{AttDir}}(\mathbb{K}'_2)$. Since we only consider direct defeat in $\mathsf{AF}_{\mathsf{AttDir}}(\mathbb{K}'_2)$, we may add two new arguments countering the brother's account:

$$k_1 : \ \blacktriangleleft_{\sf sis} n, \blacktriangleleft_{\sf sis}^{\sf rel} n, \blacktriangleleft_{\sf bro} \circledcirc_{\sf bro} a, \blacktriangleleft_{\sf bro}^{\sf rel} \circledcirc_{\sf bro} a \ \Rightarrow \ \neg \circledcirc_{\sf bro}^{\sf rel} a$$

$$k_2 : \ \blacktriangleleft_{\sf sis} n, \blacktriangleleft_{\sf sis}^{\sf rel} n, \blacktriangleleft_{\sf bro} \circledcirc_{\sf bro} a, \circledcirc_{\sf bro}^{\sf rel} a \ \Rightarrow \ \neg \blacktriangleleft_{\sf bro}^{\sf rel} \circledcirc_{\sf bro} a$$

The resulting argumentation framework has the three stable extensions highlighted in Fig. 5. On their basis, we obtain the following consequences, where $\star = \mathsf{AttDir}, \mathsf{stable},$

$$\mathbb{K}_2' \not\hspace{-2pt}\mid\hspace{-4pt}\sim_{\cap \mathsf{arg}}^{\star} \mathtt{killed(Cha, Nor)}$$
$$\mathbb{K}_2' \not\hspace{-2pt}\mid\hspace{-4pt}\sim_{\cap \mathsf{con}}^{\star} \mathtt{killed(Cha, Nor)}$$
$$\mathbb{K}_2' \not\hspace{-2pt}\mid\hspace{-4pt}\sim_{\cap \mathsf{arg}}^{\star} \mathtt{brave(Cha)}$$
$$\mathbb{K}_2' \mid\hspace{-4pt}\sim_{\cap \mathsf{con}}^{\star} \mathtt{brave(Cha)}$$

The floating conclusion $\mathtt{brave(Cha)}$ is a consequence of $\mathbb{K}_2'$ by $\mid\hspace{-4pt}\sim_{\cap \mathsf{con}}^{\star}$, but not by $\mid\hspace{-4pt}\sim_{\cap \mathsf{arg}}^{\star}$. This should not surprise us, since the former consequence relation considers the intersection of the set of conclusions induced by each extension. The latter, in contrast, considers the intersection of arguments, but no argument for $\mathtt{brave(Cha)}$ is contained in every stable extension.

4 Some Metatheoretic Insights

Ideally, we expect that the conclusions of arguments selected on the basis of a semantics form a consistent set. The next example shows that meeting this desideratum is not always guaranteed. In fact, the attack rules have to be carefully chosen in order to ascertain this property. We alter our story slightly to highlight this problem.

> **STORY 3.** *Norbert and Albert are twin dragons, only distinguished by the fact that Norbert spouts blue fire, while Albert spouts red fire. At the great battle against the underworld, the princess' brother saw her killing the red fire spouting Albert, and her sister saw her killing the blue fire spouting Norbert. However, the king saw a dragon flying over the castle right after the battle. It looked exactly like one of the twins, but the dragon did not spout fire, so he could not tell who of the two it was.*

Being not too suspicious about the reliability of the respective reports by the sister, brother, and king, we assume that at most one of them is mistaken. But who is? It could be that the sister and the brother really saw princess Charlotte killing Norbert, respectively Albert, but then the king mistook the dragon for one of the twins. Alternatively, maybe one of Charlotte's siblings is wrong and the king is right.

The story gives rise to the following knowledge base $\mathbb{K}_3 = \langle \mathcal{A}_s^3, \mathcal{A}_d \rangle$ (omitting and simplifying some details) with $\mathcal{A}_d$ as previously and

$$\mathcal{A}_s^3 = \{ \odot_{\mathsf{sis}} k_{\mathsf{Nor}},\ \odot_{\mathsf{bro}} k_{\mathsf{Alb}},\ \odot_{\mathsf{king}} \neg (k_{\mathsf{Nor}} \wedge k_{\mathsf{Alb}}) \},$$

where $k_{\mathsf{Nor}} = \mathtt{killed(Cha, Nor)}$ and $k_{\mathsf{Alb}} = \mathtt{killed(Cha, Alb)}$.

Among others, we can derive the following arguments using LK:

$a : \odot_{\mathsf{sis}} k_{\mathsf{Nor}},\ \odot_{\mathsf{sis}}^{\mathsf{rel}} k_{\mathsf{Nor}} \Rightarrow k_{\mathsf{Nor}}$

$b : \odot_{\mathsf{bro}} k_{\mathsf{Alb}},\ \odot_{\mathsf{bro}}^{\mathsf{rel}} k_{\mathsf{Alb}} \Rightarrow k_{\mathsf{Alb}}$

$c : \odot_{\mathsf{king}} \neg(k_{\mathsf{Nor}} \wedge k_{\mathsf{Alb}}),\ \odot_{\mathsf{king}}^{\mathsf{rel}} \neg(k_{\mathsf{Nor}} \wedge k_{\mathsf{Alb}}) \Rightarrow \neg(k_{\mathsf{Nor}} \wedge k_{\mathsf{Alb}})$

$ab : \mathcal{A}_s,\ \odot_{\mathsf{sis}}^{\mathsf{rel}} k_{\mathsf{Nor}},\ \odot_{\mathsf{bro}}^{\mathsf{rel}} k_{\mathsf{Alb}} \Rightarrow \neg \odot_{\mathsf{king}}^{\mathsf{rel}} \neg(k_{\mathsf{Nor}} \wedge k_{\mathsf{Alb}})$

$ac : \mathcal{A}_s,\ \odot_{\mathsf{sis}}^{\mathsf{rel}} k_{\mathsf{Nor}},\ \odot_{\mathsf{king}}^{\mathsf{rel}} \neg(k_{\mathsf{Nor}} \wedge k_{\mathsf{Alb}}) \Rightarrow \neg \odot_{\mathsf{bro}}^{\mathsf{rel}} k_{\mathsf{Alb}}$

$bc : \mathcal{A}_s,\ \odot_{\mathsf{bro}}^{\mathsf{rel}} k_{\mathsf{Alb}},\ \odot_{\mathsf{king}}^{\mathsf{rel}} \neg(k_{\mathsf{Nor}} \wedge k_{\mathsf{Alb}}) \Rightarrow \neg \odot_{\mathsf{sis}}^{\mathsf{rel}} k_{\mathsf{Nor}}$

$a' : \mathcal{A}_s,\ \odot_{\mathsf{sis}}^{\mathsf{rel}} k_{\mathsf{Nor}} \Rightarrow \neg(\odot_{\mathsf{bro}}^{\mathsf{rel}} k_{\mathsf{Alb}} \wedge \odot_{\mathsf{king}}^{\mathsf{rel}} \neg(k_{\mathsf{Nor}} \wedge k_{\mathsf{Alb}}))$

$b' : \mathcal{A}_s,\ \odot_{\mathsf{bro}}^{\mathsf{rel}} k_{\mathsf{Alb}} \Rightarrow \neg(\odot_{\mathsf{sis}}^{\mathsf{rel}} k_{\mathsf{Nor}} \wedge \odot_{\mathsf{king}}^{\mathsf{rel}} \neg(k_{\mathsf{Nor}} \wedge k_{\mathsf{Alb}}))$

$c' : \mathcal{A}_s,\ \odot_{\mathsf{king}}^{\mathsf{rel}} \neg(k_{\mathsf{Nor}} \wedge k_{\mathsf{Alb}}) \Rightarrow \neg(\odot_{\mathsf{sis}}^{\mathsf{rel}} k_{\mathsf{Nor}} \wedge \odot_{\mathsf{bro}}^{\mathsf{rel}} k_{\mathsf{Alb}})$

In our example, using the attack form of defeat in combination with stable semantics turns out to be a bad idea. In fact, there is a stable (and therefore also a preferred) extension including the arguments a, b and c (see Fig. 6, top). Clearly, their respective conclusions $k_{\mathsf{Nor}}, k_{\mathsf{Alb}}$ and $\neg(k_{\mathsf{Nor}} \wedge k_{\mathsf{Alb}})$ form an inconsistent set. When switching to direct defeat, however, the problem disappears and consistency is restored (see Fig. 6, bottom).

This poses the more general question: which combinations of attack forms and argumentation semantics are well-behaved? In what follows, we report on known results that connect logical argumentation to reasoning with *maximal consistent subsets* of knowledge bases. The method goes back to Rescher [71] and has been further developed by Makinson [50] and Makinson and van der Torre [52]. Starting with a knowledge base $\mathbb{K} = \langle \mathcal{A}_s, \mathcal{A}_d \rangle$, the idea is to reason on the basis of specific consistent subsets of $\mathbb{K}$. Since the assumptions in $\mathcal{A}_s$ are considered certain, we need to identify subsets of $\mathcal{A}_d$ that are consistent with $\mathcal{A}_s$. A subset $\mathcal{B}$ of $\mathcal{A}_d$ is *inconsistent* if $\Gamma, \Delta \Rightarrow$ is derivable for some $\Gamma \subseteq \mathcal{A}_s$ and some $\Delta \subseteq \mathcal{B}$ (recall that $\mathcal{A}_s$ is consistent). Otherwise, it is *consistent*. $\mathcal{B}$ is *maximally consistent* in $\mathbb{K}$ if it is consistent and there is no strict superset $\mathcal{B}' \subseteq \mathcal{A}_d$ of $\mathcal{B}$ that is consistent. We collect all maximal consistent sets in $\mathsf{maxcon}(\mathbb{K})$.

Let us consider again our STORY 3. Here, we have three maximal consistent sets, namely:

$$\mathcal{M}_1 = \mathcal{A}_d \setminus \{ \odot_{\mathsf{king}}^{\mathsf{rel}} \neg(k_{\mathsf{Nor}} \wedge k_{\mathsf{Alb}}) \},$$
$$\mathcal{M}_2 = \mathcal{A}_d \setminus \{ \odot_{\mathsf{bro}}^{\mathsf{rel}} k_{\mathsf{Alb}} \},$$
$$\text{and } \mathcal{M}_3 = \mathcal{A}_d \setminus \{ \odot_{\mathsf{sis}}^{\mathsf{rel}} k_{\mathsf{Nor}} \}.$$

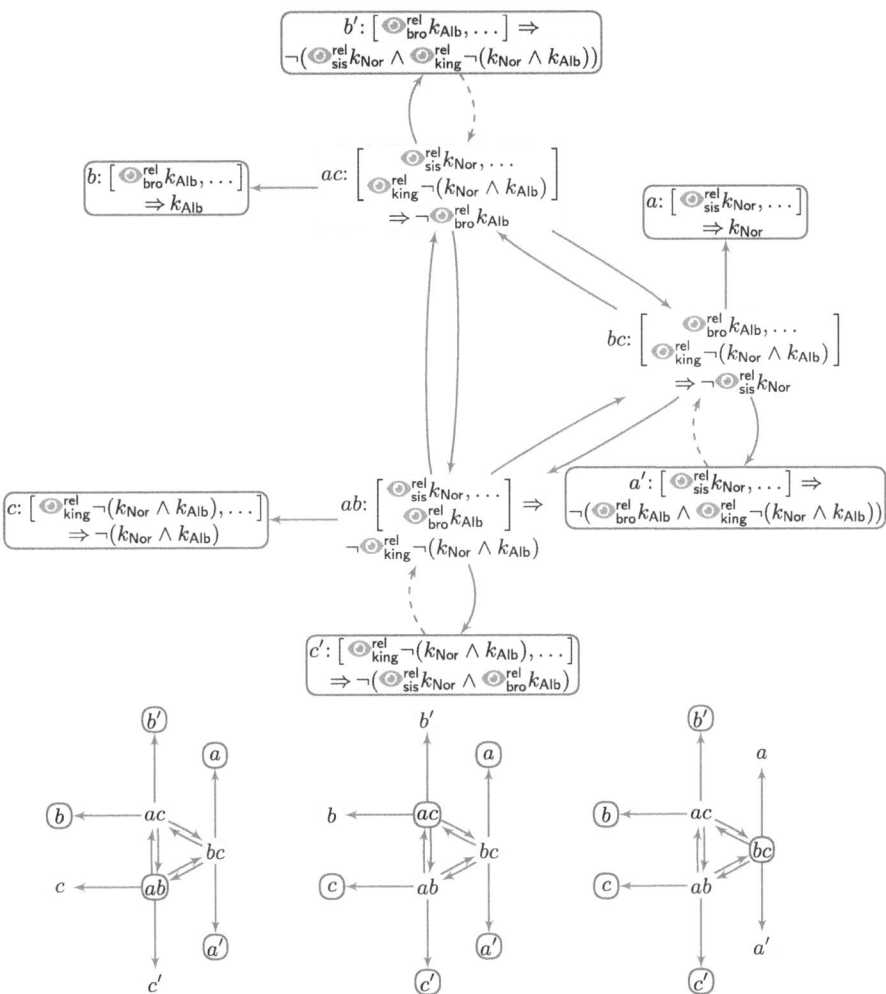

Fig. 6. An excerpt of the argumentation framework for STORY 3. Top: The framework with defeats. Highlighted is a stable extensions that gives rise to inconsistent conclusions. Bottom: The same argumentation framework but with only direct defeat and with the three stable extensions highlighted.

If we let Att ∈ {AttDir, AttDirCon}, sem ∈ {stable, preferred} and $\mathbb{K}$ be any knowledge base, we obtain a remarkable correspondence. Namely, for every sem-extension $\mathcal{E}$ of $\mathsf{AF}_{\mathsf{Att}}(\mathbb{K})$ there is an $\mathcal{M} \in \mathsf{maxcon}(\mathbb{K})$ such that $\mathcal{E}$ exactly contains those arguments whose defeasible premises are contained in $\mathcal{M}$. This also holds vice versa: for every $\mathcal{M} \in \mathsf{maxcon}(\mathbb{K})$ we can find a sem-extension that consists exactly of those arguments whose defeasible premises are contained in $\mathcal{M}$.

We can express this more formally. Let $\mathsf{sem}(\mathbb{K}, \mathsf{Att})$ be the set of all sem-extensions of $\mathsf{AF}_{\mathsf{Att}}(\mathbb{K})$ and let $\mathsf{Arg}(\mathcal{M})$ be the set of arguments $\Gamma \Rightarrow \varphi \in \mathsf{Arg}(\mathbb{K})$ for which $\Gamma \cap \mathcal{A}_d \subseteq \mathcal{M}$. We have the following result:[12]

Theorem 1. *Let $\mathbb{K}$ be a knowledge base, $\mathsf{Att} \in \{\mathsf{AttDir}, \mathsf{AttDirCon}\}$, $\mathsf{sem} \in \{\mathsf{stable}, \mathsf{preferred}\}$, and $\mathsf{sem} \in \{\mathsf{stable}, \mathsf{preferred}\}$. Then,*

$$\mathsf{sem}(\mathbb{K}, \mathsf{Att}) = \{\mathsf{Arg}(\mathcal{M}) \mid \mathcal{M} \in \mathsf{maxcon}(\mathbb{K})\}.$$

As our example based on STORY 3 shows, this result does not hold for $\mathsf{Att} = \{\mathsf{Def}\}$ and the preferred respectively, stable semantics. Still, another correspondence can be established for grounded semantics.

Theorem 2. *Let $\mathbb{K}$ be a knowledge base and $\mathsf{free}(\mathbb{K}) = \bigcap \mathsf{maxcon}(\mathbb{K})$. Then,*

$$\mathsf{grounded}(\mathbb{K}, \mathsf{AttDef}) = \mathsf{grounded}(\mathbb{K}, \mathsf{AttDirCon}) = \{\mathsf{Arg}(\mathsf{free}(\mathbb{K}))\}.$$

These theorems have valuable consequences in terms of desiderata that have been proposed for formal argumentation, and are grouped under the name of *rationality postulates* [27].

One of these postulates we already discussed informally, namely, that extensions are supposed to give rise to consistent sets of consequences. In what follows, let $\mathcal{E} \in \mathsf{sem}(\mathbb{K}, \mathsf{Att})$.

Consistency of extensions: The set $\{\varphi \mid \Gamma \Rightarrow \varphi \in \mathcal{E}\}$ is consistent.

A related property is that the set of conclusions is supposed to be closed under its own consequences. Henceforth, we denote the classical consequence set of a set of formulas $\mathcal{S}$ by $\mathsf{Cn}(\mathcal{S})$.[13]

Logical closure: For all $\psi \in \mathsf{Cn}(\{\varphi \mid \Delta \Rightarrow \varphi \in \mathcal{E}\})$, there is a $\Gamma \Rightarrow \psi \in \mathcal{E}$.

Another property relates to relevance [25,83]. Suppose we add to our initial knowledge base $\mathbb{K}$ some strict assumption γ that is syntactically unrelated (so no atoms in γ are contained in any assumptions of $\mathbb{K}$). In this case, we expect the resulting knowledge base to yield the same extensions:

Non-interference: Where γ is syntactically unrelated to $\mathbb{K}$ and $\mathbb{K} \oplus \gamma = \langle \mathcal{A}_s \cup \{\gamma\}, \mathcal{A}_d \rangle$, $\mathcal{E} \in \mathsf{sem}(\mathbb{K} \oplus \gamma)$ iff $\mathcal{E} \cap \mathsf{Arg}(\mathbb{K}) \in \mathsf{sem}(\mathbb{K})$.[14]

In view of Theorem 1 and 2 above, it can easily be checked that these rationality postulates are satisfied when using a combination of DirAtt and $\mathsf{sem} \in \{\mathsf{stable}, \mathsf{preferred}\}$, respectively of Def and $\mathsf{grounded}$.

These two theorems also give rise to alternative characterizations of argumentative consequence relations (recall page 12) in terms of other consequence relations that are well understood in the field of nonmonotonic logic.[15]

---

[12] The following results are proven in [8]. Our Theorem 1 and 2 are Theorem 3 in [8], our Theorem 3 is Theorem 4 in [8], and our Proposition 2 is Lemma 19 in [8].

[13] We note that Cn can be defined on the basis of LK by: $\mathsf{Cn}(\mathcal{S}) = \{\varphi \mid \text{there is a } \Gamma \subseteq \mathcal{S} \text{ such that } \Gamma \Rightarrow \varphi \text{ is } \mathsf{LK}\text{-derivable}\}$.

[14] A similar property can be defined for $\mathbb{K} \oplus \gamma = \langle \mathcal{A}_s, \mathcal{A}_d \cup \{\gamma\} \rangle$.

[15] For a thorough study see [16,78].

Theorem 3. *Let $\mathbb{K}$ be a knowledge base.*

1. *Where* sem $\in$ {stable, preferred} *and* Att $\in$ {AttDir, AttDirCon}:

$$\mathbb{K} \hspace{0.1em}\mid\hspace{-0.5em}\sim_{\cap\text{con}}^{\text{Att,sem}} \varphi \quad \textit{iff} \quad \varphi \in \bigcap\nolimits_{\mathcal{M} \in \text{maxcon}(\mathbb{K})} \text{Cn}(\mathcal{M} \cup \mathcal{A}_s)$$

2. *Where* sem $\in$ {stable, preferred} *and* Att $\in$ {AttDir, AttDirCon}:

$$\mathbb{K} \hspace{0.1em}\mid\hspace{-0.5em}\sim_{\cap\text{arg}}^{\text{Att,sem}} \varphi \quad \textit{iff} \quad \varphi \in \text{Cn}(\bigcap \text{maxcon}(\mathbb{K}) \cup \mathcal{A}_s)$$

3. *Where* $\star \in \{\cap\text{con}, \cap\text{arg}\}$ *and* Att $\in$ {AttDef, AttDirCon}:

$$\mathbb{K} \hspace{0.1em}\mid\hspace{-0.5em}\sim_{\star}^{\text{Att,grounded}} \varphi \quad \textit{iff} \quad \varphi \in \text{Cn}(\bigcap \text{maxcon}(\mathbb{K}) \cup \mathcal{A}_s).$$

Theorem 3 represents what is often referred to as *soundness and completeness* results, where an equivalence of the inference relations of two formal systems is shown. When an equivalence between a NML and inference in formal argumentation is shown, we call the latter an argumentative characterization of the former.

Furthermore, this third theorem ties the argumentative consequence relations closely to properties studied in nonmonotonic logic. For instance, we immediately obtain that these relations are cumulative. A consequence relation is cumulative if it is robust under adding its own consequences. More formally, where $\mathbb{K} \oplus \gamma \in \{\langle \mathcal{A}_s \cup \{\gamma\}, \mathcal{A}_d \rangle, \langle \mathcal{A}_s, \mathcal{A}_d \cup \{\gamma\}\rangle\}$, we have:

Cumulativity: A consequence relation $\mid\hspace{-0.3em}\sim$ is cumulative if, whenever $\mathbb{K} \mid\hspace{-0.3em}\sim \gamma$, we have:[16]

$$\mathbb{K} \oplus \gamma \mid\hspace{-0.3em}\sim \psi \quad \textit{iff} \quad \mathbb{K} \mid\hspace{-0.3em}\sim \psi.$$

Since the consequence relations that are based on maximal consistent subsets in Theorem 3 are known to be cumulative, we immediately obtain:

Corollary 1. *The consequence relations listed in Theorem 3 are cumulative.*

Another property frequently discussed in the context of nonnomonotonic consequence relations is OR. It is a form of reasoning by cases:

OR: If $\mathbb{K} \oplus \gamma \mid\hspace{-0.3em}\sim \varphi$ and $\mathbb{K} \oplus \delta \mid\hspace{-0.3em}\sim \varphi$ then $\mathbb{K} \oplus (\gamma \vee \delta) \mid\hspace{-0.3em}\sim \varphi$.

We start with a positive result:

Proposition 2. *OR holds for $\mid\hspace{-0.3em}\sim_{\cap\text{con}}^{\text{AttDirCon,sem}}$, where* sem $\in$ {stable, preferred}.

However, the property fails, e.g., for $\mid\hspace{-0.3em}\sim_{\cap\text{arg}}^{\text{AttDirCon,sem}}$ with sem $\in$ {stable, preferred, grounded} and for $\mid\hspace{-0.3em}\sim_{\cap\text{arg}}^{\text{AttDirCon,grounded}}$. For a demonstration consider the following extension of our story.

---

[16] The direction from left to right is known under the name of *cautious transitivity*, the one from right to left as *cautious monotonicity*. See [40,47] for a thorough study.

Story 4 Let $\mathbb{K}_4 = \langle \mathcal{A}_s^4, \mathcal{A}_d \rangle$, $k = \texttt{killed}(\mathsf{Cha}, \mathsf{Nor})$,

$$\mathcal{A}_s^4 = \{ \bigcirc_{\mathsf{sis}} k, \bigcirc_{\mathsf{bro}} k \},$$
$$\mathbb{K}_4^1 = \langle \mathcal{A}_s^4 \cup \{ \neg \bigcirc_{\mathsf{sis}}^{\mathsf{rel}} k \}, \mathcal{A}_d \rangle,$$
$$\mathbb{K}_4^2 = \langle \mathcal{A}_s^4 \cup \{ \neg \bigcirc_{\mathsf{bro}}^{\mathsf{rel}} k \}, \mathcal{A}_d \rangle,$$
$$\text{and } \mathbb{K}_4^\vee = \langle \mathcal{A}_s^4 \cup \{ \neg \bigcirc_{\mathsf{sis}}^{\mathsf{rel}} k \vee \neg \bigcirc_{\mathsf{bro}}^{\mathsf{rel}} k \}, \mathcal{A}_d \rangle.$$

We have,

$$\mathbb{K}_4^1 \mid\!\sim k, \tag{6}$$

$$\text{and } \mathbb{K}_4^2 \mid\!\sim k. \tag{7}$$

To see (6), note that $\mathsf{maxcon}(\mathbb{K}_4^1) = \{\mathcal{M}_1\}$, where $\mathcal{M}_1 = \mathcal{A}_d \setminus \{\bigcirc_{\mathsf{sis}}^{\mathsf{rel}} k\}$. By Theorem 3, (6) is equivalent to $k \in \mathsf{Cn}(\mathcal{A}_s \cup \mathcal{M}_1)$. The latter follows since $k \in \mathsf{Cn}(\{\bigcirc_{\mathsf{bro}} k, \bigcirc_{\mathsf{bro}}^{\mathsf{rel}} k\})$ by Modus Ponens and $\{\bigcirc_{\mathsf{bro}} k, \bigcirc_{\mathsf{bro}}^{\mathsf{rel}} k\} \subseteq \mathcal{A}_s \cup \mathcal{M}_1$.

However, in violation of OR we also have,

$$\mathbb{K}_4^\vee \not\mid\!\sim k. \tag{8}$$

We can again use Theorem 3 to understand why. It is easy to see that, where $\mathcal{M}_2 = \mathcal{A}_d \setminus \{\bigcirc_{\mathsf{bro}}^{\mathsf{rel}} k\}$,

$$\mathsf{maxcon}(\mathbb{K}_4^\vee) = \{\mathcal{M}_1, \mathcal{M}_2\}.$$

So, $\bigcap \mathsf{maxcon}(\mathbb{K}_4^\vee) = \mathcal{A}_d \setminus \{\bigcirc_{\mathsf{sis}}^{\mathsf{rel}} k, \bigcirc_{\mathsf{bro}}^{\mathsf{rel}} k\}$ and $k \notin \mathsf{Cn}(\mathcal{A}_s \cup \bigcap \mathsf{maxcon}(\mathbb{K}_4^\vee))$. By Theorem 3, the latter is equivalent to (8). For our present discussion the above suffices and we refer to [6] for an extensive overview and survey of properties of argumentative consequence relations.

5 Applications to Normative Reasoning

We now show how to apply the discussed formalisms to two important topics in artificial intelligence (AI): normative reasoning and explanations. Normative reasoning involves obligations, prohibitions, permissions, rights, values, and norms. It strongly influences everyday decision-making and how agents (including AI agents) shape their world. Expanding our Story, the obligation

"Promises must be kept."

might cause princess Charlotte to hunt down and kill a dragon (since Charlotte promised her brother to kill him a fierce creature for his birthday). Whereas the obligation

"Dragons ought to be left in peace."

affects whether or not Charlotte will pursue Albert in a dragon hunt or hunt some other fierce creature instead. Agents often find themselves in situations where norms conflict. In such cases, the conflict must be resolved and it must be determined which commands override others. This makes normative reasoning inherently defeasible [60]. For instance, since Albert is the only fierce creature in the kingdom, Charlotte may decide to violate her promise to her brother and respect Albert's right to a tranquil life.

Deontic Logic is the overarching term for the field that uses logical methods for normative reasoning [38]. It owes its name to the Greek word 'déon', which roughly refers to 'duty.' Since the 1950s, a wide range of deontic logics has been introduced. Traditionally, these logics are monotonic modal logics (see [45] for an overview), employing modal formulas such as $\mathcal{O}\varphi$ expressing "it ought to be that φ" (where $\mathcal{O}$ is a modality expressing "it ought to be that" and φ a proposition such as "Albert is left in peace"). Over the last decades, developments in AI and Multi-Agent Systems led to the development of classes of nonmonotonic deontic logics that are often non-modal. Deontic conflicts, such as the example scenario alluded to above, can be effectively addressed using nonmonotonic formalisms [60,62].

Recently, explanation has been gradually taking up a more central position in AI [55]. The use of formal argumentation for explanatory purposes is promising due to its closeness to human reasoning practices [54] and the field is rapidly expanding [4,24,30,73,81]. Explanation is important in ethics, mathematics, law, AI, and many other disciplines (e.g., see [10,34,55]). Very broadly, one can think of an explanation as something that answers a why question with the aim to increase our understanding of the subject in question. For an overview of these concepts in the social sciences and AI, see [55,74].

Now, in the context of normative reasoning, explanations fulfill a critical role too: to coordinate and motivate compliant behavior, agents must understand why they have to behave in a specific way (particularly if they disagree with the alleged duties). For instance, princess Charlotte may ask:

"Why am I obliged to leave Albert be, even though I promised my brother to get him a fierce creature?"

Answers to such questions are *deontic explanations* (e.g., see [17, Ch.6]). In this last section, we use logical argumentation to characterize conflict resolution and defeasibility in the context of normative reasoning. We do so by adopting a proof calculus that generates deontic arguments that facilitate explainability [18].

The first step towards realizing more explanatory arguments, is to label propositional formulas.

Labelled propositional languages: $\mathcal{L}^i = \{\varphi^i \mid \varphi \in \mathcal{L}\}$ where $i \in \{f, o, c\}$.

We consider three such languages, differentiating facts ($\mathcal{L}^f$), obligations ($\mathcal{L}^o$), and constraints ($\mathcal{L}^c$). The labelling ensures a transparent representation of the various roles these formulas play in normative reasoning. For instance, let hunt be an unlabelled propositional atom denoting "Charlotte hunts Albert," then hunt^f and hunt^o express "it is a fact that Charlotte hunts Albert," respectively "it ought to be that Charlotte hunts Albert."

Additionally, we adopt languages expressing *norms*.

Norm languages: $\mathcal{L}^n = \{(\varphi, \psi) \mid \varphi, \psi \in \mathcal{L}\}$ and $\overline{\mathcal{L}^n} = \{\neg(\varphi, \psi) \mid (\varphi, \psi) \in \mathcal{L}^n\}$.

Let prom stand for "Charlotte made a promise (to hunt down Albert)." A norm is then a pair of propositional formulas $(\text{prom}, \text{hunt}) \in \mathcal{L}^n$ which is interpreted as "if Charlotte made the promise, then it ought to be that she hunts Albert." Furthermore, due to the defeasibility of normative reasoning, we also want to express when a given norm is *inapplicable* in a given context. We express this inapplicability by putting a negation in front of the norm in question. For instance, $\neg(\text{prom}, \text{hunt}) \in \overline{\mathcal{L}^n}$ expresses "the norm $(\text{prom}, \text{hunt})$ is inapplicable".

The full labelled deontic language is then

$$\mathcal{L}^d = \mathcal{L}^f \cup \mathcal{L}^o \cup \mathcal{L}^c \cup \mathcal{L}^n \cup \overline{\mathcal{L}^n}.$$

Based on the above language, we define a specific kind of knowledge base:

Normative Knowledge Base: $\mathbb{K} = \langle \mathcal{F}, \mathcal{N}, \mathcal{C} \rangle$, where $\mathcal{F} \subseteq \mathcal{L}^f$ constitutes the factual context, $\mathcal{N} \subseteq \mathcal{L}^n$ a normative code, and $\mathcal{C} \subseteq \mathcal{L}^c$ the constraints with which the inferred obligations must be consistent. Both $\mathcal{F}$ and $\mathcal{C}$ are assumed to be consistent (i.e., $\mathcal{F} \nvdash_{CL} \bot^f$ and $\mathcal{C} \nvdash_{CL} \bot^c$).[17]

Obligations are not part of the knowledge base: they are derived. The basic idea of defeasible reasoning with such knowledge bases comes from constrained Input/Output logic, a nonmonotonic formalism developed by Makinson and van der Torre [52]. It can be expressed as follows:

Facts (input) trigger norms from which obligations (output) are detached. Constraints control the output to ensure consistency.

To illustrate, suppose that princess Charlotte did promise to hunt down a fierce creature, and that this creature is in fact the dragon Albert. Let the fact prom^f express this promise. Furthermore, assume that making a promise binds one to fulfilling that promise. Hence, we obtain the norm $(\text{prom}, \text{hunt})$. Then, the factual context prom and the norm $(\text{prom}, \text{hunt})$ provide reasons for detaching the obligation to hunt Albert, i.e., hunt^o. The above is captured by the following argument type:

$$a: \underbrace{\text{prom}^f, (\text{prom}, \text{hunt})}_{\text{reasons...}} \Rightarrow \underbrace{\text{hunt}^o}_{\text{for}}$$

Deontic arguments do not only provide reasons in support of a concluded obligation but also defend them from potential attackers. Here, we focus on undercutting attacks which are arguments expressing which norms are *inapplicable* in light of a given context (i.e., norms, facts, and constraints). An attacking argument is of the type:

$$b: \text{prom}^f, \neg\text{hunt}^c \Rightarrow \neg(\text{prom}, \text{hunt})$$

---

[17] So, comparing to Sect. 2, $\mathcal{F}$ can be seen as the set of strict assumptions and $\mathcal{N}$ as the set of defeasible (conditional) assumptions.

It expresses that in the factual context prom^f, the norm $(\text{prom}, \text{hunt})$ cannot be consistently applied since it would lead to the conclusion hunt^o that conflicts with the constraint $\neg\text{hunt}^c$. An attacking argument concluding the inapplicability of $(\text{prom}, \text{hunt})$ attacks all arguments that appeal to $(\text{prom}, \text{hunt})$ as a reason. For instance, argument b attacks argument a above.[18]

These two types of argument are derivable with a <u>D</u>eontic <u>A</u>rgumentation <u>C</u>alculus, a DAC for short. A DAC belongs to the sequent-based tradition to logical argumentation, as discussed in Sect. 3.

DAC argument: We say that $\Gamma \Rightarrow \Delta$ is a DAC-*argument* (sequent) whenever $\Gamma \subseteq \mathcal{L}^d$ is a finite set, and $\Delta \subseteq \mathcal{L}^d$ is a set restricted to at most one formula.[19]

Let us now define the DAC that we will use throughout this section.[20]

Deontic Argumentation Calculus (DAC): Let DAC consists of the rules $Ax, Detach, RC, RN, Taut, LCT$, and Cut from Fig. 7.
A DAC-derivation of an argument $\Gamma \Rightarrow \Delta$ is a tree-like structure whose leaves are initial sequents of DAC, whose root is $\Gamma \Rightarrow \Delta$, and whose rule-applications are instances of the rules of DAC.

Let us briefly discuss each rule of DAC (the Cut rule is as in Sect. 3). DAC contains three types of initial sequent rules (forming the leaf-nodes of a derivation-tree). Through the Ax rule, DAC takes labelled versions of any LK-derivable (that is, classically derivable) $\Gamma \Rightarrow \Delta$ as an initial sequent. The rules of LK are, therefore, not required to be part of DAC (see page 8 for the calculus LK). The rule $Taut$ ensures that all propositional tautologies are considered among both input (facts) and output (obligations). More importantly, the rule $Detach$ is an initial explanatory argument stating that the fact φ and the norm (φ, ψ) are reasons for concluding the obligation ψ.

The rule LCT corresponds to successive detachment, expressing that a norm may likewise be triggered by output detached from some other norm(s). Consider the following example derivation using LCT:

$$\cfrac{\cfrac{}{\text{prom}^f, (\text{prom}, \text{hunt}) \Rightarrow \text{hunt}^o} Detach \quad \cfrac{\cfrac{}{\text{hunt}^f, (\text{hunt}, \text{brave}) \Rightarrow \text{brave}^o} Detach}{\text{hunt}^o, (\text{hunt}, \text{brave}) \Rightarrow \text{brave}^o} LCT}{\text{prom}^f, (\text{prom}, \text{hunt}), (\text{hunt}, \text{brave}) \Rightarrow \text{brave}^o} Cut$$

---

[18] Recall the discussion of Toulmin's [79] argument in Sect. 1. Similarly, one can read the above sequent a in general terms: facts are premises, obligations are conclusions, and norms are warrants, namely, the objects that justify the relation between premises and conclusion. In this sense, the calculus of this section can be adopted for defeasible reasoning in general, where attacks only happen on warrants, as in argument b. If we take a norm as a defeasible assumption, arguments like b express direct defeats, if a norm is taken as a warrant the attack type is referred to as an undermining defeat.
[19] This harmless restriction comes from [18] and enables the development of calculi for a large class of underlying base logics, including but not limited to classical logic.
[20] Other calculi can be found in [18].

$$\overline{\Gamma^i \Rightarrow \Delta^i} \; Ax \text{ , for } i \in \{f, o, c\} \text{ and } \Gamma^i \Rightarrow \Delta^i \text{ is LK-derivable}$$

$$\overline{\Rightarrow (\top, \top)} \; Taut \qquad \overline{\varphi^f, (\varphi, \psi) \Rightarrow \psi^o} \; Detach$$

$$\frac{\varphi^f, \Gamma \Rightarrow \Delta}{\varphi^o, \Gamma \Rightarrow \Delta} \; LCT^a \qquad \frac{\Gamma \Rightarrow \varphi^o}{\Gamma, (\neg\varphi)^c \Rightarrow} \; RC \qquad \frac{\Gamma, (\varphi, \psi) \Rightarrow}{\Gamma \Rightarrow \neg(\varphi, \psi)} \; RN$$

$$\frac{\Gamma \Rightarrow \varphi \qquad \varphi, \Gamma' \Rightarrow \Delta}{\Gamma, \Gamma' \Rightarrow \Delta} \; Cut^b$$

Fig. 7. A Deontic Argumentation Calculus (DAC). The upper level contains initial sequents, and the lower level logical and structural rules. Side-condition (a) on LCT denotes $\Gamma \cap \mathcal{L}^n \neq \emptyset$; and (b) on Cut stipulates that $\varphi \in \mathcal{L}^d$.

The above derivation illustrates successive detachment: given the fact that Charlotte promises to her brother to hunt a fierce creature, she ought to hunt Albert. Furthermore, since it is obligatory to be brave while hunting dragons, we additionally detach the obligation that Charlotte must be brave.[21]

The rules RC and RN generate attacking arguments. Concerning RC, think of a sequent with an empty right-hand side as an argument expressing inconsistent reasons (see page 8). For instance, whenever we have[22]

$$\frac{\text{prom}^f, (\text{prom}, \text{hunt}) \Rightarrow \text{hunt}^o}{\text{prom}^f, (\text{prom}, \text{hunt}), \neg\text{hunt}^c \Rightarrow} \; RC$$

the bottom argument expresses that the fact prom^f and the norm $(\text{prom}, \text{hunt})$ (which are joint reasons for hunt^o) are inconsistent whenever the detached obligations must be consistent with the constraint $\neg\text{hunt}^c$.

Moreover, whenever an argument expresses inconsistent reasons, we know that at least one of its norms is inapplicable (recall that arguments may contain any number of norms). The rule RN captures this:

$$\frac{\text{prom}^f, (\text{prom}, \text{hunt}), \neg\text{hunt}^c \Rightarrow}{\text{prom}^f, \neg\text{hunt}^c \Rightarrow \neg(\text{prom}, \text{hunt})} \; RN$$

Namely, the bottom argument expresses that prom^f and $\neg\text{hunt}^c$ are joint reasons for the *inapplicability* of the norm $(\text{prom}, \text{hunt})$. Arguments generated by the RN rule serve as attacking arguments in the envisioned argumentation frameworks.

---

[21] This process determines the agent's obligations under the assumption that the agent is willing to comply with all her obligations.
[22] Henceforth, we often use relaxed notation writing, e.g., $\neg\varphi^c$ instead of $(\neg\varphi)^c$.

We illustrate the use of DAC by addressing a challenging benchmark scenario in Deontic Logic. Development in Deontic logic is largely driven by paradoxes and challenging puzzles [45]. Defeasible normative reasoning can adequately address many of these puzzles. We look at one of the field's central challenges: contrary-to-duty (CTD) reasoning [28]. In a CTD scenario, an agent is bound by an initial duty, but violates this duty. The agent must then find out what she ought to, not within a regular compliant situation, but given her violation. Such scenarios have proven to be notoriously difficult to formalize.

Consider the following continuation of our STORY:

STORY 5 *Earlier this year, the local dragon protection guild successfully lobbied for a prohibition on hunting dragons. Since such practices are deeply entrenched within the kingdom's culture, an additional law was adopted to ensure that if such a hunt would nevertheless take place, the hunter ought to ask the dragon for consent. However, to not frighten any dragons, if no hunt takes place, no consent should be asked either (it would be rather awkward and confusing for the dragon in question).*

The above story contains three norms: a default norm obliging the kingdom's subjects not to hunt dragons $(\top, \neg\text{hunt})$; a norm expressing that if such a hunt does take place, then the hunt should at least occur with the consent of the huntee $(\text{hunt}, \text{cons})$; and a norm obliging the subjects not to ask consent when no hunt ensues $(\neg\text{hunt}, \neg\text{cons})$. Let the norm code be defined as

$$\mathcal{N}_5 = \{(\top, \neg\text{hunt}), (\text{hunt}, \text{cons}), (\neg\text{hunt}, \neg\text{cons})\}.$$

Suppose that no factual context is given (i.e., $\mathcal{F}_5 = \{\top^f\}$) and no additional constraints beyond logical consistency are imposed (i.e., $\mathcal{C}_5 = \{\top^c\}$). Let $\mathbb{K}_5 = \langle \mathcal{F}_5, \mathcal{N}_5, \mathcal{C}_5 \rangle$. We can still draw conclusions about, for instance, princess Charlotte's duties. Following convention, a norm $(\top, \neg\text{hunt})$ with as a precondition the logical tautology $\top$ is triggered by default, and expresses a default duty.[23] An application of *Detach* yields the following argument:

$$a: \frac{}{\top^f, (\top, \neg\text{hunt}) \Rightarrow \neg\text{hunt}^o} \; Detach$$

Furthermore, we can apply the norm $(\neg\text{hunt}, \neg\text{cons})$ which is a compliant-with-duty norm expressing a norm conditional on the fulfillment of the initial duty. Then, using the rule LCT we obtain argument b.

$$b: \frac{a \quad \dfrac{\dfrac{}{\neg\text{hunt}^f, (\neg\text{hunt}, \neg\text{cons}) \Rightarrow \neg\text{cons}^o} \; Detach}{\neg\text{hunt}^o, (\neg\text{hunt}, \neg\text{cons}) \Rightarrow \neg\text{cons}^o} \; LCT}{\top^f, (\top, \neg\text{hunt}), (\neg\text{hunt}, \neg\text{cons}) \Rightarrow \neg\text{cons}^o} \; Cut$$

In other words, given a default situation (i.e., $\mathcal{F}_5 = \{\top^f\}$) we infer that princess Charlotte is under (at least) two obligations: an obligation not to hunt

---

[23] An empty factual context closed under classical logical consequences always yields the set of classical tautologies (recall the *Taut* rule). We simply write $\mathcal{F} = \{\top^f\}$.

any dragons, as supported by argument a, and an obligation not to ask consent, as supported by argument b.[24]

Like in previous sections, when reasoning with a given normative knowledge base, in this case $\mathbb{K}_5$, we are only interested in arguments relevant to $\mathbb{K}$. An argument $\Gamma \Rightarrow \Delta$ is relevant with respect to $\mathbb{K}$ if its reasons Γ are part of the knowledge base, i.e., $\Gamma \subseteq \mathcal{F} \cup \mathcal{N} \cup \mathcal{C}$. For this reason, we say that the norm $(\mathsf{hunt}, \mathsf{cons})$ is not triggered in the context $\mathcal{F}_5 = \{\top^f\}$.

Application of $(\mathsf{hunt}, \mathsf{cons})$ is conditional on the occurrence of a hunt. Hence, $(\mathsf{hunt}, \mathsf{cons})$ is a CTD norm expressing what Charlotte ought to do ("hunt with consent") in the sub-optimal situation in which she acted contrary to her initial duty ("to not hunt"). Things become more complicated once we consider what happens if a violation of the set of default obligations occurs.

STORY 5 CONT. *Keeping the promise to her brother in mind, princess Charlotte decides to initiate a hunt for Albert. She also remembers that she ought to be back on time for her brother's birthday.*

The above story tells us that Charlotte is in a situation *contrary to her duty* ("thou shall not hunt!"). What should she do? Since Charlotte needs to know what she ought to do given her violation hunt^f, we impose the constraint that the output must be consistent with the fact that Charlotte goes on a hunt for Albert, i.e., hunt^c. The resulting knowledge base of our continued STORY 5 is

$$\mathbb{K}_5' = \langle\ \mathcal{F}_5' = \{\top^f, \mathsf{hunt}^f\},$$
$$\mathcal{N}_5' = \{(\top, \neg\mathsf{hunt}), (\neg\mathsf{hunt}, \neg\mathsf{cons}), (\mathsf{hunt}, \mathsf{cons}), (\mathsf{hunt}, \mathsf{back})\},$$
$$\mathcal{C}_5' = \{\top^c, \mathsf{hunt}^c\}\ \rangle.$$

Hence, in $\mathbb{K}_5'$, the facts are set as constraints modulo re-labelling.

Given $\mathcal{F}_5'$, we can still derive arguments a and b above, but now we can derive additional arguments, some of which are problematic. First of all, we have the initial arguments

$$\frac{}{c:\ \mathsf{hunt}^f, (\mathsf{hunt}, \mathsf{cons}) \Rightarrow \mathsf{cons}^o}\ Detach$$

and

$$\frac{}{d:\ \mathsf{hunt}^f, (\mathsf{hunt}, \mathsf{back}) \Rightarrow \mathsf{back}^o}\ Detach$$

concluding that Charlotte must ask Albert to consent to the hunt, respectively, be back on time for her brother's party.

However, further DAC-reasoning yields the following problematic obligation:

$$\cfrac{b \quad \cfrac{c \quad \cfrac{}{\mathsf{cons}^o, \neg\mathsf{cons}^o \Rightarrow \bot^o}\ Ax}{\neg\mathsf{cons}^o, \mathsf{hunt}^f, (\mathsf{hunt}, \mathsf{cons}) \Rightarrow \bot^o}\ Cut}{x:\ \top^f, \mathsf{hunt}^f, (\top, \neg\mathsf{hunt}), (\neg\mathsf{hunt}, \neg\mathsf{cons}), (\mathsf{hunt}, \mathsf{cons}) \Rightarrow \bot^o}\ Cut$$

---

[24] Additional DAC reasoning yields obligations like $(\neg\mathsf{hunt} \land \neg\mathsf{cons})^o$, that is, obligations obtained by closing the set $\{\neg\mathsf{hunt}^o, \neg\mathsf{cons}^o\}$ under classical consequence.

In other words, the given violation context together with all three norms yields an inconsistent obligation for princess Charlotte. So, the central question is: what should Charlotte do? This is where the constraints in $\mathcal{C}'_5$ come in. The set $\mathcal{C}'_5$ gives us various $\mathbb{K}_5$-based arguments:

$$\cfrac{\cfrac{\overline{\top^c \Rightarrow \neg\bot^c}\ Ax \quad \cfrac{x}{\top^f, \mathtt{hunt}^f, (\top, \neg\mathtt{hunt}), (\neg\mathtt{hunt}, \neg\mathtt{cons}), (\mathtt{hunt}, \mathtt{cons}), \neg\bot^c \Rightarrow}\ RC}{\top^f, \mathtt{hunt}^f, (\top, \neg\mathtt{hunt}), (\neg\mathtt{hunt}, \neg\mathtt{cons}), (\mathtt{hunt}, \mathtt{cons}), \top^c \Rightarrow}\ Cut}{e:\ \top^f, \mathtt{hunt}^f, (\neg\mathtt{hunt}, \neg\mathtt{cons}), (\mathtt{hunt}, \mathtt{cons}), \top^c \Rightarrow \neg(\top, \neg\mathtt{hunt})}\ RN$$

This argument serves as an attacker of any argument that appeals to $(\top, \neg\mathtt{hunt})$ in its reasons. In this case, this includes arguments a and b. With similar reasoning we obtain arguments

$$f:\quad \top^f, \mathtt{hunt}^f, (\top, \neg\mathtt{hunt}), (\mathtt{hunt}, \mathtt{cons}), \top^c \Rightarrow \neg(\neg\mathtt{hunt}, \neg\mathtt{cons})$$

and

$$g:\quad \top^f, \mathtt{hunt}^f, (\top, \neg\mathtt{hunt}), (\neg\mathtt{hunt}, \neg\mathtt{cons}), \top^c \Rightarrow \neg(\mathtt{hunt}, \mathtt{cons})$$

Hence, e, f, and g express that the three norms cannot be jointly applied and these arguments mutually attack each other. Note that this threefold attack is not yet due to Charlotte's violation: it ensues because of the general consistency constraint $\top^c$. When we consider the CTD constraint $\mathtt{hunt}^c$, we obtain the following attacking argument:

$$\cfrac{\cfrac{\overline{\mathtt{hunt}^c \Rightarrow \neg\neg\mathtt{hunt}^c}\ Ax \quad \cfrac{a}{\top^f, (\top, \neg\mathtt{hunt}), \neg\neg\mathtt{hunt}^c \Rightarrow}\ RC}{\top^f, (\top, \neg\mathtt{hunt}), \mathtt{hunt}^c \Rightarrow}\ Cut}{h:\ \top^f, \mathtt{hunt}^c \Rightarrow \neg(\top, \neg\mathtt{hunt})}\ RN$$

Argument h expresses that, with the constraint of the occurred violation $\mathtt{hunt}^c$, the norm $(\top, \neg\mathtt{hunt})$ becomes inapplicable. This enables us to conclude what princess Charlotte's obligations are in the CTD scenario. We do this by *instantiating* an argumentation framework with the above derived arguments.

We saw that the central DAC-arguments are of two types: those giving reasons for obligations or those giving reasons for why certain norms are inapplicable.[25] The latter type captures the defeasibility of normative reasoning and defines the interaction among arguments: an argument concluding $\neg(\top, \mathtt{hunt})$, attacks all arguments making an appeal to $(\top, \mathtt{hunt})$ in their reasons. We instantiate argumentation frameworks with DAC-arguments to model this interaction.[26]

DAC-induced Argumentation Frameworks: Let $\mathbb{K} = \langle \mathcal{F}, \mathcal{N}, \mathcal{C} \rangle$ be a normative knowledge base. A DAC-induced argumentation framework is a tuple $\mathsf{AF}(\mathbb{K}) = \langle \mathsf{Arg}, \mathsf{Attack} \rangle$ such that:

---

[25] Other DAC arguments include arguments about facts and constraints.
[26] In [5], a nonmonotonic extension of DAC was developed, that incorporates argumentative notions of attack directly in the proof-system such that the entailment relation is sound and complete for DAC-induced argumentation frameworks under grounded semantics.

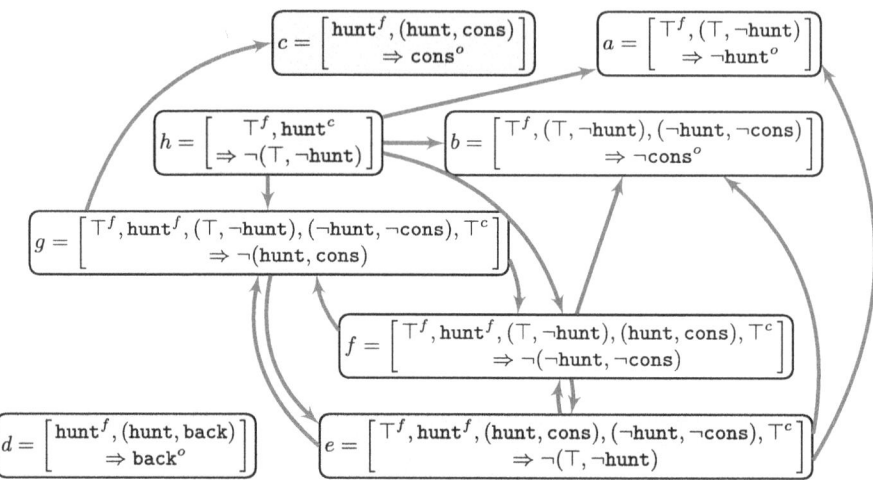

Fig. 8. Defeasible normative reasoning: A contrary-to-duty scenario (STORY 5 CONT). Arrows denote attack relations between arguments, relative to the knowledge base $\mathbb{K}'_5$. The shaded arguments (green) form the unique stable extension $\{c, d, e, h\}$, which is also the grounded extension. (Color figure online)

- $\Gamma \Rightarrow \Delta \in \mathsf{Arg}$ iff $\Gamma \Rightarrow \Delta$ is DAC-derivable and $\Gamma \subseteq \mathcal{F} \cup \mathcal{N} \cup \mathcal{C}$.
  And for each $a, b \in \mathsf{Arg}$:
- a attacks b, i.e., $(a, b) \in \mathsf{Attack}$ iff $a : \Gamma \Rightarrow \neg(\varphi, \psi)$ and $b : \Delta, (\varphi, \psi) \Rightarrow \Delta'$.

Remark 1. The calculus DAC given in this section corresponds to the system Out_3 of the Input/Output (I/O) family, which is a renowned logical formalism for defeasible reasoning. Developed by Makinson and van der Torre [51], I/O logics are suitable for normative reasoning [61], causal and doxastic reasoning [23], as well as legal reasoning [29]. In [18], a class of 16 Deontic Argumentation Calculi was developed and it was shown that formal argumentation frameworks instantiated with DAC arguments are sound and complete with respect to the class of nonmonotonic I/O logics [52]. Among others, these results contribute to the claim that formal argumentation is a uniform formalism for the characterization of large classes of nonmonotonic logics, especially those systems based on maximally consistent sets [7]. Recently [20], the DAC formalism was adjusted to capture Reiter's [70] normal default logic.

The arguments of STORY 5 CONT yield the argumentation framework presented in Fig. 8 (for the sake of readability, we omit argument x in the figure, since it is attacked by all attacking arguments $e, f, g,$ and h). Recall that argument x demonstrates the joint inconsistency of the three norms in the knowledge base $\mathbb{K}'_5$. This threefold conflict is expressed in Fig. 8 by the mutual attacks between $e, f,$ and g. Although the conflict is mutual, the outcome is in favor of e and h due to the constraint $\mathcal{C} = \{\top^c, \mathsf{hunt}^c\}$ yielding the unassailable h. Argument h is unassailable because it does not employ any norms in its reasons and can therefore not receive any attack either (in the context of undercutting attacks). Furthermore, h attacks g, the latter challenges the obligation that Charlotte ought to ask Albert for consent (concluded by c). Last, we point out that argument d does not interact with any of the arguments. Intuitively, this is because the entailed obligation is syntactically disjoint from any of the other norms (see the discussion of non-interference on page 18).

Employing the semantic notions discussed in Sect. 2 (page 6), we find that the $\mathsf{AF}(\mathbb{K}_5')$ in Fig. 8 has exactly one stable extension $\{c, d, e, h\}$ (in fact, it is also the smallest complete extension, and thus establishes the grounded extension). Since the $\mathsf{AF}(\mathbb{K}_5')$ has one unique stable extension the three nonmonotonic inference relations (page 12) equate. For instance, we have:

$$\mathbb{K}_5' \mathrel{\vert\!\sim}_*^{\mathsf{Att, stable}} \mathsf{cons}^o$$
$$\mathbb{K}_5' \mathrel{\vert\!\sim}_*^{\mathsf{Att, stable}} \mathsf{back}^o$$
$$\mathbb{K}_5' \mathrel{\vert\!\not\sim}_*^{\mathsf{Att, stable}} \neg\mathsf{hunt}^o$$

for $* \in \{\cup, \cap\mathsf{con}, \cap\mathsf{arg}\}$ and where Att refers to the notion of attack for DAC-induced argumentation frameworks, i.e., the relation Attack above.

As a consequence, given that princess Charlotte decides to initiate a hunt for Albert, she ought to ask Albert for his consent and she ought to be back on time for the party. Charlotte's initial duties (i.e., prior to her violation), expressed by arguments a and b are blocked in this argumentation framework by the unassailable h. This is due to the constraint hunt^c which is asserted as one of the reasons in argument h. In fact, the obligation to ask for consent is the desired outcome of this CTD scenario (e.g., see [61]).

DAC generates what we called a direct defeat (on norms) in Sect. 2. In fact, since we only consider stable semantics in this section, we may restrict the focus on direct defeats. In the context of grounded semantics, however, it is advisable to include consistency-attacks to avoid problems with non-interference and to obtain results similar to Theorem 2 (see [8, 18]). Using DAC-reasoning, we can derive the problematic argument

$$y: \quad \top^f, \mathsf{hunt}^f, (\top, \neg\mathsf{hunt}), (\neg\mathsf{hunt}, \neg\mathsf{cons}), (\mathsf{hunt}, \mathsf{cons}) \Rightarrow \neg(\mathsf{hunt}, \mathsf{back})$$

attacking argument d. Consistency attacks can be seen as generalized notions of defeat where, in case of DAC all the norms used in the construction of an argument are jointly attacked. Such a defeat rule is considered in [5, 19] in characterizing grounded reasoning with Input/Output logic. The rule looks as follows

$$\frac{\Gamma, \Delta \Rightarrow}{\Gamma \Rightarrow \neg\Delta} \; RNS$$

where Δ is a non-empty set of norms and Γ does not contain any norms. In other words, the rule says that if the norms Δ in a sequent together yield an inconsistency (i.e., $\Gamma, \Delta \Rightarrow$), then these norms are not jointly applicable (i.e.,

$\Gamma \Rightarrow \neg \Delta$). In the context of $\mathbb{K}_5$, we would derive the following argument using RNS

$$\top^f, \top^c \Rightarrow \neg\{(\top, \neg\text{hunt}), (\text{hunt}, \text{cons}), (\neg\text{hunt}, \neg\text{cons})\}$$

attacking the problematic argument y. Likewise, one can think of other forms of attacks expressible in DAC.

We now illustrate how DAC-induced argumentation frameworks can be employed for generating deontic explanations. We do this by adopting the notion of *related admissibility*, proposed by Fan and Toni [35] to provide argumentative explanations ([24] generalize the semantics to include more notions of argumentative explanations). This notion can be adopted to a deontic context and explains why some obligations hold *despite* certain norms to the contrary. First, let us recall some of the required definitions.

Indirect defense: An argument a *indirectly defends* b iff $a = b$, or there is an argument c that attacks b and a attacks c, or there is an argument c that is indirectly defended by a and c indirectly defends b.[27]

Related admissibility: For $a \in \text{Arg}$ and $\mathcal{A}_a \subseteq \text{Arg}$, the set $\mathcal{A}_a$ is *related admissible with topic* a iff $a \in \mathcal{A}_a$, for all $b \in \mathcal{A}_a$, b indirectly defends a, and $\mathcal{A}_a$ is admissible.

In other words, a related admissible set $\mathcal{A}_a$ identifies the relevant arguments that justify the acceptability of an argument a. Let

$$\mathcal{A}^+ = \{a \in \text{Arg} \mid \mathcal{A} \text{ attacks } a\}$$

and

$$\mathcal{A}^- = \{a \in \text{Arg} \mid a \text{ attacks some } b \in \mathcal{A}\}$$

be the set containing the arguments that are attacked by arguments from the set $\mathcal{A}$, respectively that attack arguments in $\mathcal{A}$.

In light of the above notions, we can answer Charlotte's inquiry (given $\mathbb{K}_5'$):

"Why am I obliged to ask Albert for consent, despite reasons for the contrary?"

(Reasons to the contrary being, for instance, the seeming obligation to not ask for consent as concluded in argument b.) First, argument c provides (internal) reasons for why the obligation cons^o can be concluded from the knowledge base. Then, the related admissible set $\mathcal{A}_c = \{c, e, h\}$ provides external reasons for the acceptability of c. Observe that this related admissible extension is a proper subset of the unique stable extension, i.e., $\mathcal{A}_c \subset \{c, d, e, h\}$. This is exactly the purpose of related admissibility: it collects only those arguments *relevant* for explaining the acceptance of c. Argument d does not interact with any of the other derived arguments and, so, that Charlotte ought to be back on time for her brother's party is clearly irrelevant for an explanation of c. This also shows

---

[27] Not to be confused with the notion of defense in Sect. 2.

that stable extensions are not directly suitable for the purpose of explanation. Next, let $\mathcal{A}_c^- = \{f, g\}$ be the set of attackers of related admissible set $\mathcal{A}_c$. Then, $\{f, g\}^- \cap \mathcal{A}_c = \{e, h\}$ contains the arguments e and h that defend $\mathcal{A}_c$ from its counterarguments g and f.[28] Thus, Charlotte is obliged to ask Albert for consent because of the applicable norm (hunt, cons), together with the fact and constraint that she initiated a hunt^f, respectively, hunt^c, which jointly provide reasons for why the conflicting norm $(\top, \neg\text{hunt})$ is inapplicable in this context.

For the present purpose the above suffices. We refer to [19] for an application of DAC in the context of dialogue models that create deontic explanations.

Conclusion. In this tutorial, we presented a methodology for *Argumentative Knowledge Representation and Reasoning, ArgKRR* for short, which is a subfield of KRR for argumentative approaches. Figure 9 represents, what we call, the new ArgKRR pipeline. It contains the various stages [27] in which formal argumentation deals with KRR. We note that whereas previous focus was on determining the logical consequences of the reasoning process (Stage 6 in Fig. 9) the *new ArgKRR* pipeline contains an additional explainability step (Stage 7) accommodating the need for more transparent, traceable, and explainable reasoning processes. In this respect, formal argumentation is particularly suitable since it explicitly maps the dynamics between (conflicting) arguments. This tutorial focused on Steps 2 to 7, excluding Step 1, which comprises the natural language processing and translation of text into formal databases (argument mining techniques allow for bridging between natural language representation of arguments and the formal domain, see [26] and see [36] for NLP in the context of norms). Furthermore, we used sequent-style calculi in the construction of arguments in Step 3, and argued how this proof-theoretic approach may bring several advantages to ArgKRR.

We introduced the reader to the world of logical argumentation. Our focus was on proof-theoretic methods in which sequent-calculi are employed to generate arguments and attacks. We have drawn parallels to reasoning with maximal consistent sets and identified systems of logical argumentation that satisfy key properties proposed in nonmonotonic logic and formal argumentation. Finally, we applied logical argumentation to deontic reasoning and illustrated how explanations can be obtained using proof calculi and instantiated argumentation frameworks. We hope to have raised the reader's interest in digging further into related material. Besides the cited papers throughout this article, we particularly recommend the handbook series on formal argumentation [14,37] and on deontic logic [38,39], and refer to [30,81] for an overview on explainability methods in formal argumentation. For alternative approaches to logical argumentation see [31] and, with less emphasis on proof theory, [21].

---

[28] In fact, one may argue that in this case, h suffices since the acceptability of e depends on that of h, but not the other way around (this can be straightforwardly determined by applying the same reasoning to explaining why argument e is acceptable).

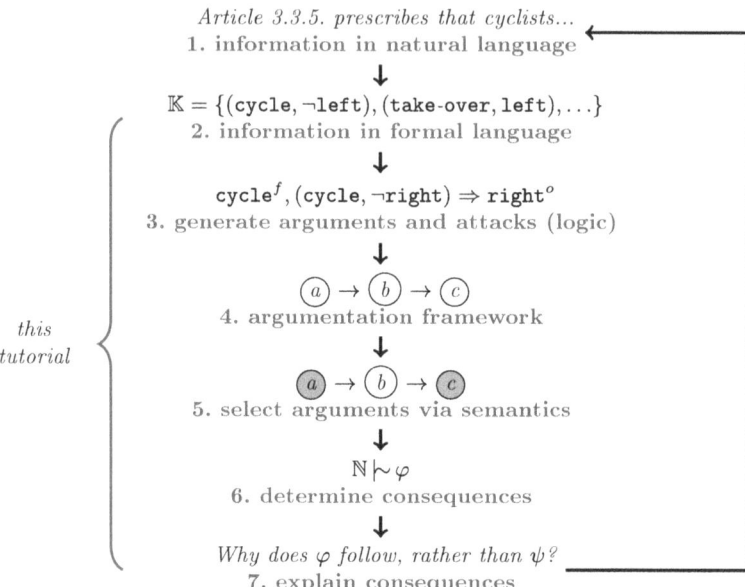

Fig. 9. The New Argumentative KRR Pipeline. This tutorial treats Steps 2 to 7 in the context of proof-theoretic approaches to logical argumentation.

Acknowledgments. This work was partially funded by the "Logical Methods of Deontic Explanations" (LoDeX) project, funded by the Deutsche Forschungsgemeinschaft (DFG, German Research Foundation) - Project Number 511915728.

Disclosure of Interests. The authors have no competing interests which are relevant to this work.

References

1. Amgoud, L., Cayrol, C., Lagasquie-Schiex, M., Livet, P.: On bipolarity in argumentation frameworks. Int. J. Intell. Syst. **23**(10), 1062–1093 (2008)
2. Amgoud, L., Cayrol, C.: On the acceptability of arguments in preference-based argumentation. arXiv preprint arXiv:1301.7358 (2013)
3. Amgoud, L., Maudet, N., Parsons, S.: Modeling dialogues using argumentation. In: International Conference on Multi-Agent Systems, p. 0031. IEEE Computer Society (2000)
4. Amgoud, L., Prade, H.: Using arguments for making and explaining decisions. Artif. Intell. **173**(3–4), 413–436 (2009)
5. Arieli, O., van Berkel, K., Strasser, C.: Defeasible normative reasoning: a proof-theoretic integration of logical argumentation. In: Proceedings of AAAI24, the 38th Annual AAAI Conference on Artificial Intelligence, no. 9, pp. 10450–10458. AAAI Press (2024)

6. Arieli, O., Borg, A., Hesse, M., Straßer, C.: Explainable logic-based argumentation. In: Toni, F., Polberg, S., Booth, R., Caminada, M., Kido, H. (eds.) Frontiers in Artificial Intelligence and Applications: Computational Models of Argument, proceedings (COMMA22), vol. 353, pp. 32 – 43. IOS press (2022). https://doi.org/10.3233/FAIA220139
7. Arieli, O., Borg, A., Heyninck, J., Straßer, C.: Logic-based approaches to formal argumentation. In: Gabbay, D., Giacomin, M., Simari, G.R., Thimm, M. (eds.) Handbook of Formal Argumentation, vol. 2, pp. 1793–1898. College Publications (2021)
8. Arieli, O., Borg, A., Straßer, C.: A postulate-deriven study of logical argumentation. Artif. Intell. 103966 (2023)
9. Arieli, O., Straßer, C.: Sequent-based logical argumentation. Argument Comput. **6**(1), 73–99 (2015)
10. Atkinson, K., Bench-Capon, T., Bollegala, D.: Explanation in AI and law: past, present and future. Artif. Intell. **289**, 103387 (2020)
11. Atkinson, K., Bench-Capon, T., McBurney, P.: A dialogue game protocol for multi-agent argument over proposals for action. Auton. Agent. Multi-Agent Syst. **11**, 153–171 (2005)
12. Barnes, J.: The Complete Works of Aristotle. The Revised Oxford Translation. One Volume Digital Edition. Princeton University Press, Princeton (1984)
13. Baroni, P., Caminada, M., Giacomin, M.: An introduction to argumentation semantics. Knowl. Eng. Rev. **26**(4), 365–410 (2011)
14. Baroni, P., Gabbay, D., Giacomin, M., van der Torre, L.: Handbook of Formal Argumentation, vol. 1. College Publications, UK (2018)
15. Batens, D.: Dialectical dynamics within formal logics. Logique et Anal. (N.S.) **114**, 161–173 (1986)
16. Benferhat, S., Dubois, D., Prade, H.: Some syntactic approaches to the handling of inconsistent knowledge bases: a comparative study. Part 1: Flat Case **58**, 17–45 (1997)
17. van Berkel, K.: A logical analysis of normative reasoning: agency, action, and argumentation. Ph.D. thesis, TU Wien (2023)
18. van Berkel, K., Straßer, C.: Reasoning with and about norms in logical argumentation. In: Toni, F., Polberg, S., Booth, R., Caminada, M., Kido, H. (eds.) Frontiers in Artificial Intelligence and Applications: Computational Models of Argument, Proceedings (COMMA22), vol. 353, pp. 332–343. IOS Press (2022). https://doi.org/10.3233/FAIA220164
19. van Berkel, K., Straßer, C.: Towards deontic explanations through dialogue. In: Proceeding of the 2nd International Workshop on Argumentation for eXplainable AI (ArgXAI 2024), pp. 29–40. CEUR-WS Workshop Proceedings (2024)
20. van Berkel, K., Straßer, C., Zhou, Z.: Towards an argumentative unification of default reasoning. In: Proceeding of COMMA 2024, pp. 313–324. IOS Press (2024)
21. Besnard, P., Hunter, A.: A review of argumentation based on deductive arguments. Handb. Formal Argumentation **1**, 435–482 (2018)
22. Black, E., Hunter, A.: A generative inquiry dialogue system. In: Proceedings of the 6th International Joint Conference on Autonomous Agents and Multiagent Systems (AAMAS 2007), pp. 1–8 (2007). https://doi.org/10.1145/1329125.1329417
23. Bochman, A.: A Logical Theory of Causality. MIT Press, Cambridge (2021)
24. Borg, A., Bex, F.: A basic framework for explanations in argumentation. IEEE Intell. Syst. 25–35 (2021). https://doi.org/10.1109/MIS.2021.3053102

25. Borg, A., Straßer, C.: Relevance in structured argumentation. In: Proceedings of the Twenty-Seventh International Joint Conference on Artificial Intelligence, pp. 1753–1759 (2018). https://doi.org/10.24963/ijcai.2018/242
26. Budzynska, K., Villata, S., et al.: Processing natural language argumentation. Handb. Formal Argumentation **1**, 577–627 (2018)
27. Caminada, M., Amgoud, L.: On the evaluation of argumentation formalisms. Artif. Intell. **171**(5–6), 286–310 (2007)
28. Chisholm, R.M.: Contrary-to-duty imperatives and deontic logic. Analysis **24**(2), 33–36 (1963). https://doi.org/10.1093/analys/24.2.33
29. Ciabattoni, A., Parent, X., Sartor, G.: A Kelsenian deontic logic. In: Schweighofer, E. (ed.) Frontiers in Artificial Intelligence and Applications, Legal Knowledge and Information Systems, vol. 346, pp. 141–150. IOS Press (2021). https://doi.org/10.3233/FAIA210330
30. Čyras, K., Rago, A., Albini, E., Baroni, P., Toni, F.: Argumentative XAI: a survey (2021). https://doi.org/10.48550/ARXIV.2105.11266
31. D'Agostino, M., Modgil, S.: Classical logic, argument and dialectic. Artif. Intell. **262**, 15-51 (2018). https://doi.org/10.1016/j.artint.2018.05.003
32. Dung, P.M.: On the acceptability of arguments and its fundamental role in non-monotonic reasoning, logic programming and n-person games. **77**, 321–358 (1995)
33. Dung, P.M., Kowalski, R.A., Toni, F.: Assumption-based argumentation. Argumentation Artif. Intell. 199–218 (2009)
34. Dutilh Novaes, C.: A dialogical conception of explanation in mathematical proofs. Philos. Math. Educ. Today 81–98 (2018)
35. Fan, X., Toni, F.: On computing explanations in argumentation. In: Bonet, B., Koenig, S. (eds.) Proceedings of the Twenty-Ninth AAAI Conference on Artificial Intelligence (AAAI 2015), pp. 1496–1502 (2015)
36. Ferraro, G., Lam, H.P.: NLP techniques for normative mining. J. Appl. Log. - IfCoLog J. Log. Appl. **8**(4), 941–974 (2021)
37. Gabbay, D., Giacomin, M., Simari, G.R., Thimm, M.: Handbook of Formal Argumentation, vol. 2. College Publications, UK (2021)
38. Gabbay, D., Horty, J.F., Parent, X., van der Meyden, R., van der Torre, L.: Handbook of Deontic Logic and Normative Systems, vol. 1. College Publications, UK (2013)
39. Gabbay, D., Horty, J.F., Parent, X., van der Meyden, R., van der Torre, L.: The Handbook of Deontic Logic and Normative Systems, vol. 2. College Publications, UK (2021)
40. Gabbay, D.M.: Theoretical foundations for non-monotonic reasoning in expert systems. In: Logics and Models of Concurrent Systems, pp. 439–457. Springer (1985)
41. Gelfond, M., Lifschitz, V.: The stable model semantics for logic programming. In: ICLP/SLP, Cambridge, MA, vol. 88, pp. 1070–1080 (1988)
42. Gentzen, G.: Untersuchungen über das logische Schließen I, II. Math. Zeitschrift **39**(176–210), 405–431 (1934)
43. Hansson, B.: An analysis of some deontic logics. Nous 373–398 (1969)
44. Hart, H.L.: The ascription of responsibility and rights. In: Proceedings of the Aristotelian Society, vol. 49, pp. 171–194. JSTOR (1948)
45. Hilpinen, R., McNamara, P.: Deontic logic: A historical survey and introduction. In: Gabbay, D., Horty, J.F., Parent, X., van der Meyden, R., van der Torre, L. (eds.) Handbook of Deontic Logic and Normative Systems, vol. 1, pp. 3–136. College Publications (2013)

46. Koons, R.: Defeasible reasoning. In: Zalta, E.N. (ed.) The Stanford Encyclopedia of Philosophy. Metaphysics Research Lab, Stanford University, Summer 2022 edn. (2022)
47. Kraus, S., Lehman, D., Magidor, M.: Nonmonotonic reasoning, preferential models and cumulative logics. **44**, 167–207 (1990)
48. Lehmann, D.J., Magidor, M.: What does a conditional knowledge base entail? Artif. Intell. **55**(1), 1–60 (1992)
49. Lewis, D.: Counterfactuals. Harvard University Press, Cambridge (1973)
50. Makinson, D.: Bridges from Classical to Nonmonotonic Logic, Texts in Computing, vol. 5. King's College Publications, London (2005)
51. Makinson, D., van der Torre, L.: Input/Output logics. J. Philos. Log. 383–408 (2000)
52. Makinson, D., van der Torre, L.: Constraints for input/output logics. J. Philos. Log. **30**(2), 155–185 (2001)
53. McBurney, P., Parsons, S.: Dialogue games for agent argumentation. In: Argumentation in Artificial Intelligence, pp. 261–280. Springer (2009)
54. Mercier, H., Sperber, D.: Why do humans reason? Arguments for an argumentative theory. Behav. Brain Sci. **34**(2), 57–74 (2011)
55. Miller, T.: Explanation in artificial intelligence: insights from the social sciences. Artif. Intell. **267**, 1–38 (2019). https://doi.org/10.1016/j.artint.2018.07.007
56. Modgil, S., Caminada, M.: Proof theories and algorithms for abstract argumentation frameworks. In: Argumentation in Artificial Intelligence, pp. 105–129. Springer (2009)
57. Modgil, S., Prakken, H.: The ASPIC+ framework for structured argumentation: a tutorial. Argument Comput. **5**(1), 31–62 (2014)
58. Moore, R.C.: Semantical considerations on nonmonotonic logic. **25**(1), 75–94 (1985). https://doi.org/10.1016/0004-3702(85)90042-6
59. Negri, S., Von Plato, J., Ranta, A.: Structural Proof Theory. Cambridge University Press, Cambridge (2008)
60. Nute, D.: Defeasible Deontic Logic, vol. 263. Springer, Heidelberg (1997)
61. Parent, X., van der Torre, L.: Input/output logic. In: Gabbay, D., Horty, J.F., Parent, X., van der Meyden, R., van der Torre, L. (eds.) Handbook of Deontic Logic and Normative Systems, vol. 1, pp. 499–544. College Publications (2013)
62. Parent, X., van der Torre, L.: I/O logics with a consistency check. In: Broersen, J.M., Condoravdi, C., Shyam, N., Pigozzi, G. (eds.) Deontic Logic and Normative Systems, 14th International Conference, DEON 2018, pp. 285–299. College Publications (2018)
63. Pollock, J.: A theory of defeasible reasoning. **6**, 33–54 (1991)
64. Pollock, J.L.: Defeasible reasoning. Cogn. Sci. **11**(4), 481–518 (1987)
65. Prakken, H.: Coherence and flexibility in dialogue games for argumentation. J. Log. Comput. **15**, 1009–1040 (2005)
66. Prakken, H.: An abstract framework for argumentation with structured arguments. Argument Comput. **1**(2), 93–124 (2010)
67. Prakken, H.: Historical overview of formal argumentation. In: Baroni, P., Gabbay, D., Giacomin, M., van der Torre, L., et al. (eds.) Handbook of Formal Argumentation, vol. 1, pp. 75–143. College Publications (2018)
68. Rathjen, M., Sieg, W.: Proof theory. In: Zalta, E.N., Nodelman, U. (eds.) The Stanford Encyclopedia of Philosophy. Metaphysics Research Lab, Stanford University, Winter 2022 edn. (2022)
69. Reiter, R.: A logic for default reasoning. **1–2**(13) (1980)

70. Reiter, R.: A logic for default reasoning. Artif. Intell. **13**(1–2), 81–132 (1980)
71. Rescher, N., Manor, R.: On inference from inconsistent premises. Theor. Decis. **1**, 179–217 (1970)
72. Ross, W.D.: The Right and the Good. Oxford University Press, Oxford (1930)
73. Saribatur, Z.G., Wallner, J.P., Woltran, S.: Explaining non-acceptability in abstract argumentation. In: Giacomo, G.D., et al. (eds.) Frontiers in Artificial Intelligence and Applications, 24th European Conference on Artificial Intelligence - ECAI 2020, vol. 325, pp. 881–888. IOS Press (2020)
74. Šešelja, D., Straßer, C.: Abstract argumentation and explanation applied to scientific debates. Synthese **190**(12), 2195–2217 (2013)
75. Shoham, Y.: A semantical approach to nonmonotonic logics. In: Ginsberg, M.L. (ed.) Readings in Non-monotonic Reasoning, pp. 227–249. Morgan Kaufmann, Los Altos (1987)
76. Stalnaker, R.F.: A theory of conditionals. In: Reischer, N. (ed.) Studies in Logical Theory. Basil Blackwell (1968)
77. Straßer, C., Antonelli, A.: Non-monotonic Logic. In: Zalta, E.N. (ed.) The Stanford Encyclopedia of Philosophy. Metaphysics Research Lab, Stanford University, Summer 2019 edn. (2019)
78. Straßer, C.: Nonmonotonic Logic. Elements Series. Cambridge University Press (202x). Forthcoming
79. Toulmin, S.E.: The Uses of Argument. Cambridge University Press, Cambridge (1958)
80. Van Fraassen, B.C.: The logic of conditional obligation. **1**, 417–438 (1972)
81. Vassiliades, A., Bassiliades, N., Patkos, T.: Argumentation and explainable artificial intelligence: a survey. Knowl. Eng. Rev. **36**, 1–35 (2021). https://doi.org/10.1017/s0269888921000011
82. Walton, D., Reed, C.: Diagramming, argumentation schemes and critical questions. In: Anyone Who Has a View, pp. 195–211. Springer (2003)
83. Wu, Y., Podlaszewski, M.: Implementing crash-resistance and non-interference in logic-based argumentation. J. Log. Comput. **25**(2), 303–333 (2014). https://doi.org/10.1093/logcom/exu017

Author Index

C
Cima, Gianluca 54

L
Lembo, Domenico 54

M
Marconi, Lorenzo 54
Murlak, Filip 23

O
Ozaki, Ana 61

R
Rosati, Riccardo 54

S
Savo, Domenico Fabio 54
Straßer, Christian 78

T
Thomazo, Michaël 1

V
van Berkel, Kees 78

The manufacturer's authorised representative in the EU is Springer Nature Customer Service Centre GmbH, Europaplatz 3, 69115 Heidelberg, Germany. If you have any concerns regarding our products, please contact ProductSafety@springernature.com

Printed and bound by CPI Group (UK) Ltd, Croydon, CR0 4YY

26/03/2026

02078935-0016